A CASE FOR JUSTICE

RECOVERING LOST BLESSINGS

MARJORIE COLE

Dedicated to my Family including my Brothers and Sisters and the many generations that have gone before us in this War.

PREFACE

A CASE FOR JUSTICE

A Case For Justice addresses the 'crisis of faith' that we, as believers, often experience regarding the goodness and justice of God. If God is so good; and we have been forgiven and set free through His work of salvation; and our sins are 'under the Blood' - as the Word of God tells us – then, why do we suffer from as much tragedy as unbelievers and why does injustice still plague us? Why do bad things continue to operate in our lives even after we are saved? How can the many difficult things we are going through be the will of God or the work of the Holy Spirit when God told us that He would never leave us or forsake us? (Deut.31:6, 8; Josh. 1:5; Heb. 13:5) Is God for us, or is He mad at us? Am I being chastened? Is this a consequence for my sin, or is it a curse?

The Bible is very straightforward about the existence of curses. The fact that they are transferred down through the generational bloodlines - even in the life of a believer - is also straightforward, though not well understood. *A Case For Justice* examines the truth of God's Word which underlies the internal and unseen workings of Divine Justice, the functions of the Law, the Court of Heaven, and the ongoing work of the Accuser - in order to bring deeper understanding to these troublesome and frequently asked questions.

This book examines how the shed Blood of the Lamb of God - as opposed to living a perfect and sinless life - is the only remedy for sin. It examines the confusion between Law and grace. It reveals the battle for our redemption and sets our journey for righteousness within the context of the Spiritual War and the Court of Heaven. It sets our quest for understanding the will of God and the restoration of justice within a context of the Gospel of Grace.

The fact that God has an Enemy who challenges His every move in regard to us is an often overlooked and under-emphasized part of the paradigm of the Spiritual Warfare in which we live and seek to find justice. *A Case For Justice* not only clarifies how the Blood of Jesus Christ takes away our sin and breaks the curses; it also shows us the way to rest in Him in the very midst of the battle for recovering our lost blessings.

God's system of Divine Justice operates in the Court of Heaven. Its purpose is to enforce the victories of the Cross and make it possible for us to live the life Jesus died to give us. The Death and Resurrection of Jesus Christ takes away our sin and its effects - in truth, not just in theory. "For all the promises of God are 'Yes', and in Him 'Amen', to the glory of God through us." (II Cor. 1:20) God established us and anointed us. He has sealed us and given us the Spirit in our hearts as a down payment. We are more than conquerors in and through Him Who loves us. We are more than conquerors through His Word, and His Holy Spirit.

The revelation that old things have passed away and all things are become new and we are new creatures in Christ is both an instant fact, and a progressive revelation. But because we do not always realize these truths immediately, we are targets, even after salvation, the harassment and the exploitation of the Enemy. This makes uncovering the 'mysteries of iniquity' which have been buried deep within our bloodlines more obscure. If the Devil is a defeated foe, why all of this resistance and difficulty?

To answer that question and many like it, we must first discover the roots of the agreements which have been made with the Enemy. The Thief has stolen countless blessings from us and committed heinous crimes against us and our people. As we follow Jesus, the Holy Spirit begins to reveal to us the places of the ancient battles and the everyday assaults. By walking in the Spirit and practicing discernment, (Heb. 5:14) we will begin to see the deliberate and recurring patterns of loss and thus, identify the places of the Enemy's original demonic attack in our lives which may have occurred before we were born. God desires to bring these crimes committed against us and our people to justice. To do that, we must release those crimes back to the Judge.

Our Heavenly Father desires that the years of spiritual wickedness which have deprived His Children of justice and freedom be exposed by the Light of His Truth and brought to justice. The groundwork for freedom and new life in Christ has been laid. His victory must now be legally enforced through the Church, which is His 'Kingdom-of-Light-Liberation-Force' here on earth. (Eph. 3:10-12) We have an exciting and tremendously important part to play in setting the captives free, (Is. 42:22-23). Part of the advancement of the Kingdom of God comes through the advancement the truth which comes through the repentance and confession of the sins of the generations. This breaks the ancestral agreements which were made with the Liar. These lies must be canceled out, and the 'body of death' software, (Rom. 7:23) which has been operating in our souls deleted - in order for the life Jesus died to give us may be manifested in us in its fullness.

A Case For Justice unveils the agreements and exposes the arguments which the Accuser of the Brethren has been using to build his century-old case against us all our lives. It teaches us to recognize the power of *Guilt's indictment against us, and the patterns of demonic judgment he has been using to 'swallow up' our blessings and destroy our Godly inheritance. It brings us hope and deliverance through the revelation of Jesus Christ and His Gospel of grace and good news.

Please note: From time to time throughout this book, certain words are capitalized and used as proper names, for the purpose of naming the demons. We can name and identify them by what we see them doing. They are real spiritual entities that can be named, They have distinctive personalities and specific demonic skill-sets that allow them to be identified by what they do. We see Jesus using this method in addressing the demons and evil spirits. They responded to His interrogation (Mk. 1:23-26; Mk. 5:6-13), and the fact that Jesus named the demons by what they were doing (See Mk. 9:17 & 25; Lu.13:11-12) leads us to do the same.

TABLE OF CONTENTS

PART I

IN SEACH OF JUSTICE

INTRODUCTION

THE SPIRITUAL WARFARE PARADIGM

The life of Jesus Christ was given in exchange for ours. Many often quote the Bible referencing the guilt and sinful behavior of man. Romans 1:18-3:20 describes the lawlessness of those who reject God and concludes that all who are under the Law, which is everyone, is guilty, "that every mouth may be stopped, and all the world may become guilty before God." (Rom. 3:19). Another worthy translation of the word "guilt" given in the English Standard Version (ESV) says "and the whole world may be held accountable to God. For by the works of the law no human being will be justified in his sight." Being "accountable" is actually good news as it makes us all "eligible" for the justification laid out two verses later.

Since verse 20 takes away all hope of our flesh being "justified" by the "deeds of the law, for by the law is the knowledge of sin", we see God is stripping away any notion that we can earn our salvation. He is making it crystal clear that our sinful behavior and the ensuing feelings of guilt will never be remedied by the keeping of the law. Then God tells us a wonderful thing, (though verse 21-22 are rarely quoted as the qualifier and context for the more commonly known and burdensome verse) "all have sinned and fall short of the glory of God." (Rom. 3:23). (I suspect this is also a deliberate design by the Enemy to isolate us from the hope and goodness of God, Who longs to justify us, and to get us to focus on our sins and not on the work of the Son.)

In verse 21 God says, "But now, the righteousness of God apart from the law is revealed, being witnessed by the Law and the Prophets, even the righteousness of God which is through faith in Jesus Christ to all and on all who believe. For there is no difference; for all have sinned and fall short of the glory of God, being justified freely by His grace through the redemption that is in Christ Jesus, whom God set forth to be a propitiation by His blood, through faith, to demonstrate His righteousness, because in His forbearance God had passed over the sins that were previously committed, to demonstrate at the present time His righteousness, that He might be just and the justifier of the one who has faith in Jesus." (Rom. 3:21-26). "Therefore we conclude that a man is justified by faith apart from the deeds of the law". (Rom.3:27-28). Our justification clearly does not come from the law. It is very clear! The new law is the law of faith.

Jesus took the death penalty that belonged to us and paid in full all that the Devil had demanded of us. In God's book of reckoning we are forgiven if we have faith in Jesus Christ. Our guilt is gone! Jesus Christ is our righteousness. He fulfilled the demands of the Law and did what the Law could not do in bringing us to Salvation. The righteous requirements of the Law have been satisfied. We who believe are not guilty. We are forgiven. We are free to know who we are and who He is and be who He created us to be!

Salvation is not about adding another thing to the list of things we need to do to be good enough to get to heaven. Being saved is about following Jesus. Jesus died to rescue us, to redeem us from the auction block of Hell. He removed us from the place of slavery and shame and gave us a place in His family because of His love. Through the substitution of His life for ours, Jesus Christ "Himself took our infirmities and bore our sicknesses" (Mt. 8:17). Through His substitutionary death, He gathered up the broken pieces of His children's lives that had been scattered on the desolate battlefields of "many generations" (Is. 61:4). He came to heal the brokenhearted, including those who lived before us who had been struck down and captured in battle.

Through the finished work of Jesus Christ we are shielded from the furious judgment of the Accuser who seeks to try our faith and bind our souls with Confusion and Condemnation. According to his diabolical rendition of justice defined as "an eye for an eye and a tooth for a tooth", we are all still guilty. He therefore, seeks to persuade us that our guilt and the undoing of it are our most pressing issues in the unfinished business of sin. Jesus cried out from His Cross, "It is finished". It behooves us to stand on the Word of God!

The accumulation of generational junk left behind becomes the Enemy's stockpile of accusations. All of our ancestor's agreements made with the lie, the open doors of unforgiveness, the unreconciled accounts, the unconfessed sins, the accumulation of generational iniquities, the bitter root judgments, the vows and oaths, and the deals made with the Devil, including the patterns of fear, loss, and guilt provide the Accuser plenty of material to work with in building his case against us. Even in our "saved state", the evidence of sin remains abundant, allowing him to move the power his demonic judgments forward through the Court of Heaven to ruin and ravage our lives.

Because we misunderstand the paradigm of spiritual warfare, our true position as believers in Christ and the power of our agreement with the lie, we often overlook the generational list of sins and iniquities as a probable cause for problems in our lives. Any concerns are quickly over-ridden by the idea that "I'm a new creation" and "It's all under the Blood". We fail to see our agreements with fear, guilt and sin or those made by our ancestors, as the cause for the curses the Enemy is using to afflict us. The

Accuser uses these agreements to set up countless acts of violence to destroy us and our descendants. He uses the unjudged crimes committed by those who lived before us, as well as those committed by us and against us, to justify his demands to punish us. We do not realize these agreements with iniquity are the reason for our constant collisions in the spiritual world.

The simple definition of iniquity is the accumulation of sin. It comes from adherence to a lie that piles up to produce a pattern of difficulty over a long period of time. The result of believing a lie creates a long-standing agreement with sin. This agreement with the sin creates an agreement with Guilt and a path for Pain. Sin gives the Enemy the justification he needs to make a pact with Guilt which opens the door to punishment, pain and penalty. The Enemy baits us with either promises of vengeance upon our enemies or finds us guilty of judging them and thus, deserving of punishment ourselves.

Our failure to regain justice using the Enemy's solutions clears the way for injustice that only opens the door wider to Satan's demonic judgments. The Enemy declares his claims are legally justified by his religiously rigid rendition of scripture. Using his twisted interpretation of the Word of God and the very Law God gave us to protect us and warn us about the dangers of sin, the Enemy finds us guilty of sin.

Satan ultimately makes no pretense about his hatred for us or our relationship with our Heavenly Father. He finds us guilty, echoing again the scripture that says, "The soul that sins shall die." (Ez.18:4b). God is clarifying only those who sin shall die, and not those who are descendants of those who sin. The Enemy, as he did in using scripture on Jesus in the wilderness, rendered it according to his own purposes, not as it was intended by the Spirit. He finds us guilty of death for the sin he tricked us into committing. He is the hypocrite who mocks us for judging, admonishing us to "judge not" as he sits usurping the seat of the Eternal Judge!

Regret, condemnation and loss are patterns the Evil One has always used to shape, not only the lives of our ancestors, but also the lives of their future generations. Unbelief, the adherence to the lie rather than the promise of God, creates a pattern of despair and destruction down through our bloodline. Unconfessed iniquity acts as both an open door and a demonic thrust to drive the activity of the Kingdom of Darkness deeper into our souls. A pattern has been cut through our bloodline that perpetuates the generational curses down into the lives of our descendants (See Lev. 26:39-40).

Identifying those iniquities and disempowering the familiar spirits who have use them to create the patterns of death and destruction to continue to lie, kill, and steal from each successive generation is the work of the Holy Spirit. Sanctification moves forward through the revelation of Jesus Christ as given to us by the indwelling Holy Spirit Who has been sent to lead us into all truth, to sanctify and eradicate sin from our households and our souls. Obedience is essential in removing the power of the curses that have come out of the agreements we or our ancestors have made with the Evil One. Knowing the truth stops the Enemy in his fraudulent claims in usurping our right to our lives; lives he technically has no more legal right to once we are saved. Our only recourse for justice against this blatant violation of truth and the insidious accusations and crass denial of the Evil One is God.

God is a God of Justice. He has given us free access into His Court, the Court of Heaven, where we are invited to come boldly, to make our requests known and present our case before Him. His Court is the place of victory, vindication, restoration, justice, and deliverance from the ruthless accusations of the Accuser. It is the place where Satan's defeat, accomplished at the Resurrection, is executed and enforced. This is also the place where the Accuser works day and night to present his case against us using the very agreements we have made with his lies to justify his demand for the right to test us. In the testing of us, he seizes a perfect opportunity to test God that he might prove God wrong for choosing us and foolish for making us. He places his demonic judgments of guilt and punishment upon us for sinning against God.

God's Court is the place where we can receive God's forgiveness. God's forgiveness unhooks us from feelings of guilt and wrong-doing and overrules the objections Satan is making against us. *A Case for Justice: Uncovering the Mysteries, Recovering Lost Blessings,* gives us a deeper understanding of how the trial of our faith plays out in the context of Spiritual Warfare set within the legal system of Heaven's justice. When we understand what has already been done to defend us and defeat our Adversary, we begin to know the grace and goodness of God. Recovery and restoration of our spiritual legacy and the completion of our destiny begins with our renewed confidence in God's love for us and His desire to set us free.

1

THERE WAS A GREAT HOUSE

*O*NCE UPON A TIME...

I was born into a family whose last name has two meanings in German. The first carries the connotation of a 'judge'; the second means 'to make right'. At first glance, these two definitions appear to be synonymous. Upon closer examination, however, they can be seen to be contrary to each other. 'To act as a judge', or to judge, is not always the way to 'make things right'! In order to make things right, we must actually <u>refrain</u> from judging and <u>release</u> the judgment of the situation over to God, Who is the one and only Righteous Judge over all.

When we fail to take the plank out of our own eye (Mt. 7:3-5) before we extract the speck from our brother's eye, it can have the disastrous effect of setting up more offense. Presumption, pride, hurt, and misunderstanding are no strangers in family feuds, civil wars, longstanding silences, and generational bitterness within German families, - although German families are by no means an exception to the rule with regard to human conflict and contention.

Many of the German clans began as individual kingdoms. One of the most notorious of those was the ancient Germanic tribe known as the Vandals, from which we get the words vandal and vandalism. The Vandals swept through the Roman Empire ravaging Gaul, Spain, and northern Africa during the third and fourth centuries, and ended up ransacking Rome in 455 AD! They were defeated in 533 at Carthage, but the spirit of the Vandals still roams the earth through the activities of their offspring. We have seen this in their stubborn determination to instigate the only two world wars we have had since that time.

Little did I know how the power a curse can be carried in a name! Little did I realize how binding are the actions and agreements made by our ancestors, or how their actions and decisions can continue to plague their descendants - even for those of us who have been redeemed from the curse. Self-righteousness, spiritual blindness, fear, control, strife, and a bullheaded determination to be right - using their own opinions to define what was 'right'- had cut many of them off from one another and destroyed the mercy and peace within family relationships. Efforts to establish right-eousness by being right had opened countless physical and spiri-tual doors to injustice and offense. Even to this day, conflict, jealousy, pride, misunderstandings, insecurity, and relational breakdowns continue to plague family members.

Heartless and foolish strife within families only served to make them victims of even more injustice. The perpetuation of unfor-giveness and stubborn belligerence continued to fuel the perpetu-ation of ongoing injustices, depriving them of the very mercy they refuse to give others. Judgmentalism, criticism, spiritual blind-ness, self-righteousness, anger, bitterness, religious deception, rejection, pain, guilt and depression had set the foundation for a stronghold which had imprisoned my people long before I was born.

As a child, I was completely unaware of the insidious and serious ramifications of agreements, or how judgments befall those who judge others. The seeds of injustice, fighting, greed, gossip, jealousy, control, holding grudges, bitterness, paranoia and insecurity had already been planted, though they laid dormant within my bloodline. All that was needed for these poisonous pods to germinate was for them to be watered through my own agreement.

These 'word seeds' had already developed into a strong and virulent strain, full of lethal poison. 'Virulent' is a close cousin to the word 'virus', from which comes the word venom, as it relates to a snake. The snakes have bitten all of us with their venomous, extremely injurious stream of bitter and hostile words. The effects of these harsh words upon the fragile souls of the young are caustic and spiteful. The powerful toxins of striving and sin begin to eat away one's worth and validity. As a result, healthy bones become brittle, beaten down with negative, critical words. Bright little souls cringe under the religious burdens and heavy mandates to be good, work harder, do more, and get it right. Few are able to overcome the predatory nature of the poisonous invasion.

My family was raised under the influence of the group decisions of the Germanic tribes with their traditions and cultural practices. As with most families, we did not perceive the latent danger or deep roots of a spiritual plot that even then already existed. Most of the troubling evidence was submerged beneath water that had long since gone under the bridge, washing away any record of wrongs, of which there were many. All that could be seen of the painful past was the deadly presence of the jagged tips of the lofty and unforgiving icebergs still anchored in the turbulent sea of our relationships, holding us in the grip of unforgiveness and longstanding bitterness.

A SIDE BAR ON WORDS AND SOLVING MYSTERIES

I find that the dictionary, which was once a reliable and wonderfully unbiased second source for collaboration of the fuller meaning of words used in the Bible, has been pirated by the

Enemy. At one time it would have brought clarity to the meaning of words such as God, justice, sin, grace, judgment, etc. More recently, however, the dictionary seems to have undergone some sort of mysterious, spiritual alteration. It seems that there is a concerted effort to remove distinctions of meaning by making descriptions of words softer and all inclusive - part of a larger, more politically correct agenda which has succeeded in changing the meaning of words altogether! This strategy reduces the potential for human conflict by undermining the precision and integrity of words in order to reduce the risk of offending others. The pendulum seems to have swung in the other direction, from when words were used to define meanings to now being used as weapons.

The compromise of the meaning of words is not restricted to just the dictionary. The attack on the Scriptures began with words that were used to introduce the unsettling doctrinal debates regarding systematic theology which has now drifted down into our modern churches. The redefining of the Words of Sacred Scripture has given way to a sinister agenda designed to create confusion and call into question both the truth of God's Word and His intentions. New definitions which fit within the political bias that favors the schemes of the god of this world began to appear. New versions of the Bible, new translations, and colorful paraphrases began to populate our book shelves.

Tainted manuscripts began to replace once-concrete words, changing their meanings and, with them, our values. Twisting truth has always been a specialty of the spirit of Perversion, which means 'to twist'. Original words were stripped of the power of their intended meanings, and dressed up in their politically correct garments as an agenda to further promote pretense and more perversions. New words made way for new doctrines. We must understand this to be one of the critical premises the Enemy uses to popularize his position and catch us off guard in this spiritual war of words. Because our words and our confessions give power to the words we speak, it behooves us to be aware as the scripture warns, "For by your words you will be justified, and by your words you will be condemned." (Mt.12:37)

We underestimate the devices of the Evil One who is both a counterfeiter and a cunning foe. As the Deceiver, semantics is critical to his 'I' dotting 'T' crossing tactics in winning the argument for your soul. The fine print gives him permission to lie, and becomes the basis of his alibi. He chooses his words with diabolical precision for the express purpose of misleading the listener. By getting a listener to think he knows what the words mean, the Liar captures an agreement before the 'fine print' of his devious plan becomes clear, before the agreement being made is fully understood by the one who made it.

Words can be used to either tell a lie or speak the truth. Since the power of death and life are carried within words, they are one of hell's most used weapons. Words are essential in the diabolical programming and propaganda which are heavily used in spiritual warfare so as to bind and confine the hearts and souls of humankind. They can be twisted and misinterpreted. As you read these words, let them be protected by the Blood of Jesus. Let their true meaning be preserved, and may the truth of God's Word be rightly divided. (II Tim. 2:15) May *A Case for Justice* be correctly understood and protected from the manipulation of the Enemy in the hearts and minds of those who read it. And, finally, may the words of this book adequately describe the thoughts and intents of the inspired Scripture as set forth by the Holy Spirit, to bring freedom from the snare of the Fowler.

THE CONSPIRACY

Everything we see and do not see operating in and around us is connected. Just as we do not have a random third arm operating from outside our body that can be used to explain how the body functions to move something - and all that happens to us must fit within the context of having a human body with two arms - so too, our worldview must provide the answers and explanation for things from that which exists within it. Though the things operating within that system may not be visible, (see Heb. 11:3), those things are nonetheless real and part of all that exists. In other words, the spiritual dimensions of our tangible world are as real and part of the explanation of things that happen as are the physical parts. The whole, with its many visible and invisible, intricate and seemingly contradictary parts, is one.

If we use the 'causal theory of things' we must reject the theory that everything is random and accidental. There are only two options here, an accidental explanation which offers no meaning or solid explanation for life or our experiences in it, and the theory of cause and effect. These two theories cannot co-exist within the same system, - though we suspend the integrity of the whole when we mix the ideas of something being an accident with the idea of there being a reason for everything. Mixing the two worldviews leads to madness (insanity), futility (a pointless existence) and confusion.

Holding the 'causal' worldview, and observing the consistent, general disposition of instability and conflict we see going on all around us, we must conclude that this is a war. A war must have two sides. Though one or both of those sides may seek to remain hidden, it cannot be denied. There is a power struggle going on for domination between the opposing forces. Let us name those forces 'good' and 'evil'. This leads to the logical and reasonable conclusion that if this is a war, then there must also be a conspiracy going on against God (who we will call good) and His intentions for the functioning of His creation (which includes us) and one who opposes Him. This one we will call Evil or the Evil One.

Within the worldview of this being a conspiracy, we are now able to make logical, reasonable explanations for what appears to be 'accidental'. Because our premise does not allow for things to have come into existence as random, accidental, non-connected events, we conclude, (as the Bible also tells us), there must be a cause for things that both do and do not appear. We have also agreed using the 'causal theory of things" that these things must fit together with other events and causes. Therefore, we conclude, everything is connected and nothing comes from out-of-nowhere.

In solving a mystery, as with putting anything back together, all pieces must be assembled and accounted for. The same is true when explaining things in the Bible. It cannot contradict itself, although there appear to be opposites within its pages. Within the context of the Bible, it is also true that in making an explanation of any part of the whole - or any specific passage of scripture - the explanation must remain consistent with the intentions of the whole itself, which includes the will and intention of its Author.

Although there can be various layers of meaning, the levels complement and complete each other; they do not compete or conspire against one another. Any interpretation of the Word of God used to explain a specific human experience, which is part of the whole spectrum of human experiences, must adhere to this rule of the integrity of the whole, as well. God does not contradict Himself, nor does He act in opposition to His own Word when dealing with us or His Enemy, His justice, or His mercy.

Accepting the premise that this creation was set up to exist within an orderly fashion as designed and created by the One Who made it, we can safely conclude that nothing exists outside of His sovereignty, and since we call that One God the Creator, all things must submit to the general operating principles He set forth in His Word. There are no such thing as accidents, fate, or bad luck. All explanations must be consistent with the principles of truth as set forth by the God of Creation. And since one of the first tenets of faith is to believe that what God says is true and that He cannot lie, we know the Word of God is, by the confirmation of His Spirit, bearing witness with our spirit, the source of absolute Truth.

Therefore, when Jesus, Who is the Word of God - Incarnate – tells us that the truth will set us free, we can conclude that all bondage comes from not knowing or believing the truth. In other words, behind every bondage, there is a lie. The explanation of the various and seemingly oppositional experiences within the realm of human experience must be understood within the context of the whole Word of God and be consistent with His character. In order for any spiritual explanations to work, they must include an understanding of spiritual warfare which would logically include the Enemy's continued and intentional misuse of the Word of God; and the Law, which though now obsolete in the believer's life, still remains one of the Enemy's primary means for finding fault, assigning blame, and setting up confusion, discord and bondage in people.

If we are willing to set aside our dysfunctional and mixed world-view and reexamine our sacred opinions and religious traditions within the context of there being a war on the truth, we will begin to understand how blessings and curses work. Judgment and justice and spiritual warfare do not make sense outside the context of the paradigm (a model that forms the basis for a methodology or a theory), in this case, the Paradigm of Spiritual Warfare. All we seek to understand must fit within the context of God's Word, including His admonitions about sin, the Gospel of Grace, the Law, the curses, and suffering persecution for right-eousness sake.

BURIED IN THE PAST

Most of us are speechless, clueless, or silent, (without words) when it comes to describing what is or has gone on in our life. Both below and above the surface of our existence, the search for truth compels us to dig deeper. We sift through the rubble of the past, much like archaeologists, searching for clues to our origin, meaning, and destiny. Words and deeds handed down - some-times preserved, sometimes hidden in the folds of time - remind us once again that there is nothing new under the sun and there is nothing that has not been done before.

The Scriptures provide the compass, the plumb line from which to measure the history of our past, as well as the place from which to make observations in the present. The Word establishes the absolutes of truth as defined in Jesus Christ. It provides the essential information both in the identification of our present location and our historical past (where we came from) - although many of the specifics may yet be hidden in the past, even as they are as yet unknown and overlooked in the present.

The Word of God is invaluable when attempting to identify the spiritual makeup of the Snake Pit, the very place into which we have been born. The truth of God's Word is a light unto our path, and essential for exposing the unseen works of darkness, including the roots of offense and the cause of the malignancy of any family curse. These crimes and curses empower the Enemy's thrust against us and move some more readily into becoming susceptible to Hell's thugs and bullies.

Why it is that some seem to be marked for certain calamities or benefits, while others are more vulnerable to the spirit of hurt and offense and accept their plight without putting up a fight? This makes both those who suffer wrong and those who wrong them susceptible to injustice. Both those with the 'judging gene' - and those whom they judge – are vulnerable to the ever expanding realm of destruction, while insensitivities to injustice cause more pronounced cases of spiritual blindness, anger, self-righteousness, bitterness, and hardness of the heart.

Even to this day, the only remedy for injustice and offense are the same as those prescribed by Jesus two thousand years ago. Forgiveness and turning the crimes (both real and perceived) over to the One Who Knows our hearts and the truth about what really happened, is the only way to obtain justice and absolution. Freedom begins when we release the judgment of those who have hurt us, ripped us off, and stolen that which is rightfully ours, back over to the Righteous Judge to defend us. Only He can right the wrong. (1 Peter 2:21-23; James 2:12) Trusting Him to bring justice is the faith-action that God requires in dealing with the matters of offense and injustice in bringing us to the place of rest and restoration.

REST releases us from the grip of anger, bitterness, offense, and the temptation to take matters into our own hands. Someday we will be called to give an account of our lives. Someday we will be called on to judge angels. Someday the truth will be known by all. But for today, we must satisfy ourselves with knowing that God's promises to defend us, deliver us, acquit us, redeem us, and keep us from the Evil One, are true. He will deliver us from the relentless demands of the Accuser to prosecute the Innocent. God's mercy and justice are our portion and our protection.

ONCE UPON A TIME, THERE WAS A GREAT HOUSE

And so our birth, like many great stories, continues to be part of a larger story of the human generation. We were all created by God to be an expression of His image, and placed, by His will, into specific families. And just as we were born into a specific time and created for a unique purpose, made in the 'image of God', each one of us is one-of-a-kind. We were fashioned from the spiritual DNA of God Himself, and knit together in our mother's womb from the physical elements which belonged to the gene pool of our respective families.

As each new member of any particular family bloodline appears, their spiritual and physical aptitudes and vulnerabilities begin to take shape and form patterns similar to those of both past and current family members. Thus, each new individual, though unique, is designed from the collective gene pool of traits drawn out of the same set of unseen generational codes and determinants that had shaped their particular family line since the beginning.

Every aspect of our being, both spiritual and physical, is coded on our DNA - including our aptitudes and their development. The codes on our DNA are activated and influenced by our epigenetics. The epigenetics define the environmental conditions to which our DNA is exposed, and determine the final outcome of our creation/modification depending on the toxicity of the environment to which we are born. Exposing our DNA into certain negative or positive solutions, (situations) or environments can literally change the DNA. In other words, our DNA responds to what is present and or missing in those environments. Ex. Fetal Alcohol Syndrome Babies come from a toxic exposure to alcohol. The power of our thoughts, whether positive or negative, the power of words, and misperceptions also create an epigenetic situation that influences and shapes the development of our original, 'starter' DNA.

Our Enemy also has ways of 'speaking' into our world, our perceptions and our experiences as generated from within a paradigm of conflict and danger (war). He creates an environment in which he can recondition (program) us through the processes of learning and experience. This develops and holds us in a vicious cycle that reinforces the lies. This is especially true if the environment and our interactions with others does not provide an alternative to the lies. We just get used to them, familiar with things the way things are.

We are placed within the context of countless forgotten spiritual agreements that were made by those who have gone before us. We may never have considered those agreements relevant to our personal lives or even suspect they existed. But even though we may brush them off as 'no big deal', the Enemy works to keep them 'hidden in plain sight', under the 'spiritual radar' of the average person. We are influenced by the recycling of our own ever evolving concept of life and the world until our decisions become the automatic decisions we make every day.

Our spiritual agreements, though automatic, give the 'soul-shaper' the permission he needs to systematically and psychologically recondition us. Beginning at conception, the 'god of this world' shapes our experiences within the controlled environment he has set up - in order to project his worldview onto our soft, impressionable minds and hearts. The Enemy uses our inner thoughts and feelings - often generated by him - as a tool with which to persuade, manipulate, and control us.

The truth is, God is the Divine Potter. He formed us in the matrix of our mother's womb. Fashioned from clay and made in the image of God, our humanness and the genetic material that forms us makes us and our DNA Satan's most insane obsession and greatest target. As disembodied spirits seeking bodies for themselves, the demons eagerly risk the discomfort of dwelling within us for the express purpose of destroying us.

This battle to overthrow us and corrupt the image of the divine Creator which is manifested in us, is fought within every sphere of our existence - our body, soul, mind, will and emotions, even to the very core of our spiritual being. This is the battle between the eternal omniscient Creator and the invisible powers of Darkness, over our will. They must have our consent (permission) to influence our lives. The question of control and our eternal destiny is determined by our consent. It all simply reduces down to one matter: whose report are we going to believe?

As we grow, the power of our agreements begins to create a particular set of experiences. The Enemy perverts and filters our perceptions of those experiences in such a way as to convince us that our experiences are real. He begins to program our souls using those perceptions to define our self-concept. The things that happen to me form the experiences that I use to define who I am. As I process those experiences and respond accordingly, a brain pathway is formed which determines how to handle the next situation. They form the blueprint for my life. Patterns and habits of behavior begin to emerge.

Many of the unseen agreements that undergird these concepts were crafted long ago by the Enemy who first introduced them to our ancestors as ideas with which to solve similar issues of survival. Those agreements generated the traditions, religions, superstitions, belief systems, and patterns which we have come to believe are good and desirable in maintaining our safety and producing internal righteousness. These agreements, once made, become the hidden contracts and fine print the Enemy uses to direct our lives, ever so slowly, toward the cliffs of destruction.

The reasons for the decisions our ancestors made are often lost to us and we are unaware of their specific agreements. Any agreements they made with the lies Fear told them would cause them to turn away from the commandments of God. Disobedience would, therefore, open them up to the Devil's judgments. In many ways, our lives are the product of our parents' faith and obedience unto blessings - or their fear and disobedience unto curses.

Even as we are shaped by our parents' experiences, their experiences become ours. We end up looking and living a lot like people we have never seen. And even though we have not met them, their choices influence and dominate our choices in unseen ways, making their preferences, habits and tendencies, our own. Our blind and impulsive agreement with the Liar's rendition of life, either knowingly or unknowingly, gives the Enemy permission to reconstruct their past as our present.

Our passive agreements with, 'It is what it is', and our compliance with whatever is going on, begins to shape our experiences. These experiences form the mindsets which create the beliefs by which we live. These belief systems, in turn, build and reinforce the filters and craft the lenses through which we see the world. We believe our perceptions are correct; and thus, they reconfirm and reinforce our belief systems, which determine our actions. We get caught in the vicious circle of mindless assumptions and automatic responses and behaviors without even realizing it.

We are held fast and stay stuck, influenced to repeat the same things, even though we do not understand why we did them and have often tried to change them. And so the demonic life patterns move down the bloodlines with deliberate, although unseen, precision held intact and left fairly unaltered and undisturbed from one generation to the next.

Hence our inheritance, both physical and spiritual, is a unique result of both things we have received and things we have learned, including those things that were part of the innate and divine collection of genetic instructions originally used by God in defining us. In his subtle efforts to obscure and distort the truth about me being made in the image of God, however, Satan combines the elements of both nature and nurture to conceal the truth about my divine nature and who I really am by redefining me into being who I think I am.

The informational record of the bloodline and its survival are thus carried through hundreds of years of ancestry on the human strands of DNA. Each successive generation influences the next. A person's generational house and individual wellbeing are determined by what they have done or not done; by what they have left behind or what they have carried down; by what agreements they have made with Darkness; and by what choices and decisions they have made to follow God.

AS FOR ME AND MY HOUSE

As part of our family, we become responsible for the continuance and the quality of what is being passed on down to our children. The only hope for the restoration of the blessings of God in our generational legacy is in allowing the Holy Spirit to draw a line between us and iniquity and reestablish our declaration and commitment to the truth, as Joshua did when he said, "As for me and my house, we will serve the Lord." (Josh. 24:15)

What we do ultimately affects what will be passed on to our children and becomes the foundation upon which they build. And even as we share the same spiritual house with those who have gone before us, we rarely realize it. Rather, we simply begin to live in the house as we find it. And though the mansion may be filled with hundreds of rooms where people have lived and died, the legacy left behind is often a spiritual mixture of blessings and curses, a difficult mess for the children to sort out.

Some have lived in the house, dwelling according to the Word of God. They were righteous and conscientious about the condition in which they left the house. They passed down a good and Godly inheritance for their children and grandchildren. They took care of the business of sin and walked in the truth of God's love and forgiveness. They overturned the agreements made with Darkness by those who had preceded them.

Others chose to walk in the light of their own imagination, carelessly leaving the spiritual doors of their house open to danger and allowing strangers to enter who were not at all interested in the truth or given to following it. Their disregard for truth, passive oversight, and lack of desire for holiness and truth open the doors to the invasion of unclean spirits, spiritual varmints, angels of light and physical plagues.

The patterns of destruction are set. Rats begin to feed on the garbage left lying around. Lies and chaos begin to take over the house. The sins of the fathers were "visited onto their children to the third and fourth generation". (Ex. 20:5) When no one renounced the sins, the familiar spirits that inspired them were allowed to stay. (Familiars are ancient spirits that are familiar with the work that has/is being done in the bloodline to which they have been assigned. They come into each new generation by pretending to be old 'friends of the family').

These visitors are instrumental in bringing the sins and the consequences of sins of the fathers down onto the heads of their children. These familiar spirits became long term occupants long before the current generation arrived. Their negative presence is often undetected as they present themselves as butlers and maids, caretakers and false benefactors. The occupants of the house grow up with them, unaware of any reason for concern or suspicion.

At first those living in the house do not notice anything different or out of place. They are glad they don't have to do all the work to keep things in order or be diligent to do the tedious chores required to maintain a safe living environment. They get used to being taken care of and waited on; content to let someone else do the heavy lifting, content to procrastinate in making their dwellings clean and upright.

Eventually the fight for survival is replaced by a complacent dependency on the systems created to govern and care for them. The pursuit of pleasure and the escape from the harsh reality of the Snake Pit fill their days. They love to play games of pretense, live in fantasy worlds, and be entertained. They only want to relax and do fun things. Neglect and lost opportunities are not met with regret or alarm, if there is even any awareness of them.

An atmosphere of chaos and the clutter of unfinished business begin to fill the house because no one wanted to take out the garbage or deal with pending spiritual matters. Strife distracts those who live in the house and gives them justification for their own actions. Dysfunction slips in the side door and soon prevails in every relationship. Apathy and aggressive passivity entertain silence and shut down communication between them, with strife having the last word in every conversation. Injustice and iniquity break out in the hallways as abuse fills the bedrooms with secrets and shame.

The children are the most affected. They feel angry and unsafe. They become rebellious, anxious and confused. Life is overwhelming and they struggle, unable to learn and grow up rightly. They cannot concentrate. They become hyperactive and sullen. Thankfulness is forgotten. They feel afraid and unloved. They are torn between feeling unprotected by their caregivers or entitlement to have everything they want. Everyone yells at each other. Strife and contention rule, and evil works settle like dust into every corner.

Betrayal and bitterness consume relationships. Lawlessness prevails as the love of many grows cold. (Matt. 24:12) Some become unruly and calloused, while others became fearful and hide. Anxiety and loneliness fill the house with pain and obsessions. Not even perfection and performance can bring lasting order to the fear and anxiety that seeps in from the foundation and oozes in through the walls.

No one took responsibility for the garbage that filled the house as the iniquity grew. The dreadful state of deterioration becomes more pronounced with each passing generation. Those born into the mess never even know anything different, including what the house could be or had once been. The sins of the fathers are eating up the children's lives and no one seemed to care, or notice, or discern the need to do anything differently.

And, although some didn't like the situation, others just accepted it as normal or yelled at someone else to do something to fix it. Everyone tried to adjust. Some tried harder to do better, but things only grew worse. Not only did the house fall into general disrepair, but some very serious problems began to develop. The health of the dwellers began to deteriorate, yet they could not seem to discover the source of the problem or its solution. The water pipes that had been clogged with sin began to burst.

No one seemed to desire the fresh water of the revelation of God's Word. The prophecy of Isaiah had come to pass: "Therefore they could not believe, because Isaiah said again: 'He has blinded their eyes and hardened their heart, lest they should see with their eyes and understand with their heart, lest they should turn, so that I should heal them.'" (Jn. 12:39-40)

Time moved on. No one bothered to fix the pipes, although the water lines had burst many generations ago. The house that had originally been plumbed with the wonders of hot and cold running water now had no water at all. As things continued to deteriorate, those living in the house began to spend more of their time running out to the well for water. They worked every day to carry in water that once ran freely through the house.

The younger ones learned to drink from a pail with a tin dipper, never even realizing that the house had once been plumbed for running water. No one ever told them about the broken pipes, nor did anyone know how to fix them. They came to accept pumping water and carrying it inside, never suspecting the provision God had given them for "Living Water". Religion and sin had washed away the knowledge of God's provision for meeting their daily needs for strength and refreshing. They had grown accustomed to the idea of carrying water, and began to spend most of their lives working to earn a living just to survive.

Trusting God had been replaced by self-preservation and striving. Life had become a matter of works for those who live inside the house. They had learned to rely upon themselves, and had become so busy taking care of themselves that they did not realize His presence had left them.

And yet, for all their hard work, the inhabitants of the house remained thirsty and unsatisfied. The great house that had been built by the generations to bring safety and comfort to those within, no longer affords protection or peace. Sadly enough, no one even seemed to care or believe that things could be any better.

The sickness and disease that plagued their bodies became a common thing. Cracks in the foundation had left their relationships broken and without a firm understanding of love or truth. Holes in the roof allowed every wind of doctrine and promiscuity to blow in at the will and whim of the elements. Clutter and chaos filled the rooms with confusion and futility. Those who dwelt in the house had become increasingly more anxious and exhausted. They are overwhelmed with the tasks left to them and the limited resources for repairing things. Hostile words and angry curses filled the very air the occupants inhaled, and though none was free from its deadly poison, most were not aware of it.

The ancestors had given little thought to those who would follow. All seemed to be caught up in their own struggle, which had left them little time for concern or care for their descendants. Unfortunately, as with many things, those who followed after had little to say about how things had been handled and what things had been handed down to them.

As the foundations were set, so they stood. What had become one generation's lifestyle became the next generation's legacy. The only hope for the house was in the coming of the Carpenter, the return of the Master Builder. Through His labor of love, He would re-teach the inhabitants how to rebuild their houses and restore peace and purpose to their descendants. Only He would be able to reinstate truth and bring back the joy of salvation in knowing the love and goodness of God.

IT'S YOUR HOUSE NOW

Some houses are almost vacant. Their families have died out. Others are still filled with all kinds of aunts and uncles and cousins. The house may be full of laughter, or silence. Those living in the house may or may not be speaking with one another. They may not agree on who is responsible for what and who is to blame. They may not agree on who's in charge or who are permitted to visit as guests.

New family members may be cherished, or cast off. Some are discarded and sent away to fend for themselves while others are prized and paraded, full of their parents expectations. The older residents may be kind and nourish the souls of their children, or they may ignore their young in pursuit of their own comforts.

As we enter our house, we have no choice as to how or when we come into the family or which house will be ours. We learn to adapt and adjust to our living conditions as best we can. We may never feel safe, or we may do well in the house. We may feel welcome, or be victims of abuse.

The power to fashion the soft, malleable life of the innocent little child who lives unaware of his or her own vulnerability, is as astonishing as it is terrifying. When a child finds no one to trust, he/she subconsciously appoint themselves to be responsible, not only for their own safety, but also for the emotional and physical happiness of those around them. Children begin to parent their parents. Self-preservation and Selfishness become the driving forces behind their decisions. Fear and Control turn them inside out and thrust them into conflict with themselves, as well as with those around them.

Even as we learn to rely on ourselves for safety, we look to ourselves for guidance. 'It's up to me', and 'I can do it myself' become the motto, as the Devil's philosophy of survival rules our life. He uses pain and fear and the desire to be right as a way to intimidate us and manipulate us in his ever intensifying endeavor to 'catch us on the hooks of sin' and enslave us forever.

As he secures his grip on our lives, the Enemy rules with relentless precision in crafting the snares for our souls. The subtle seduction of our minds and hearts allows the Evil One to prevail in his agenda to divide the house. Lawlessness covers our lives with Shame, as Violence waits outside the gate, and Hopelessness and Horror prepare to pay the child a visit.

The Enemy is looking for an invitation to come in. Ignorance opens the door and rolls out the welcome mat. Love and human kindness no longer serve as the norm, but rather are seen as a call to Suspicion and Alienation. In order to protect ourselves from others, goodness and intimacy are exchanged for space and isolation. Loneliness claims the lost, while Sadness breaks the heart and Sorrow breaks the spirit, covering our emotions with a mask of Numbness and Indifference.

Some have worked hard trying to get everyone to pitch in and clean up the mess. They think that control and increased performance will bring peace and safety to the house. In an attempt to administer order, they become bitter and hurt, angry that some are not helping. Other family members begin to blame each other, hold grudges, and refuse to forgive one another.

Some are insecure. They have learned to work harder to gain the love and approval of family and friends. Others retreat. Some walk away. They disown their family, vowing not to trust anyone, committed to doing it on their own. The irony is that no one who leaves really ever escapes; the delusion only serves as a temporary delay of the fruit of the lie.

When a family works together within a context of biblical unity, health and life are restored. It is a wonderful thing. When they do not, broken relationships become one of the greatest sources of pain and anxiety known to the human heart. When a generational house is left in disarray, it makes the life of each consecutive generation more difficult and cumbersome. And if staying alive becomes the main occupation of the occupants, the hope of living beyond the urgency of the moment becomes dim and faded.

We are demoralized by the Enemy who works to destroy us in this greatest of all wars, using our own hands to do it. The lies we have believed and the actions we have taken as a response have created the prison of darkness we live in. The light dims just when we need it most. The invasion of the Kingdom of Darkness presses in on us from every side.

GENERATIONAL INIQUITY - HOT SPOTS FOR THE CURSE

Some of us try to make improvements to the house of our birth, while others simply accept things the way they are. Bound by tradition, doing things the way they have always been done seems to be the norm. Until the Plunderer, the Strong Man (Mt. 12:29, Lu. 11:21-22) who has come to divide our house is discovered, God's blessings will continue to be stolen, spilled, and lost.

Our lives will not be fixed with things or accomplishments! We will not experience any real or lasting changes in our lives until the foundations are restored. "If the foundations be destroyed, what can the righteous do?", David asked. (Ps. 11:3) Isaiah calls this generational dysfunction and breakdown the "desolations of many generations."(Is. 61:4)

These desolations are the open doors, the unconfessed sin, the family secrets and the garbage left, rotting in the smelly hallways. They breed neglect and atrocities. The unsolved crimes against love have been left unresolved. Standing agreements with blood-guilt and the betrayal of love have left us defenseless against the accusations of the Evil One. Idolatry claims its worshippers and demands the shedding of more innocent blood. Iniquity disrupts the flow of God's favor and destroys the blessings He meant for those who live in the house.

If we do not bother to address the issue of truth and lies, the 'generational junk' will continue to come crashing down, like an avalanche of evil, to swallow up the hope and life of our family. The debris of broken relationships brings more hurt and bitterness and confusion. Each passing generation is forced to bear, not only its own pain and desolation, but also that of the ones who have gone before them. This is the story of human desperation and the desecration of, not only our own souls, but also those of our precious children. So what can be done? Let us gather the courage to examine the lie and call for the restoration of truth in our lives, that healing may begin!!

2

IN SEARCH OF JUSTICE

*S*IMPLE JUSTICE

In its simplest definition, Justice is the resolution of injustice. Justice re-establishes equilibrium within the systems, and satisfies our desire to 'make things fair and right'. Justice, and the pursuit of it, are part of the 'universal desire for justice' which God has written into the heart of every one made in His image. And yet Jesus warns us against allowing our internal desire for justice, and striving for it, to overtake us - lest our search for justice becomes the undoing of it, and our own unwillingness to forgive sets us up in the unlawful place as a judge.

Jesus knew it was inevitable that "offenses" would come (Lu. 17:1) and that the opportunities to forgive each other would abound. Yet He did not command us to pursue fairness at the expense of forgiveness. Rather, even while He commanded us to forgive, He also warned us of the severe judgment that would come to those who denied justice and withheld the forgiveness due their fellow man.

Jesus instructed us to forgive those who 'trespass against us' rather than go after them. We are taught to trust Him and <u>wait</u> on

Him to make things right, whether He takes immediate action, or wisely reserves the right to delay His judgment. Forgiving others demonstrates our faith in the faithfulness and justice of the Righteous Judge to keep His Word and make things right.

Our trust rests in the fact that God will never compromise His own commitment to truth and justice to do wrong. He instructs us to 'release from our judgment' those who have wronged us - by turning the 'crimes' and injustices they have committed against us over to Him for judgment. He is asking us to let Him be the Judge, and trust Him to completely address and redress the wrongs and compensate us for all the losses we have suffered. (1 Pe. 2:21-23)

"Woe to those through whom [offenses] would come," Jesus cautioned (Matt 18:7). He assures us that the offenses do not go unnoticed, although the Enemy presses upon us and tempts us to take matters into our own hands and strike back. The Enemy has no shame in exerting his vindictive and vicious desire for the destruction of order and safety. By using revenge and accusation, he turns the victim into the next perpetrator, and the perpetrator into the next victim. In the spirit of insanity, a wrong is not righted by initiating another wrong to make the first wrong right.

The Enemy's hatred for humans and his perversion of justice has created a hostile environment that makes justice both impossible to find and difficult to defend. His web of lies has served to 'catch us up' in an incredible tangle of anger and bitterness. Confusion, and the perversion of justice have left no one safe from the fury of the Enemy's accusations. Even those who have lived out their innocence for only a brief moment in their mother's womb have not escaped the assault of Satan's insatiable rage and contempt for human life.

The Devil's crimes committed against us, however, often go undetected because he hides them behind the long list of charges he has made against us. We get so caught up in either trying to defend ourselves against his accusations, or justify ourselves in our sin, that we do not stop to consider what is really going on. We unwittingly fall prey to the feelings of Guilt, which the Accuser of the Brethren is using to put the blame on us for what he has done. We are deceived into believing it is our fault; or become bitter for being blamed for something we have not done.

Persuading and manipulating us to - consciously or unconsciously - take on the guilt and blame ourselves or others for what he has done, becomes one of the Enemy's most effective means of destroying us. Guilt and Condemnation are a great source of confusion and 'point of pain' for all who desire God, but still live under the thumb of the god of this world.

How can I prove my innocence when I myself agreed to participate in an act which I now find repulsive? How can I prove my innocence when his temptation to get me to accept the guilt is so embedded within my own mind that I cannot tell the difference between my thoughts and his?

Some suffer from the sins and injustices committed against them by those who were under the sway of the Evil One. They struggle all their lives with feeling guilty for being angry for things that happened to them, things which they did not want and could not stop, currently bound by consequences they do not deserve.

Others suffer from those injustices, believing that they are to blame and that the lies which have been spoken over them are true. They survive as victims and martyrs, needlessly tormented under the relentless accusation of the Accuser of the Brethren. Others live in shame for what they did, never finding a way to forgive themselves or be restored.

THE FIRST ACT OF INJUSTICE

For all of our human efforts to restore justice and fully satisfy the demands of the Law, many never feel fully justified or forgiven. There is always something more that must be done, could have been done, should have been done. Nothing ever seems good enough to satisfy the demands of the Evil One (Matt 18:7). When trying to keep the Law, some are left feeling lost and 'ripped off', while others feel unworthy of any justice at all.

Neither the attempts of social justice to remedy the tragedies of our lives, nor the strict adherence to the Law, have been able to restore peace or replace what has been stolen from us. From the very beginning, human efforts to attain justice have failed miserably. The first act of violence recorded in the Bible was the killing of Abel by his offended brother, Cain. The offense sprang from a perceived injustice.

Cain judged God for being partial and unfair in accepting his brother's sacrifice and not his own. Misunderstanding the rejection of his gift created a transgression between Cain and Abel. The offense set up a point of tension between the two brothers. Cain's anger was stirred up against Abel, which resulted in violence, bloodshed, and manslaughter.

Murder is intentional. At this point, neither Cain nor Abel would have been deliberate in their intention to kill the other, as no one as yet understood that the human body could be killed. And though ignorance brings no absolution or release from the consequence of the act, it proved the futility of our own attempts to 'fix things' by force.

How many times has this scenario been repeated in human relationships? The balance between fair and unfair gets upset. Expectations are not met. Control and anger set up a power struggle. Tension mounts. We become angry and take matters into our own hands; and, like Cain, we reject the counsel of the Lord and misunderstand His chastening. (Heb. 12)

We get mad and become offended. We either bury the hurt deep within our own heart and vow to get even later, which drives the fires of bitterness deeper into our souls; or we choose to live as victims. Bitterness smolders, sometimes for years, affecting our lives in countless ways which rob our health and steal our blessings. We feel we have been cheated; or we feel like we deserve the abuse and had it coming. We fail to keep the law of love. The Lord's command that we love one another and bear one another's burdens is completely lost in 'keeping track' of the other person's sins, and our desire to get even.

The multitude of opportunities given within the context of human relationships to mistreat (or be hurt); misrepresent (or be lied to); misperceive (or be deceived); misunderstand (or make assumptions); and be misjudged (or get offended) by someone are as many as they are endless. Love and forgiveness are not usually our first response to hurt and injustice, nor are they our first choice in resolving our differences.

The Enemy comes in and takes advantage of the opportunity to tear apart our relationships, create grudges, isolate individuals, and open the doors to strife and contention. That strife permeates society and builds a mountain of offense from one generation to the next. Not realizing the danger we are in, or the diabolical plot that is being set up against us, the Enemy takes full advantage of our human differences to stir up a perfect opportunity for his demonic intervention which often comes to us under the guise of 'helping' us 'get justice'.

Ongoing injustice and unresolved offenses destroy our sense of safety. Our willingness to love one another grows cold (Matt. 24:12). Our efforts to restore 'Justice' and the safety and sense of wellbeing outside of the context of God's truth only results in creating a greater opportunity for the Enemy to bring division and pain.

It is amazing to note that all of the human conflict over justice can be traced back to worship. Whom will you worship? Whose report will you believe? Cain and Abel's sacrifices were both made as an act of worship offered to God. Their pursuit of righteousness, one through works (Cain), and the other through the lamb's blood (Abel), became Satan's starting point for setting up a division between them and God - which gave way to a never ending stream of religious strife and tension in human relationships.

From that day to this, the Enemy has used the issues of worship and injustice to set us up in opposition to ourselves, to each other, and to God - even to the place where some would justify killing the Son of God or the followers of Jesus Christ "thinking they are offering God service" (Jn.16:2). Satan has used our desire to worship God to practice idolatry (the worship of false gods) and has cloaked his intentions to deceive us into looking like worship. His express purpose is to misled the people into following their own paths to righteousness. Deception, and misperceptions, and the whisperings of the Evil One, have seared and saturated our human conscience with reasoning, and programmed our souls with lies until only the scattered fragments of truth and love remain.

GOD PROVIDED THE REMEDY

God has provided a remedy for our sins in the death of His Son. When we come into agreement with and accept His plan of salvation, we are born again. We are now citizens of heaven, even though we may continue to live on earth for many more years. We now <u>have</u> forgiveness of sins. We are now made righteous and saved through the shed Blood of Jesus Christ.

Being saved, however, does not mean we will never sin again, or be tempted or fooled into choosing to believe a lie which leads to sin. Salvation does not make us immune to the trickery and deception of the Evil One. <u>Salvation is the starting point in making us eligible to address the issue of sin. Salvation grafts us into the Vine</u>. We are adopted into the family of God and made citizens of heaven.

With salvation comes the power to overcome sin's power to

destroy us, if we repent (change our minds) and confess the Enemy's lies as sin, and believe what God says. The question of our salvation is not contingent upon our being perfect or sinless. We did not get saved because we stopped sinning and were finally perfect; therefore we cannot lose our salvation by sinning if we continue allow the Jesus. Salvation and sanctification are two different things.

Salvation sets us free from the final judgment of eternal damnation which forever separates from God those who reject Jesus Christ and His work on the Cross. Christ's sacrifice procured not only our pardon and His forgiveness, but brings us into the place of life and purpose which is part of the dispensation of grace. Sanctification is the work of the Holy Spirit in us to deprogram us, to transform us, to teach us to love one another, and to make us more like Jesus.

The message of God's good will and intention toward us is to know His love for us. This is the message of Good News! This is the heart of God and the true Gospel of Jesus Christ given to the church. Our assignment is to preach the Gospel, heal the sick, cleanse the lepers, raise the dead, cast out demons, and love one another. Our job of bringing the Good News to those still lost will be finished at the culmination of the Church age when Jesus comes back.

The residual matters of justice and judgment from that point on are reserved for the Lord Himself, Who will conclude all the unfinished business of sin - including the rejection of the Gospel of Jesus Christ - at His Second coming with the Last Judgments. Justice will prevail, and mercy will stand to resolve the bitter battle between the truth and the lie, and establish His righteousness in the creation of a new heaven and a new earth.

For now, the New Covenant written in the shed blood of the Lamb of God fulfills all the requirements of the Law and brings forth the promise of the redemption of all things. It releases us from the curse of the Law. The remedy for sin has been given. The power of sin has been broken. Death has been defeated, and we are restored to life eternal!

Technically, the grip of the curse is broken, although we are still being persecuted for righteousness sake and indicted under the judgments of the Evil One. Although the work of Salvation is finished, Guilt will continue to lay condemnation and punishment for sin upon any who do not understand the full provision of their salvation. Residual feelings of guilt over remitted (forgiven) sin can open the door wide for us to judge God for 'not being fair'; when it is, in fact, we who do not understand that our request for forgiveness and freedom, as blood-bought sons and daughters of God, has already been granted.

Jesus said, "But if you had known what this means, 'I desire mercy and not sacrifice,' you would not have condemned the guiltless." (Matt. 12:7) Only through the revelation of the Holy Spirit, and the application of Christ's finished work to our situations and our souls, will our healing and the freedom He died to give us be fully manifested.

THE BATTLE BETWEEN HUMAN EFFORT AND THE BLOOD

The Scriptures identify the conflict between right behavior and righteousness, to be the same issue as that between Cain and Abel. The battle has always been between works and grace. Romans 9:30-33 explains the manifestation of the offense as a full-blown war between works of the law (good works); and the Law of Love, which is, faith in the finished work of Christ (grace).

"What shall we say then? That Gentiles, who did not pursue righteousness, have attained to righteousness, even the righteousness of faith; but Israel, pursuing the law of righteousness, has not attained to the law of righteousness. Why? Because they did not seek it by faith, but as it were, by the works of the law. For they stumble at that stumbling stone. As it is written: 'Behold, I lay in Zion a stumbling stone and rock of offense, and whoever believes on Him will not be put to shame.'" (Rom. 9:32-33)

In obedience, Abel offered the blood of the lamb, which provided the appropriate retribution for the death penalty that sin required of humans. Cain had hoped to appease death with a fruit basket filled with his own works. Given the fact that "the life of the flesh is in the blood" (Lev. 17.11), and that the only satisfactory solution for justice under the Law is "an eye for an eye, and blood for blood", God's only remedy for the death sentence we faced had to come through the shedding of blood.

Rather than permitting the Devil to take our own blood as payment for our sin - and until a sinless human could be found - God had instructed Cain and Abel to offer the blood of a lamb to stand in the gap to bring temporary atonement. Cain's offering of fruit and vegetables was no more a satisfactory retribution for death than giving a basket of bananas would be in making amends for deliberately taking the life of someone's child.

Cain's hard work, although sincere, was not sufficient to satisfy the demands of sin or pay its wages (death). The Law required the shedding of blood. Blood was necessary in making atonement for the sin (crime). Only blood could satisfy the demands of death and restore righteousness. The basket of fruit, therefore, had to be rejected. The decision was not made out of bias or favoritism. The brutal facts of the horror of sin were clear. In the Law of Reciprocity, innocent blood was shed, and innocent blood must be given.

The theological dispute between works and grace is one based on our own self effort versus faith in the promises of God. This debate has created a raging war that has called the grace and goodness of God into question since the very first acts of worship outside of Eden. God's desire to satisfy the requirements of death, by paying the price demanded by sin with the innocent blood of His Only Begotten Son put Him at risk of being misunderstood and rejected. He knew that - in paying the penalty demanded by sin Himself - the Judge would become the accused, and the accused would become the judge!

The first clash between Law and grace ended in the shedding of innocent blood in the meadow outside of Eden. That conflict created the bloodguilt that still covers every man, and has carried the seeds of conflict since that time to this. Bloodshed bound mankind with a cord of violence and murder that brought a curse upon all of us. (For a more in-depth discussion of God's requirement of the lamb's blood and not a basket of vegetables, listen to Episode 7 & 8 of "God on Trial – Opening Arguments" available at www.liferecovery.com).

Since then, the field of human experience has been filled with bloody wars fought in the name of God against the people of God; including the most bloody of them all, the battle fought on Golgotha's hill. Offense and Self-justification have provided both the impetus and excuse for countless crimes committed in the name of God, all justified as His will.

The most profound irony of justice in all of this is that the greatest perversion of justice, the greatest injustice of injustice, has been suffered by God Himself. Every day, even still, He must witness countless acts of violence committed against the innocent, done in His name. Every day He is accused of being responsible for the outcomes of the brutal and heartless choices made by others - all while Satan, the god of this world, claims his own innocence and provokes the ignorant to judge God for being unfit to rule and unfair.

The Evil One is not satisfied with the suffering and destruction of the masses. His disgust for the humans made in the image of God drives him to scrutinize the loyalty of his own followers. He fetters them with unreasonable demands and leads them to fight against each other in the name of their specialty-gods; all while the one true God's message of love and devotion is mocked and trampled into the ground as contemptible. Satan has no intentions of mercy or pity for the weak. He delights openly in their destruction.

"These things I have spoken to you," Jesus said, "that you should not be made to stumble." (Jn. 16:1) Jesus warned us that the chief place of stumbling among us would come out of demented service to God offered by those deceived into believing that it is (was) His will to "kill [others] and think that [they] offer God service." (Jn.16:2) The profound strength which faith demonstrated in the face of this grievous injustice arises out of the mouth of the Lamb Himself as He submitted to being baptized by one of His own creations, when He said, "Permit it to be so for now, for thus it is fitting for us to fulfill all righteousness." (Mt. 3:15) "Who, when He was reviled, did not revile in return; when He suffered, He did not threaten, but committed Himself to him who judges righteously;" (I Pet. 2:23) By faith we also stand and wait with confidence, for the final righteous judgments of the Lord God when all the wickedness will be sorted out and the righteous stand in the goodness of their Father forever.

THE CONSEQUENCES OF BLOODGUILT AND THE CURSE

God's warning to Cain gives us the first glimpse of the consequences for shedding innocent blood. "And He said, 'What have you done? The voice of your brother's blood cries out to Me from the ground. So now you are cursed from the earth, which has opened its mouth to receive your brother's blood from your hand, when you till the ground, it shall no longer yield its strength to you.' " (Gen. 4:9-11)

The very thing Cain had relied on for sustenance and survival, the very thing that gave meaning and purpose and justification to his life was the ground. His identity and self-reliance had come from his own hard work and his horticultural skills, in bringing forth the fruit from the ground. Food was necessary for life. Now it was cursed. The bloodguilt of his brother's innocent blood covered the ground, demanding to be heard.

God, in a swift act of justice to spare Cain's life - permitted the very thing that the Enemy had used to steal Cain's affection away from God, the work of his hands - to be cursed instead of Cain. Thus God averted, for the moment, the Devil's diabolical demands for retribution in the form of Cain dying for his own sins. The curse was God's 'stay of execution'. In his stead, the ground would be cursed. The fruit of his labors would no longer yield to him the blessing of food. The things that defined Cain's life were gone. His dream was lost. The place of his blessing had been cursed. Bloodguilt had turned his blessing into a curse and his gifting into a snare. His life had suddenly morphed into a nightmare. Futility and dread drove Cain out from his place. He was reduced to the status of a vagabond and a fugitive, haunted by the fear of being killed himself.

In a split second Cain's sin, his choice to let anger and offense rule over him, had opened the door to death and alienation. Peace and goodness left him. The Serpent's venom had found its way into his mind. Now the Devil had a reasonable argument to present to God in building his case against all humans. Now he could strip them of their lives and livelihoods legally. All he would have to do would be to get them to agree with him that they were guilty; and he could use the shedding of innocent blood to call for his demonic judgments against them any time he wanted to.

Cain's emotions broke under the weight of the perceived injustice, and he was overtaken in his soul. The spiritual chain of events that caused judgment to fall in the natural had been set in motion. The strength of the ground, which had been at his command, was taken from him. The source of his joy and livelihood was replaced by bitterness and exile. Because he had taken the matter into his own hands and judged the perceived injustice himself, his own life was judged and he was ruined.

Jesus knew that offenses would come. He knew that the Enemy would tempt us to take matters into our own hands and become angry when things did not seem to be fair. He knew how vulnerable we would be to 'getting even'. He knew how clever and quick our Enemy would be in seducing us into believing his logic and accepting his lie. That is why Jesus said, "Blessed is he who is not offended in or because of Me." (Mt. 11:6)

And because we are created in the image of God to love what He loves and hate what He hates, we are in even greater jeopardy of becoming angry at injustice and wanting to set the record of wrongs straight, by the very fact that God hates injustice too! When we judge, however, we step into the place of the Judge in determining what is right and fair. According to the unbendable law of 'an eye for an eye', we take on God's job 'of making things right'. God calls us to trust Him and rest in knowing that He is the Righteous Judge, that He will make things right. "Vengeance is Mine, I will repay, says the Lord." (Deut. 32:35)

Even though we know that, in a human court of law, justice can never be obtained by one who acts as both the Judge and the Plaintiff in the same case, we are continually tempted to act as both the judge and the petitioner in the very matters where we most stand in need of justice. If acting as the Judge on our own behalf carries no weight in a human court, how much less will our judgments be valid in the Court of Heaven? And how can there be any righteous settlement or justice in this twisted conflict of interests where we get judged for wanting justice? We fall headlong into the Devil's trap of judging us for judging one another! Satan's master plan is to create war and violence on the earth, and to embroil man in the treachery and indignation of that war by tempting them to right the wrongs in their own strength!

Pain and bloodshed are the Adversary's first round in taking the 'spoils'; his second round comes when he can entice us into taking matters of justice into our own hands. This yields to him yet another windfall in unresolved offenses and relational breakdowns and bitter root judgments. The Bible clearly tells us that "we do not wrestle against flesh and blood, but against principalities, against powers, against the rulers of the darkness of this age, against spiritual hosts of wickedness in the heavenly places." (Eph. 6:12)

What a brilliant and insidious twist the Enemy brings in plotting against the innocent by using their pursuit of the truth and their innate desire for justice to 'bait his trap'. What a clever and perverted rendition of justice the Devil has in condoning the use of violence to promote harmony. Whatever could be our hope of righteousness and vindication when Tyranny guards the gates of peace, and Guilt becomes the purveyor of justice?

SETTLING OUR DIFFERENCES

How presumptuous to think we can redefine God's righteousness according to our own, or reword His declarations according to our own selfish, short-sighted ambition. How ignorant and arrogant to think we have a right to define truth by our standards! There is no greater folly than to judge another man for the things we are guilty of ourselves (hypocrisy); or to believe our ideology or 'ism' (delusion) is a match for or can ever replace God's truth.

This pervasive deception in the re-defining of truth is, at its most basic level, what Jesus referred to when He said "If therefore the light that is in you is darkness, how great is that darkness!" (Mt. 6:23b) How hard and difficult it is to persuade a person to let go of the lie if he believes it is the truth, and especially if he believes it is God's truth!

God's Word says that "the soul that sins shall die." (Ez. 18:20) At the Fall, Adam and Eve's spiritual understanding was darkened. The agreement they made with sin stained the souls of all humanity. It opened the door for the Devil to download his 'body-of-death-operating-software' not only into their souls, but for all who were to come from them. This software allowed him to create within each of us a state of deception, which permits our human nature - the old man, which is our 'second nature' - to operate as our 'first nature'.

'The body of death' operates out of our souls: that place where our mind, will and emotions come together to interpret experiences, form thoughts, and make decisions. It processes the stimuli and initiates the plan of action, including specific thoughts and directives which are sent throughout the body to form a response.

Although we are not usually aware of the deeper workings of the soul, the gift of Salvation brings with it a 'quickening' of our spirit. "But God, who is rich in mercy, because of His great love with which He loved us, even when we were dead in trespasses, made us alive (quickened us) together with Christ, (by grace you have been saved)". (Eph. 2:4-5) This 'quickening' of our human spirit, and the ensuing process of sanctification and conversion, lights the candle of our "spirit man" (Pr. 20:27), which illuminates the ongoing work of the Holy Spirit in our lives. It qualifies us to leave the confines of living under the dictates of our human nature, with its corrupt belief system and demonic indoctrination; and return to living in our divine nature, which is our original first nature, the one which God gave to us when He created us in His image.

3

THE FOUNDATIONS OF JUSTICE

USTICE IS SIMPLE

Justice is simple. It is not mediation, arbitration, manipulation of the system, lobbying for a different outcome, or engaging in complicated legal battles. It is not wrangling for legislation that legalizes sin, or negotiating a court settlement that favors our own personal interests. It is not plea bargaining or bribing the judge. It is not pacifying offended parties nor settling out of court. It is not acquired by well-paid lawyers or high powered attorneys working for well-established special interest groups. It is not a luxury of the rich secured at the expense of the poor or innocent. It is not a complicated rendering of the record by legal architects looking for loopholes, nor rewriting the facts to justify one's own personal interpretation of the law or what is right.

Justice is the restoration of that which is right and fair. It restores truth to the place of honor according to the righteous judgments of God. Justice empowers righteousness. It strips wickedness of its terror, and exalts love and truth. It addresses the crime and rightfully calculates individual losses. It vindicates the righteous, restoring safety and goodness to the downtrodden and forsaken.

Justice is the administration of what is right and fair, assigning merit and reward, or punishment, according to God's righteousness. It is the literal expression of God's righteousness applied to every situation, including the past, present, and future, to bring all things back into order and alignment with His holy will and divine purpose.

On earth, Justice maintains fairness and safety in human conduct and activity, through a due process of law based upon the adoption and social interpretation of those laws as instituted by individual communities. In Heaven, Justice rests on the Biblical Code of Law and Order, which some have described as the Universal Code of Justice (see Paul Billheimer, *Destined for the Throne*).

The Universal Code of Justice is literally expressed in the moral plumb line of an "eye for eye, tooth for tooth, hand for hand, foot for foot, burn for burn, wound for wound, stripe for stripe." (Ex. 21:23-25) When the Universal Code of Justice is broken or misinterpreted by the corruption of man under the influence of sin, injustice and iniquity prevail.

Because of sin and offense, and because the instigator of all sin and offense is the Evil One, a 'counter remedy' to sin must be found - which not only takes into account the weighty matters of the violation of law and justice, but also the deliberate and malicious treachery of the Enemy as well. <u>The counter measure to sin is forgiveness and mercy, summed up and given to us in the gift of God's grace.</u>

Unfortunately, most of us hold on to the traditions of sin and guilt. We have been "cheated through philosophy and empty deceit, according to the traditions of men, according to the basic principles of the world, and not according to Christ." (Col. 2:8) We have been indoctrinated in the benefits of "self-imposed religion and false humility." (Col. 2:23)

Satan has enticed us. We have become thoroughly invested in the counterfeit remedies for guilt and sin by substituting the do-it-yourself traditions of men for the commandment of God, which is defined as loving our neighbor as ourselves. As Jesus demonstrated in His question about the legality of doing good on the Sabbath, declared by the Law to be the day of rest, religion and law were overriding love. (Matt. 12:9-13)

Without grace and forgiveness, offense, injustice, immorality, and unrestrained evil prevail. Safety and harmony among the creatures is disrupted or cut off altogether. The due processes of justice in the fair exchange of the things necessary in the care of life is lost, causing life to be dangerous, difficult, greedy, fearful, unfair, and painful.

ADAM'S TRAGIC FAILURE

Before we can understand the power of sin and its grip on the inhabitants of Eden - or comprehend its tragic effects on Adam and Eve - we must understand the context of the world in which they functioned. Before we can play any game, we must understand the rules of the game. These are war games. This war has continued on to this present day unabated - although, in the end, it will be fully resolved. The stakes are not a trophy, a medal or a famous name. The stakes are the souls and eternal destinies of men.

Paul Billheimer, in his book *Destined for the Throne*, describes well, not only the state of the affairs of earth, but also the rules used to determine a fair victory. "The entire universe is governed by law. Redemption from beginning to end is based upon a system of divine jurisprudence. It has a legal foundation. God's granting of authority and dominion over the earth to man was a *bona fide* gift. This authority and dominion became *legally* his". (Billheimer, p. 73)

Billheimer went on to say that God gave man the free will to administrate that authority as he best saw fit. If, so to speak, he 'fumbled the ball' and lost it, God could not lawfully step in and repossess it for him. Without a doubt, Omnipotence had the power to block Satan's conquest of Adam and his attempt to steal his inheritance. But this would have violated His own Word in setting up the moral principles of government, in giving man a free will. "If God had gone over man's head and had forcibly repossessed the lost title to the earth from Satan, that would have been done without due process of law." (Billheimer, p. 73)

THE GAME

Without 'due process of law', no victory is valid or title secure. After the Fall of man, God's position in the Garden of Eden became like that of the head coach whose team is playing in the Super Bowl for the world championship. His team has just lost the ball and is down by 20 points in the fourth quarter, with the other team in possession.

The coach could step into the game and onto the field to recover the ball himself; but if he did, he would have to forfeit the game because his participation in the game is illegal. He did not qualify to enter the game as a player. He is the coach. In that scenario, even if His team wins, they would be disqualified from taking home the trophy because the rules of the game have been broken. The points, the recovery, the win, would all have been gained unlawfully. In order to win the game, the coach, as well as the team, must 'play by the rules' or there is forfeiture. Whomever the coach sends in as a replacement must also be qualified to play, an authorized member of the team and in good standing with the sports league.

Likewise, in order to play, any substitute brought into the 'spiritual game of life' must be a bona fide member of the human race. He must be a human being. In order to compete in this game, he must also meet a second set of qualifications: he must be a free man, free from any other binding contracts or obligations. That includes any agreement made with sin, which would enslave him and put him under the authority of the god of this world. In that case, his life and his blood are not his to give.

If Jesus would have been born only as an ordinary man like all the rest of us, He would have been disqualified from playing in the game, because He would have already been bound under contract of sin and enslaved by Hell. Jesus would have been unable to compete. And yet, the dilemma is that he must be a human in order to compete! In retrospect, we again see that - according to the law of reciprocity - it was a human that sinned (Adam); and therefore, it had to be a human that died (Jesus Christ, the second Adam). Before Jesus Christ became the Incarnate Son of God, no such human existed!

Adam and Eve had yielded to the Serpent's lie and had become slaves of Satan. In that one fatal moment, "Adam lost all of his legal rights, not only to his personal life but also to his domain. His agreement with the lie gave way to the sin which separated Adam from God and gave Satan legal authority to rule over both him and his domain which was earth and its contents. If Satan's dominion was to be revoked, a way had to be found to redeem fallen man and recover his lost authority without violating the universal principles of justice." (Billheimer, pg. 73)

Jesus Christ was both the Son of Man and the Son of God. As the Son of Man, He was a *bona fide* member of the human race, and as such, qualified to participate in the playoff game. As the Son of God, He was sinless. He was not enslaved under Satan's author-ity, although He entered the game late in the fourth quarter. In His battle with Hell, He not only fully recovered the ball, He took possession of it. He carried it, through His death on the Cross, all the way back to the "end zone' of death and the grave - in order to score the winning touchdown in taking captivity captive! (I Pet. 3:18-22 & I Pet. 4:6)

Through the Cross and the Death of His Son, God made a legal move against Satan's demand for the death of His children. The

Enemy was not able to defeat nor disqualify Jesus Christ or His Father's solution. His strategy to pay the penalty for sin Himself was a brilliant legal move permitted within the rules of engagement.

The wages of sin is death. Sin required Death to satisfy its demands, according to the Law of Reciprocity. Nothing in the Law, written or implied, disqualified God Himself from paying the penalty for sin which His Justice demanded. The work of the Cross both began and finished the ongoing work of redemption and restoration, in rediscovering freedom and victory for 'whosoever' would call upon His name.

THE UNIVERSAL CODE OF JUSTICE

We are supernatural beings made up of body, soul and spirit. As such, we must draw our life from both the natural and the spiritual worlds. We are born into one, and destined to dwell forever in the other. Being ignorant or unaware of the specifics of the paradigm of spiritual warfare - as we live in the natural world - does not make it any less deadly, or cancel out its existence, or make it any less critical in determining the final outcome of our eternal destiny. Just as ignoring the natural laws of the physical world does not exempt us from the consequences of breaking them; disregarding the spiritual laws, including the war that is part of the spiritual world, will not protect us from becoming a casualty in the spiritual war that rages between God & Satan.

The universe was created to operate under a code of harmony and balance, which requires that each part be freely given what it needs to enjoy optimal life and functioning. The code of love and justice define the standards that provide each member with the right to the things it needs to sustain the goodness of its life. God's intention is that love and justice work together in unity to run the universe, including all the necessary exchanges carried on within it. Any violation of love is a violation of justice; and any violation of justice is a violation of the Law of Love. Thus, love and justice are bound together in inseparable unity. We call that Law the Universal Code of Justice.

The indescribable complexity of Creation, however - with its intricate ordering, and diversity of kinds, and its generous variety of organisms, all of which have different needs and dependencies - make Creation extremely vulnerable to the infiltration and intentions of the Evil One. Because its' marvelous but fragile systems must all function as an integrated whole, of systems within systems, the quality of that life must depend the harmony between love and justice. Those who refuse to embrace justice, or reject the Law of Love it promotes, violate the Law of Love. Withholding, defrauding, and cheating others out of the things they need to live and do well is the source of injustice. Injustice opens the door to vulnerability, deprivation, anger, hatred, dysfunction, loss of dignity, disease, danger, and death.

Justice preserves order and the continuance of the things needed for the survival of life and safety. Even in physics, justice can be seen in its demand of an equal and opposite reaction in response to every action taken. The interdependence and interlocking which links members of the natural world together offers us a tangible understanding of the vulnerability of each individual member and their dependence upon the other members for their mutual survival. By examining the multifaceted systems and intricate ordering of operations as manifested in the physical realm, we better understand how spiritual systems and hierarchies operate in the unseen world.

The mutually beneficial dynamics of justice which work through the Law of Love can be seen in something as ordinary as supply and demand, where the dignity for each part is integrated within a meaningful relationship with the whole. And even as creation itself testifies to the wisdom and power of God by its vast and deliberate design, all who realize the incomprehensible function of it must also acknowledge the necessity of God's justice in maintaining it.

God's matchless love for us requires that each one both freely give and be given what it needs to live well. Living within the standard of justice, which works by love, allows the order of the natural laws to function to protect and sustain the Universe and its ability to support human life. When the laws of love and justice are broken, so is creation. When the Law of the God Who is love, and the Creation He made, covenant to live justly and love one another, life is honored and goodness preserved.

God's justice and God's love are inseparable! Even as He gave us His Love, His Love for us causes us to give to one another the very thing we need ourselves. Love reflects the true nature of the Creator in doing that which is right. Even the most uncomely part, the most insignificant member of God's creation, is of measureless value to God - a priceless and necessary part in the bigger scheme of His Divine Plan.

Justice in our relationships with one another includes living in harmony with each other and walking in agreement with the truth. Truth causes us to do what is right and honorable. Justice is the demonstration of love in action. God's Word declares, "Righteousness and justice are the foundation of Your throne; mercy and truth go before Your face." (Ps. 89:14) God built the foundation of His throne with truth and love. He guards it with justice. His righteousness provides the standard and the atonement for His Creation to keep order and provide safety for all of His Creation.

Regardless of what we know or believe, God's correction and judgment in response to injustice are acts of love. Love and forgiveness are His 'measuring rod' and method for resetting the balances of justice and truth for the safety and dignity of both the individual and the world as a whole. God intends for every part to have respect and be needed.

Therefore, the enforcement of justice becomes the demonstration of God's love in the preservation of His Creation.

NO EXCUSES

Justice becomes the mandate for the fair exchange of all things necessary for the preservation and protection of life. God has not left us without understanding regarding His expectations. He calls us to live in good will toward one another. To embrace the revelation of God's love and justice as expressed in His creation of us, we must also embrace the depth of our inexcusable 'folly' in resisting that revelation.

The Scriptures are without error. The path is clearly marked, although some would excuse themselves. "Because, although they knew God, they did not glorify Him as God, nor were thankful, but became futile in their thoughts and their foolish hearts were darkened. Professing to be wise, they became fools and changed the glory of the incorruptible God into an image made like corruptible man – and birds and four-footed beasts and creeping things. Therefore God also gave them up to uncleanness, in the lusts of their hearts to dishonor their bodies among themselves, who exchanged the truth of God for the lie…" (Rom. 1:21-25)

In spite of His love, God has stepped aside to allow us to exercise the 'free will' which He gave us. He permitted those who had given themselves over to the unclean and unholy behavior of sin to be overtaken by their choice to embrace the lie. This explains why a 'good God' does not stop all the 'bad things' from happening in the world. God has both chosen to share His power and authority with us; and has given us the freedom to use it to reject Him. He does not force anyone to love Him any more than you would grab your fiancée around the neck and force her/him to 'love' you.

DOES GOD GET EVERYTHING HE WANTS?

Despite the truth that God's perfect will is always to bless His children, He must, for now, operate in His permissive will, in order to allow us to operate within our free will. He has given us the authority to manage His properties on earth. With that authority, we can spoil and exploit His creation if we so choose. Exploitation of others causes pain; it promotes a system of lawlessness and injustice, which makes it necessary for Justice to call Wickedness to give an account.

Love is the standard by which God judges wickedness. The justice of God, therefore, promotes the love of God and insures the safety of His creatures in their pursuit of life. When His justice is overthrown and truth is fallen in the streets, lawlessness prevails. Refusing the love of the truth opens up the door to being given over to a debased mind, which leads to "being filled with all unrighteousness, sexual immorality, wickedness, covetousness, maliciousness, full of envy, murder, strife, deceit, evil-mindedness; they are whisperers, backbiters, haters of God, violent, proud, boasters, inventors of evil things, disobedient to parents..." (Rom. 1:29-30)

Rebellion creates injustice, which creates perilous times, which blinds the eyes of those who practice lawlessness, "Knowing the righteous judgments of God, that those who practice such things are worthy of death, not only do the same but also approve of those who practice them." (Rom. 1:32) Injustice is a well-integrated strategy in the Devil's plan to destroy the world. For even though, "we do not wrestle against flesh and blood," (Eph. 6:12) and "the weapons of our warfare are not carnal", (2 Cor. 10:4) the Enemy seeks to pit human against human in a relentless attempt to provoke them to get even with each other. This is, ultimately, all about Satan's vendetta against God, knowing that God is forced to watch His own children being influenced by him to kill one another. The manifestation of this wickedness brings Satan his sweetest moments of revenge against God for interfering with his plans to rule (ruin) the world.

Lawlessness is the outcome of hatred and lovelessness. Human rebellion is the demonic manifestation of Satan's war against God's law of love. Lawlessness and lovelessness open the door to lies, separation, and destruction. Believing lies and refusing to abide in the truth creates a spiritual blindness which sets the stage for the increase of rejection abandonment, hardheartedness, murder, violence, rage, hatred and anarchy.

If we refuse the love of the truth, God Himself will send us a strong delusion that we will believe a lie. (II Thess. 2:10-11) God must permit what we choose; He tells us to choose life! If we refuse the love of the truth, we have chosen the lie (by default), even though many times we do not even realize it is a lie or that we have made an actual choice for or against anything. The very nature of the delusion and the deception is for us to think we are right when we are not! This delusion presents a real, yet hidden, danger and major obstacle to all who have refused the love of the truth and walk in rebellion and disobedience, in that they cannot see the error of their ways.

If it is no big thing for Satan himself to <u>appear</u> as an angel of light and his ministers to <u>appear</u> to be ministers of righteousness, (II Cor. 11:14-15) is it any big deal for deception to appear as truth? Jesus said, "If the light that is in you is darkness, how great is that darkness!" (Mt. 6:23) In other words, if the thing you believe to be true is not true, but operates as truth within you, how great and impenetrable is that darkness? If we do not perceive the light that is in us - and the fruit of that light is a perversion of truth - darkness will appear as light and truth. We will continue to believe that the lies we believe are true. The end of such delusions will be destruction.

4

INJUSTICE AND THE LAW

IT'S NOT FAIR

Inscribed in the very DNA of our original divine nature is the innate desire for justice, and the ability to recognize when something is not fair. The concept of fairness is intrinsic, both to God's nature and the nature of children He has created in His image. The inherent knowledge of justice is written in the heart of every infant, and expressed in the cry of every human.

Even before a child is three years old, they have usually already learned enough language so that they can articulate their reaction to injustice: 'It's not fair!' Even without the benefit of formal or informal education, the concept of justice and 'fair-ness' surfaces as an automatic response to life. We get hurt, and feel angry. We learn to 'hurt back' and stay angry. We get defensive and distrust the very ones put in our lives to protect us. Offenses become an ordinary and ongoing part of everyday life.

Christ assures us that "offenses must come" (Mt. 18:7). When something is 'not fair', the injustice sets up the offense. Similar to the concept of injustice, the idea of being offended does not need to be taught, nor is it easily surrendered. Therefore, given the fact that everybody is born knowing what is 'fair'; and given the fact that everybody is going to be treated unfairly and become offended, the occurrence of injustice is absolutely inevitable.

Injustice and unfairness are an inherent part of the godless system in which we live. This is exactly what we would expect, given the nature of the god of this world who runs it. Sin and offense establish the fact that injustice will continue to mix and mingle with our thoughts and desires to move us ever closer to taking action ourselves, even to the point of war if necessary. The Enemy uses this agitation and the hostility it generates to set up his 'divide and conquer' strategy among us. His agenda of injustice and offense is woven into the very fabric of the relationships we must form with each other in order to maintain order and interact in the business of life. And because God has already voted for truth and goodness, the Devil's desire to destroy everything cannot go forward except for one thing: he must have our consent (agreement) to do it!

On the other hand, justice is silent and impenetrable, like the sands of the seashore that hold the great tides of the oceans in place; it is the guardian of safety that holds the boundaries of one of earth's most daunting forces in place to insure the protection of life's tiniest and yet necessary interactions. Justice sets the standard for truth, freedom, and peace - even in the face of Hell's most intimidating forces.

Justice also holds us in a state of conscious and unconscious awareness of having to someday give an account of our actions to God. Justice secures our safety, and keeps hope alive that there is, indeed, a final vindication where truth and justice are fully restored. We will be vindicated through faith, as demonstrated by our reliance upon God. The wrath and fury of the Evil One, who has accused us of wrongdoing day and night, will ultimately be silenced.

When Justice is hindered, sin prevails. Hardness of heart is allowed to operate. Iniquity accumulates. Like plaque building up inside the arteries, iniquity clogs up the generational bloodlines to prevent the flow of God's love and blessings down through the family. As iniquity accumulates, the flow of love and goodness becomes more restricted. Lack creates opportunity for more resistance and injustice. Trust and hope are replaced by betrayal and greed.

The prophet Micah describes what happens in the world when faithful and fair men perish from the earth. "They all lie in wait for blood; every man hunts his brother with a net." They "do evil with both hands... the judge seeks a bribe, they scheme together... Do not trust in a friend; do not put your confidence in a companion; guard the doors of your mouth from her who lies in your bosom. For son dishonors father, daughter rises against her mother, and a man's enemies are the men of his own house." (Micah 7:2-6)

When Justice fails, love is lost. Control rises, and trust in God is for the foolhardy. The world trembles, trapped under the weight of the 'free-for-all' created by sin. Iniquity moves rampant and unchecked. The more we hide our sin and deny our need for justice, the more susceptible we become to sin and the pain of its curse. Just as Justice is given to protect love, true love promotes justice. When justice falls, society collapses. When the house of human habitation is divided, the spiritual foundation is unable to sustain the structure. The lives of those who dwell therein become a prey to both their own sin and the sins of those who preceded them. The sins of the fathers have left unfinished business that must be dealt with by the children, or it is sure to bring upon them a curse.

God's whole intention and desire in His dealings with His children has always been to bless and restore them, and bring them back "to the land which their fathers possessed." (Deut. 30:5) His desire was to prosper them as a nation and keep His promise to Abraham. Redemption and recovery of all that has been stolen from us has always been God's plan for all of His children. As a result of the sin of our first parents, however, we are still caught in the middle of Adam and Eve's decision to disobey God. Their sin forced God to go to war to save all of His children. God was compelled to switch from operating in His perfect will to His permissive will, which permits us to function in the exercise of our free will. By giving us a free will, He was compelled to operate in the context of His permissive will. In giving us the freedom to choose, God knew that He would eventually have no choice but to intervene in the affairs of men Himself.

Operating in our free will has opened us up to endless opportunities to be deceived. Every moment we live on this planet, we live in jeopardy of believing the lies Satan has 'dressed up' to look like solutions to the problems we are facing. These problems have been deliberately designed by the Evil One to take advantage of our vulnerabilities. He creates a physical lack or an emotional vacuum, and then presents a reasonable solution to the problem. If we yield to his suggestion, he is allowed to drag us into his stronghold, where we will be forced to pay for his 'help'. We are trapped: caught in the crossfire of an insidious, unseen, and ongoing war which began in the Garden and ends up at our kitchen table or in our back yard. It is the same war our parents and grandparents fought. Some overcame. Some died in captivity as prisoners of war. For us, the task remains.

What are the decisive factors for realizing a victorious outcome? Our lives and our legacies continue to be determined or undermined by the decisions, choices, and agreements we make. Many of our decisions were made by those who lived before us. The Enemy uses the permissions they gave him as a way to claim operating privileges in our lives. This allows him to make his claims just as boldly and frequently in the life of a believer (even though that one has been redeemed and is no longer technically under his dominion), as it does in the life of the unredeemed.

IT IS ALL UNDER THE BLOOD

This point confuses many believers who are taught to believe that they are free from the curses because the Devil is a defeated foe. If that is true, why do we continue to experience the effects of the curses, even after we are saved? If we are freed from the curse of sin and death through the Blood of Jesus Christ, then why does sin and death still operate in believers' lives? Why do things like disease and divorce, loss and misfortune, calamity and trouble, continue to happen just as frequently to the believer as they do to the unbeliever - if, in fact, 'it is all under the Blood' as most would believe?

It is true. We are new creatures. We have been "raised up together, and made to sit together in the heavenly places in Christ Jesus." (Eph. 2:6) This truth, however, does not keep us from having to go to the dentist or prevent us from getting caught in rush hour traffic, both examples of un-heavenly places. Neither does being saved keep us from experiencing the effects of sin or the consequences of the curse in our natural life down here. Why not?

Many believers struggle with believing in the idea of a real, active and involved Devil who is still in hot pursuit of his goal to 'be like God'. They are tempted to take a 'Pollyanna' approach to Christianity. We either deny what is really going on, proclaiming, 'it's all under the Blood'; or we live in fear that it is all up to me to make this world right and safe and just - or both. We say we believe in the power of the Blood; but we live in powerlessness and defeat.

There is no dispute that the promises of God are absolutely true. Our sin is forgiven and under the Blood. But it is also true that there is more to the story. Just as when the Devil tempted Jesus to jump down from the pinnacle of the Temple, (Mt 4:5) telling Him the angels would catch Him (which was written in Scripture), Jesus - knowing the right context and application of the verse -

called the Devil out on it and said, "You shall not tempt the LORD your God." (Mt. 4:7)

If 'it's all under the Blood', which implies that the battle is over, then why is every book of the New Testament filled with instruction on how to "fight the good fight and lay hold of eternal life"? (I Tim.6:12) If it is all 'under the Blood', why are we given spiritual authority over all the powers of the Enemy? (Lk.10:19; Mk.16:17; Mt. 10:1 & 8) If the Enemy is a defeated foe, and is under our feet, and the battle is already won, then why are we still fighting?

Ephesians 6:11-12 in the Amplified Bible tells us to "Put on God's whole armor (the armor of a heavily-armed soldier which God supplies), that you may be able successfully to stand up against (all) the strategies and the deceits of the devil. For we are not wrestling with flesh and blood (contending only with physical opponents), but against the despotisms, against the powers, against (the master spirits who are) the world rulers of this present darkness, against the spirit forces of wickedness in the heavenly (supernatural) sphere."

If the victory is complete, why does Ephesians 3:9-10 commission the church to "make all see what is the fellowship of the mystery, which from the beginning of the ages has been hidden in God who created all things through Jesus Christ; to the intent that now the manifold wisdom of God might be made known by the church to the principalities and powers in the heavenly places"?

The confusion lies in the fact that, even though our sins and transgressions are under the Blood, the power of that forgiveness - and exemption from the power of the curses brought on by sin - resides in the appropriation of His Blood to our everyday lives by the Holy Spirit. The finished work of Calvary is completed as it is being applied through faith to our everyday issues, by submitting to God and resisting the devil. (Ja. 4:7)

FAITH AND THE RESISTANCE

Our faith is demonstrated through our obedience. That obedience is demonstrated in doing what God has told us to do, no matter how strong and devious the resistance the Enemy exerts in our lives and relationships. Clearly, the Accuser will continue to accuse us, in spite of the fact that we are no longer his.

As believers, we are called to act in faith, by appropriating the power of the Blood and the finished work of the Cross to our current situation! Through our faith we are enforcing what it means when we say that it is all under the Blood. The gift of freedom from sin and its' consequences, given in salvation, will be of no more benefit to us than someone who would make a deposit of a million dollars in our bank account, unless we used it by making a withdrawal from that account. The Blood of the Lamb of God has already paid for our release and our justification.

The Blood of Christ cancels out any liens Satan has on our souls including the legitimacy and legality of the curses. He wants us to be confident in His finished work, which legally has released us from the control of His Enemy. Jesus wants us to know that we can know that we are no longer rightfully held under the curse of sin, nor do we have to suffer death as the slaves of Satan.

For the most part, modern Christianity has misunderstood the nature of Christ's finished work on the Cross. Because we have failed to comprehend and acknowledge the spiritual battle that continues to rage against us, including the Devil's real and ongoing attempts to snatch our souls, the effectiveness of the Kingdom of God on earth has been compromised. This makes it an even more essential and fitting work for the Believer to ascribe the power of the Blood as the evidence of our freedom!

Jesus Christ gave us power and authority over "all the power of the enemy". (Lk. 10:19) If we fail to use that power and authority because we think there is no need to so engage the Enemy, we have already been deceived and undermined. We cannot win the victory in a battle we do not believe exists, or do not feel a need to fight. And, although the battle is the Lord's, and it has already been won, He has invited His Church to join Him in enforcing that victory.

The church cannot fully enter into the depths of the righteousness and riches of Christ without a fight - which is to declare the manifold wisdom of God to the hostile forces, the principalities and powers, and nests of evil lodged in the heavenly places!! Under the direction of the Holy Spirit, through faith in the power of the Blood, we stand; and having done all, we stand. Our faith in the promises of God becomes the testimony of Christ's power to make known to the Enemy the eternal purposes which God accomplished in Jesus Christ (Eph. 3:9-10). Our stand is essential in the realization of winning this battle that has already been won.

Satan's relentless accusations and false claims against us do not just automatically go away once we are saved. He will actually increase his accusation and assault, and even more so if we do not deal with him. We are told to "Submit to God. Resist the Devil, and he will flee from you." (Ja.4:7) There is a divine reason for this. If we let the Evil One usurp our authority without challenge or resistance, he will continue to ravage both our lives and the world we live in. His oppression and thievery strives to hold us in the grip of the terrible (Is.49:24-25). Being held hostage, chained by doubt, uncertain about the love of God, and stripped of our confidence in His goodness, offers neither the world nor the Devil a convincing testimony of our deliverance, or evidence of our liberation or the power of God to keep us.

Our testimony in this dispute, this war, is essential to settle the issue of dominance. Jesus said, "You shall be witnesses to Me..." (Acts 1:8) If Satan can silence the testimony of the witnesses through intimidation, or blackmail, or bribery; or kidnap them so that they cannot show up in court to testify; if he can rig the jury with godless men; or bring unsubstantiated objections before the bench, he thinks he can still win a verdict of not guilty for himself!

The spiritual conflict has left us feeling confused about why God, in His sovereignty, would continue to 'let' such bad things happen to us. The Enemy uses this Confusion to raise huge questions about the goodness of God, and what He expects from us. We are left feeling angry, bitter, and weary, ripped off and abandoned by a Father we had been told would never leave us or forsake us. We are mad at God for not helping us. We have fallen for the 'smoke and mirror' tricks of the Deceiver and forgotten that "the just shall live by faith, not sight" (Rom. 1:17, Hab. 2:4)) or feelings!

As long as the invisible hosts of wickedness continue to raid and invade our lives and legacies, they will attempt to shift the blame for these ruthless attacks against us onto God. The forces of evil that work to shift the focus back onto God often gain our acceptance and agreement by concealing themselves as our own thoughts and feelings.

Temptations to feel bitter against God - and feeling guilty for thinking those thoughts and feeling those feelings - holds us in a double-minded position of indecision. Embracing those thoughts and feelings as our own is a ploy of Satan to keep us from discerning the real spirit behind what is going on in the spirit world, lest we should rise up to resist it (II Tim. 2:24-26). We must take a stand by using the Word of God and taking back ground for the truth.

Another way the Devil thwarts our resistance is by challenging our very right to be here. By questioning us on our right to exist, he is tearing away at the very fabric of our identity and our authority. We must be secure in knowing who we are before we can begin to resist the Devil. Knowing that we know that we are not our own idea, and that it is God Who gave us the right to be here and that we are made to be humans through the very act of

His creation of us, is our justification for having the right to be here and exist.

He did not have to create us. There was no compulsion that forced Him to make us. We are completely His idea! We are justified and altogether genuine, in that it was His will and His desire for us that brought us forth in the first place. We have been created and called forth by God! Being created by God offers us the ultimate, authentic, and indisputable validation that qualifies us to participate in the gift of life which He chose to give us. "You did not choose Me, but I chose you..." (Jn. 15:16) is true on so many levels. We have been authorized and qualified to conduct the business of heaven in the affairs of earth.

We do not need to be ashamed of our existence, nor feel the need to justify our existence, or prove that we have a right to be here. Neither does the justification of our existence need to be the focal point of our activities here. We do not need to apologize for our birth, the time of our arrival, the place where we were born, our gender, or the delight or dismay we may have brought to others. We are not responsible for something over which we had no control, or how someone else feels about us and our being here. These things were determined by God, Who works all things together for our good. These things are God's responsibility - though the Enemy uses them to create distractions and debates within us concerning our worthiness.

OFFENSE AND INJUSTICE

For restoration to the place of living in our 'new nature', the crimes and injustices committed in the past must be addressed. Both sins committed by us, and against us - including those we have committed against one another, when we were "yet dead in sins and trespasses" (Eph.2:1) - can now be brought to justice. Under the guidance of the Holy Spirit, Who directs our human spirit, we can deal with these sins and their negative effects in a godly manner.

Jesus clearly addresses the subject throughout Matthew 18 where He instructs us on how to handle offenses, which are the outcome of believing lies and taking matters of justice into our own hands. "Moreover if your brother sins against you, go and tell him his fault between you and him alone. If he hears you, you have gained your brother. But if he will not hear you, take with you one or two more...." (Mt.18:15)

We are admonished to embrace reconciliation and the restoration of peace between ourselves and the other party. Why? Because bitterness, injustice, unresolved conflicts, and unforgiveness are the 'battering rams' which Hell uses to break down the unity and strength of the Kingdom of God. Forgiveness is the key to both justice and unity. Unity is the key to strength and safety. We are directly admonished to "keep the unity of the Spirit in the bond of peace". (Eph. 4:3)

Forgiveness regains the opportunity for divine justice to be granted - because we have let go of the control of the only thing we had left, the right to be mad and stay mad until things were made right. When we turn our 'right to judge' the criminal and the crime back over to the Righteous Judge, we feel like we are allowing ourselves to be in a vulnerable position, fearful of being hurt or used again. It takes courage, and trust in the faithfulness of God to 'make things right', that He will indeed restore justice and lift the burden of fear in being taken advantage of again. Only when we forgive can we be free from condemnation ourselves. Forgiving the offender protects us from the demonic accusations and ensuing judgments the Enemy would like to put on us for taking the sacred matter of justice into our own hands.

In believing that "God is a just Judge" (Ps.7:11) we demonstrate our faith in His Justice. We live our personal life in the peace and confidence of knowing He will make all things right. We avoid

becoming a casualty of bitterness, which is the spiritual and physical killer of life, health and goodness. Forgiving, and accepting
forgiveness, promotes the unity of the Spirit and the bond of
peace which knits the members of Christ's Body together as a
force against evil and injustice in this present wicked world. Love
and forgiveness are the hallmarks of the Kingdom of God on
Earth. "By this all will know that you are My disciples, if you
have love for one another." (Jn.13:35)

THE LAW CANNOT JUSTIFY US

It is evident, according to Galatians 3:10, that "no one is justified
by the Law in the sight of God", for "the just shall live by faith."
In this passage, we see that justice becomes divinely tied to faith.
The simple definition of faith is to believe that God will do what
He has promised to do, including restoration of all things to their
proper order and function. This means that justice will be re-
established in the lives of those who live by faith and allow Him
to be Judge on their behalf.

Faith in God's promises - not the Law - becomes the foundation of
our relationship with our Father, and the grounds for recovering
the losses we have incurred while living here on earth. Faith is
being sure of what we hope for and certain of what we do not yet
see (Heb.11:1). Faith, and the certainty of the accomplishment of
those things hoped for, are completed simply by abiding in Him.
Just as the branch abiding in the vine is sustained by the life of the
vine, and brings forth its fruit through that abiding relationship;
abiding in Christ brings forth the fruit of the Spirit - righteousness, peace, and joy.

The fruit of our faith is the works that come as a result of our relationship with Him. Contrary to popular teaching, these works are
not good deeds done to prove ourselves worthy of heaven, but are
an expression of our love for the Father and evidence of our faith

in Him. The good works and words are the <u>fruit</u> of our abiding in Him.

PAID IN FULL

Christ's death on the Cross satisfied the requirements demanded by Justice and the Law that "the soul that sins shall die". He willingly paid the death penalty for our sin, and gave His own life as a substitute for ours. By allowing His blood to be shed to atone for our sins, the sentence of death could no longer be legally applied to those who accepted the substitutionary death of Jesus Christ as their own. Punishment could no longer be inflicted, nor payment extracted from the penitent - unless the penitent could be manipulated and tricked into surrendering his blood-bought right to freedom and pardon.

Jesus settled all of Hell's accounts. Our debt was 'paid in full', as indicated by His own words: "It is Finished." Jesus took our transgressions, trespasses, and residue of guilt - as calculated and accumulated against us under the Law, "having abolished in His flesh the enmity, that is, the law of commandments... (Eph.2:15) - and paid the debt of our sins Himself. Faith in the finished work of Christ allows us to embrace that Atonement as just recompense for our sins, and sets us free from the curse that still rests upon 'whosoever will not' accept the free gift of Salvation.

Those deceived into thinking they still have to pay for their own sins are inclined to add works and law-keeping to the finished work of Christ. They have insulted the Giver of grace and complicated the issue of God's pardon and forgiveness. They are still in jeopardy of being pulled back into slavery to the Law and Satan's tyranny - through the curse of the Law and the requirements it makes on those who subscribe to it as the means for justification.

For those who mix Law with Grace, the consequences are just as bad. Still believing they must now do both, the believer is caught in the diabolical net of failure set by Guilt and Accusation. Failure to keep the Law in all of its requirements allows the Enemy to continue to inflict the consequences of sin and judgment upon them. He is technically justified in doing this, because they have accepted the accusation of Guilt by making an agreement with the lie. This agreement (often made by implied agreement, one of the ways the Devil deceives us into making an agreement) allows the Enemy to bring curses upon his enslaved subjects for their infractions against the Law.

He justifies his actions by using the Scriptures (as he often does). "For as many as are of the works of the law are under the curse; for it is written, 'Cursed is everyone who does not continue in all things which are written in the book of the law, to do them.'" (Gal. 3:10) The Enemy uses our agreement with Guilt and our Rejection of the ransom Jesus Christ paid for us to 'lawfully' bring those consequences and curses upon us as a means by which to enslave us. He is then able to detain us as his subjects until we are able to pay our debt in full.

Unfortunately, for those who want to 'do it themselves', there is no other legitimate payment plan for sin, no other means or Mediator between God and men other than the one made and given by God Himself: "For there is one God, and one Mediator between God and men, the man Christ Jesus." (1 Tim. 2:5) Though the Enemy would mock those eager for freedom by inspiring them to 'try harder' to get out from under their load of sin - their debt of sin -'by being perfect', there is no lasting remedy for sin found in good works or perfection. In fact, practicing good works apart from the shed blood of Christ's Atonement only supplies more evidence for the justification of the curse, which is tied to one's failure to keep the Law. Galatians 3:11 warns us, "...no man is justified by the Law in the sight of God...for, the just shall live by faith."

The divine promise given in Galatians 3:13, however, gives us hope and a new promise: "Christ has redeemed us from the curse of the law, having become a curse for us...." He took the beating and embraced the shame, suffering the death which His Own Justice demanded to 'clear the record' and, by Himself, fulfill the righteous requirements of the Law. The death of Jesus - the Lamb of God Who takes away the sins of the world - satisfied God's justice and allowed Him to reinstate His mercy, so that peace and the fellowship of good-will between Him and us might flourish yet again. That peace reconciles us to God so that we no longer live as His estranged sons and daughters. The power of sin to separate us is forever broken.

God never intended to abandon us or leave us without a remedy for the curse. That is why Jesus Christ became a curse for us. His body absorbed all the ill effects of sin and pain; and ultimately, the death intended for us individually. Because of His sacrifice, we are free. Released from the prison within, we can now live in full fellowship with Him. Our relationship with God, ourselves, and others, is one of peace and joy and freedom, living the abundant life Christ died to give us.

THE LAW – A FORCE TO BE RECKONED WITH

God knew it was not possible for us - with our limited perspective and our finite understanding - to live by the black and white letter of the Law. "All have sinned" and fallen short of even the most elementary and basic requirements of law and justice. (Rom. 3:23) There is none righteous in himself. We are all in need of redemption. No one who chose to live outside of the Atonement was exempt from the curse of the Law. Satan had the plans for our eternal destruction fully laid out; we had all been found guilty under the Law, and no one was qualified to save himself.

Under the Law, the curse was a force to be reckoned with. The Law could not save us (Gal. 5:4) nor keep us from sinning (Rom. 8:3-4). Sin and iniquity had cut a canyon-sized gorge between us and God that provided a readymade riverbed for carrying the consequences of generational sins down through every human bloodline. Unforgiveness and bitterness held the gates open as the surge of death and destruction flooded through the city souls of those living in the path, and along the banks of the angry river of sin.

The Accuser of the Brethren stood ready to fish for the souls of men being swept down the river of life. He set his hooks deep into our DNA, and stretched his nets with confidence over the birth of each successive generation. Tampering with our lives and snatching the souls of men was as easy as shooting fish in a barrel. The ongoing curses, the consequences of sins that had accumulated as the iniquities moved like sludge down through each successive generation, created the Snake Pit into which their children would be born. The Law Breaker used the unconfessed sins and unfinished business of crimes committed by and against the previous generations as a way to justify the transfer of the sins of the fathers onto the children. Their agreements with Unforgiveness and Guilt activated the curses and made a way for judgment to press hard against the doors of each new arrival born into their respective bloodlines.

The debris from the destruction of those unconfessed sins and ancient agreements allowed Satan to 'hack into' our Personal Identity Information Code. The information coded into our genes was being turned into a cesspool of generational junk and misinformation. The marks of iniquity and trauma had been etched onto our DNA, leaving it damaged and vulnerable to pain and weakness. Sin had corrupted us, bankrupting us both physically and spiritually. Through the curse of sin and the Snake Pit, Satan was able to tamper with what God had created - which was perfect and good and divine - to psychologically recondition us and obscure the truth about our divine nature, making us more susceptible to his lies.

As a result, the gifts and relationships given to us by God - which were meant to be a blessing - have been twisted to become one of the greatest sources of pain and temptation for us. Division and isolation tear families apart and shred the fabric of human interactions, leaving us unprotected and afraid. Our relationships are at the mercy of a brutal, merciless Hater. The very thing God intended for comfort was twisted to become the source of our greatest pain. Shame and Rejection replaced love and acceptance, and we became more alone and afraid than ever.

The Enemy enforces his interpretation of justice on us by exacting from us the full measure of law's most minute demands. He then insures our failure to keep the Law by tempting us to choose his solutions to the 'problem' he set up. Choosing the Enemy's solutions brings us into an agreement with the lie, and ultimately brings forth death. (Ja. 1:14-15) Satan uses the very Law he breaks himself to declare himself innocent and pronounce judgment upon us!

We are declared to be hypocrites, guilty and deserving of punishment. He either gets us to agree that we broke the Law and are guilty so he can pronounce judgment on us; or he tempts us to blame and judge someone else for doing something wrong so he can catch us on the technicality of judging them. "Judge not, lest you be judged" (Matt. 7:1) leaves us wide open to being judged ourselves.

Only God's grace can reopen our access to God's strength and the blessing which sin has denied us. The confusion comes in attributing the judgment of our sin to God. "God did not send His Son into the world to condemn the world but that the world through Him might be saved. He who believes in Him is not condemned; but he who does not believe is condemned already, because he has not believed in the name of the only begotten Son of God." (Jn. 3:17-18)

Jesus did not come to judge or condemn us, although it is to the Devil's great advantage to alienate us from the grace and goodness of our Heavenly Father by convincing us that the consequences we are suffering are a punishment from God for breaking

His Law. Because we automatically associate the Law with God, it stands to reason that breaking the Law makes God mad. We are convinced that our present difficulties are the result of God's anger with us for disobeying His Law.

Though His admonitions to keep the Law were sobering and seemed harsh, His warnings are for a different purpose than we might at first suspect. God knows that Satan's true intentions are to set a snare for us, that he might go to God and demand our destruction. He knows that this will make God look bad and make His love for us appear to be biased and 'conditional'. Not realizing that God's admonitions are for our good to protect us from the Devil's plan creates separation and confusion. We feel guilty and alienated from God, and turn our efforts back to the task of making God happy with us again. This further promotes the Devil's religious advocacy of good works which results in corrupting our concept of both the Gospel of Jesus Christ and the goodness of God.

The truth is that the Enemy has used our own agreement with him, i.e., that we have sinned, to persuade us that we deserve to be punished. This is often a subconscious agreement that, nonetheless gives him permission to "steal, kill, and destroy" us legally. He must, however, have our agreement with Guilt, which agrees that 'it is my fault', before the Enemy can inflict and afflict us with his demonic judgments. He implicates God as the One responsible for our 'trials', calling God's intentions and goodness into question at the same time he gets us to accept the placement of the blame and guilt upon ourselves. That way, He gets to punish us and make God look mean and angry all at the same time!

He plants questions in our minds such as, 'If God is so good, then why did He let those bad things happen?', etc. The Enemy sets up arguments in our minds that lead us to the conclusion that God is the One who cannot be trusted and His love for us is conditional. We fail to "cast down the argument" or "take captive every thought" (II Cor. 10:4-6) - so we draw a wrong conclusion. Jesus said the truth sets us free. (Jn.8:32) The lie tightens its grip around our life and freedom to kill us, as our relationship with God is once again undermined by the very Law God originally gave to protect His people.

"Behold, I lay in Zion a stumbling stone and rock of offense, and whoever believes on Him will not be put to shame." (I Pet. 2:8) Part of our faith in God is not only to believe He is good, but that He will right the wrongs and address the injustices in our lives. Part of our test is to believe that what God said is true; that He will do what He said; and that He can be trusted, no matter what it feels or looks like.

Our faith in God is lived out whenever we reject the temptation to believe a lie, including the lie to be offended at God. We commit back to Him the revelation of the truth and the restoration of justice. We ask for forgiveness for believing the lie, for judging God, ourselves, or others. We choose to forgive those who sinned against us, and turn the injustices, violent acts, assaults, and offenses committed against us, back over to the Righteous Judge of all the earth, Who we know will vindicate us.

Faith which works through love (Gal. 5:6) is the fulfillment of the Law. The Law does not work contrary to the Holy Spirit. The problem is that the Enemy gets us to misuse the Law to fulfill our own righteousness. There is nothing wrong with the proper use of the mirror to show us our spots; it is when we attempt to use the mirror to wash off the spots that the mirror fails us. So it is with the Law of God.

Just as the "letter kills, the Spirit gives life" (2 Cor. 3:6), Law and order flow naturally from the gracious operation of the Law of love. Love not only fulfills the Law; it supersedes it. Love turns the issues of injustice over to God. It removes the complications of getting justice, by making it a simple matter of trusting in the goodness of God to do that which is right and needful to make

things fair. The Law requires that we walk within the legal parameters of certain preordained boundaries and religious
observances.

Love rejects the boundaries that fear and Law would place around
it. Even as it risks being rejected and destroyed, love lives on
unafraid, willing to become the expression of goodness to others
at its own expense - eg., the Good Samaritan (Lk. 10:25). Love
builds no rules around itself. Our love and forgiveness for others
is nothing the Law could demand of us, because the Law cannot
make us love one another. It could only keep us civil and
command us not to murder or defraud one another. Our love for
one another is the continuation of what Jesus began to do on the
Cross. It is the Law of Love written, not on stone tablets, but upon
our hearts.

5

STUCK IN DEMONIC JUDGMENTS

*M*AKING GOD THE BAD GUY

In taking a closer look at the connection between sin, and the generational patterns of iniquity - we can see, from the loss of blessing and the accumulation of curses - that the Enemy has robbed many of us of God's intended benefits. This war between God and Satan for the souls of men has put God in a very difficult and dubious position as both the Judge and the judged.

The Devil's strategy has always been to make God look like the bad-guy. To that end, the Enemy has worked to discredit, disconnect, and destroy every relationship God would desire to have with His Creation. In Satan's typical bait- and-switch, truth-twisting approach, he uses the very Law that God had given His children - so as to protect and identify them as His own - as a way to separate them from Him.

The Law that God meant for good has become - in the hands of His Enemy - an instrument of torment with which to inflict fear, separation, confusion, and wrath upon the deceived and unsuspecting. The Bible says, "…the law brings about wrath; for where there is no law there is no transgression." (Rom. 4:15) Conversely, where there IS a law, there IS transgression. Satan needs the Law as a means by which to accuse us of transgression; call forth his judgment against us as sinners; and petition for the right to bring down his demonic judgments upon us, via the curse.

Satan uses the very Law God has given us - whose intention is for maintaining justice and peace - as a means with which to charge us with transgression as 'law breakers'. Sin and transgression could not be defined without the Law. When we sin, the Enemy pronounces us 'guilty' and deserving of punishment. The sin we commit allows him to press charges against us. Our agreement with the lie Guilt tells us allows the Enemy to justify calling for his demonic judgments as punishment in our lives. Since we have (in error) come to believe that these judgments are divine punishments - and thus part of the sanctification process - we accept both the judgment and the consequence of that judgment as something we deserve. We agree that we 'have it coming'.

This allows the Enemy to perpetuate a lie and confusion about the goodness of God. It opens the door to needless pain through generational curses; and causes us to suffer under the weight of regret in the anticipation of God's wrath. It brings discouragement and fear of divine disapproval and disappointment.

Satan also uses the Law of God as the 'centerpiece' to his false, counterfeit gospel, in order to scramble the message of the one true Gospel. Christ came, preaching love, forgiveness, and the grace of God - as given to us through the Gospel of Jesus Christ. Through the Law and adherence to it, the Enemy has shifted the core concept and foundational principal of the gospel - from grace and atonement for our sins through the death of Jesus Christ - to having to make atonement for our own sins, through a system of merit and earning wages through good works.

The vital and unalterable truth is that the Gospel is not to about our sin or how to get rid of it. It is all about what we do with the

Son of God, Who delivered us from sin. The simple vowel difference in the two words, 'sin' and 'son', illustrates well how closely Satan cuts his counterfeits to match the real. We see, in this case, that the Gospel of Jesus Christ is being subverted by the Gospel of Good Works for the eradication of one's own sin.

Satan offers us any one of a thousand rigorous religious rituals with which to assuage our guilt. Using any one of those recommendations, however, will bind us to the spiritual authority that issued those declarations. Coming into agreement with the Devil's remedies for sin gives him power and control over us. To use any other means than the one provided by Jesus Christ to mediate our eternal destiny is a blasphemous rejection of the Lord Who died in our place. In so doing, we have taken the matters of righteousness into our own hands and have fallen short of the grace of God, swapping it for a counterfeit gospel.

When we surrender ourselves to the dictates and condemnation of someone (who we consider more qualified to determine our relationship with God than we ourselves), we get tangled up in spiritual abuse. Religious 'gurus' manipulate our free will. We become confused, anxious, and overburdened by pursuing a salvation based on works - and the performance of complicated rituals and religious rigors - as opposed to the simple Gospel of Jesus Christ, the power of His Blood, and the forgiveness of God.

The fruit of the complicated gospels are failure, stress, and striving. Their fruit indicates that these efforts are not from God; therefore, they do not come from the Holy Spirit. Nor do these counterfeit paths bring us to peace with God or reassurance of His love. Because we do not understand the power that original sin had in cutting us off from God; or what Justice demanded as the remedy for sin; we do not recognize that the only and absolute solution for sin is in the Blood of Christ. It is the only effective cure for sin and death.

We are easily persuaded by the religious arguments of Hell that we must deal with our sin and overcome our sinful habits in order to really be forgiven. Because we do not fully understand that the only requirement for atonement for the shedding of any blood is blood, and in the atonement for sin, the Blood must be of the innocent Lamb of God. What if we are no match for the strength of an addiction; or what if we have worn ourselves out trying to be perfect to the point of physical illness, exhaustion, and unbelief, with still no relief or rest? If our salvation rests upon our own efforts, what happens to us when our efforts fail? Does that mean we are lost or the salvation of God rests on conditions beyond our acceptance of it?

The fruit of truth is rest. The fruit of the lie becomes a never-enough, never- ending pursuit of our own goodness. This comes out of our innate desire for goodness, which is part of our divine nature in being made in the image of God. The Enemy persuades us that the way to return to our original state of innocence is through penance and the pursuit of excellence by 'being good'. Being good cannot remove the original sin or restore us to our original state of goodness and purity or holiness which has been obscured through sin.

Trying to return to our original state of goodness by being good and doing good works, is like Watchman Nee describes someone who is struggling to get into a room they are already sitting in! We are already sitting in the room, though we may still be dirty and in desperate need of washing. Getting dirty with sin does not change the fact that we were already built by God to love goodness, because goodness is what we were built to be. The real challenge is to believe that sin cannot change our original divine nature!

Being born in a stable did not make Jesus any less the Son of God. Being born into the Snake Pit of sin does not make me less precious or change my original, innate, divine origin or identity. What I do or what is done to me does not change my identity, although it may cause me to change my opinion of myself. Being born the King's daughter does not change if I rob a bank. I am still the King's daughter, although now I am the King's daughter who robbed the bank and has brought shame upon both me and my Father.

We are eternal beings, not 'doings'; although Satan relentlessly attempts to persuade us to agree that we are human Doings defined by what we Do. Even as robbing a bank does not change my royal identity, it does tarnish my reputation and others' opinions of me. We are still created in the image of God - no matter what we do or what happens to us - we are still good and worth saving! For any of you who have children, this is not difficult to understand. We do not throw away our child because they played in the mud puddle. We do not abandon them, even if they did it in disobedience. We save them, and wash them, and put clean clothes on them, and teach them to understand the dangers of the Snake Pit.

Basing our salvation upon the merit of our good works (merit-based salvation) in order to qualify for eternal life throws faith in the promises of God in the 'back seat' and puts us in control of our own destiny, we think! When faith based upon the promises of God is replaced by performance and perfection and the 'be good' gospel; God's love is perceived to be conditional, and our relationship with Him is tentative and insecure.

Satan needed a way to neutralize the power of the Cross of Christ. By promoting the idea of us having to get rid of our sin ourselves, Perfection and Performance were promoted to a new level of importance. Satan made the gospel all about earning-and-deserving the right to be saved. He deceived us into believing that we needed to get control of our spiritual lives, and that our eternal destiny was all up to us. This perverted shift in the thrust of the Gospel allowed Satan to use our sin and 'how to deal with it, as the foundation of his 'modern-man-made' gospel; the gospel we have come to believe is the Gospel of Jesus Christ. Satan has twisted the Law into a deadly blade to hack up the hungry and tear us away from the truth about the love of God. By switching the primary focus of the gospel and God's love for us into an 'it is up to us', 'we have to do it ourselves' mode, he moved the center of the Gospel over to getting rid of our sin ourselves.

The Enemy has thus marginalized the finished work of Christ on the Cross and tossed it into the 'ditch of self-improvement and self-deification'. We have been taught to live by our own definitions of truth and salvation. We have boldly declared our 'own ways' to be indisputably correct. Using emergent theology to redefine the truth, we have been persuaded to believe that truth is whatever we say it is, and 'all roads lead to Heaven'.

'GUILTY AS CHARGED'

In every matter of the transgression of the Law, Satan wants to assume the position of judge. His arguments against us are always the same: we are guilty. We are guilty because we have come into agreement with his accusation of us - which makes us 'guilty as charged'. By agreeing with the accusations of Guilt and Fear, we have inadvertently voted against ourselves. Satan uses the Law of God to push his agenda against us.

Using his clever arguments as the Prosecutor, the Great Hypocrite, (the biggest Law breaker of all) persuades us to agree that we are bad because we broke God's Law. And - because God is good, and because God's Law is good and breaking God's Law is bad - we conclude that we are bad. We have come into agreement with the lie of the Accuser through implied consent. We have sinned and broken God's Law. Therefore, we assume that God is angry with us for breaking the Law and we conclude we deserve to be punished for our sin.

We see the Enemy is using something that is true; Knowing that the Law is good, and given by God, to open the door to feeling guilty for sinning and accepting the consequence of sin. Believing that we are what we do (or have done) gives weight to both of the

Devil's argument, that God is mad at us, and that God is the One punishing us for our transgressions against the Law. Guilt, and feelings of Guilt, convince us that God is mad at us because we broke the Law and 'have it coming'. We agree that we deserve to be punished, and accept the judgments of Guilt, Pain, Poverty, and Infirmity thinking they are the judgments of God and are suitable consequences of God's wrath and judgment.

Satan has deceived us into believing four lies: first, 'I am bad'; secondly, 'It is up to me to be good'; thirdly, that God is harsh and unreasonable and finally, 'I had it coming'. Coming into agreement with these lies causes us to break the Law by trying to fulfill the Law ourselves. In essence, by believing that we are responsible for securing our own righteousness, we have rejected the Law of righteousness that comes only from surrendering ourselves to Christ, Who shed His blood for us. Truly, the modern-man-made gospel is an affront and an insult to the Cross of Jesus Christ and the work He finished on it!

Satan knows that - according to the Law of Reciprocity - an eye must be given for an eye taken. He also knows that good deeds and fruit baskets do not satisfy the Law of Reciprocity, nor make up for a grievous transgression, nor satisfy the Law of Retribution (making something right or fair by getting even). The Law of Sin and Death required the death penalty; the taking of life required the giving of life.

Satan knows that when we take matters into our own hands and try to 'be good' in our own strength, we have actually sinned! We have transgressed the Law in rejecting the very point and purpose of the Law, Jesus Christ. By refusing the sacrifice Jesus made to take the death penalty for us, we have rejected the only means to salvation. Only death could fully pay the debt sin demanded and make a way for the implementation of God's salvation.

Trying to live a perfect, sinless life actually allows Satan to legally inflict his demonic judgments on us for failing to be good enough.

This does not mean we advocate a lifestyle of reckless and loose living for the believer. Abusing the Grace of God is not one of the fruits of the Holy Spirit. The _fruit_ of the Holy Spirit which comes from abiding in the Vine is righteousness, peace, and joy. It simply means that we are guilty for breaking the Law when we use keeping the Law as our means for righteousness. We fail to realize that, in choosing the Law as our preferred means of salvation over the atonement God has provided, we have fallen short of the grace of God.

All have sinned (Rom. 3:23). God knows that. He knew we would all be tempted, accused, fail, make bad choices, feel responsible for those choices, and be pressured to try harder. He knew we would be 'sitting ducks' for the hounds of hell who hunt the souls of men. He knew we were no match for the 'wiles' of the Evil One who cheats at every turn to bully and oppress and trample the created sons and daughters of God.

In an odd sort of twisted way, Satan has always wanted to be our "savior". Therefore God knew He would have to deal not only with sin but with Satan for trying to usurp His rightful position as Savior and Lord over His creation. The Enemy deliberately misconstrued the purposes of the Law to alienate us from God and get us to judge Him for being unreasonable, controlling and difficult to please.

Satan will manipulate and corrupt our minds through Deception - in order to project his own ideas about salvation and good works onto our hearts, confusing us as to the integrity of God's intentions. By 'offering' his panacea of remedies in every assortment of good works and religious deeds, The Deceiver has confused and complicated the matter of Salvation making it into everything God never intended! This is all part of the great deception that takes us away from trusting, loving, and surrendering to the finished work of God though the obedience of His Son.

DIVINE PROTECTION AND IDENTIFICATION

God had two reasons for giving the Law to His people. It provided both Identification; and Protection (as a covering) for His children against the accusations of the Accuser of the Brethren, (Rev.12:10). God's children were clearly identified through their obedience to the Covenant which He had made with them through Abraham. That Covenant was re-established four hundred years later, through the Ten Commandments and the pattern of worship given in the Tabernacle. Their obedience to the Covenant confirmed their relationship with God. It was based on trust and faith in the Promises God as originally given to Abraham.

That Covenant was based upon Abraham's faith in the promises of God; the sign of that Covenant was circumcision. Circumcision was not the means of salvation, nor could it save anyone. It was only the sign of the Covenant which God had made with Abraham. Later, the Ten Commandments were given to further define and identify the people of God. God needed to clearly identify and distinguish the nation which desired that He be their God - as opposed to the rest of mankind, who were held under the sway of paganism and superstition.

The Law was not given because He wanted to control the people; rather, it was a means of protection from the Accuser. It also became the means of distinguishing the fledgling Nation of Israel. Through obedience to the commandments, they would distinguish themselves as belonging to God. Their obedience gave Him the means through which to protect them from the constant accusations of the Evil One, who was claiming them for himself. That is why obedience to the commandments and statutes of the Law were of such paramount importance to the safety of the children of Israel, and brought such devastating consequences when they broke them.

EVEN TO THIS VERY DAY

Because of the hostile relationship between God and Satan, Satan is constantly attempting to find fault with the Redeemed so that he might number us among the transgressors. Because of his constant accusations, there needed to be a clarification between the definition of sinful behaviors and transgressions, which means 'to cross the line'. The Law drew the lines and set the limitations for the permitted and expected behavior of God's people.

Part of Jesus' mission in coming to earth was to establish the dispensation of the New Covenant. His Death would institute a divine change, thereby bringing the temporary work and purpose of the Law to a satisfactory conclusion. His death did what the Law could not do; Mosaic Law was to be replaced by grace, and faith in the promises of God. The dispensation of Grace was an 'upgrade' to the Ten Commandments. Whereas the Ten Commandments forbade killing our neighbor, the new Law of the Kingdom commanded us to love even our enemies, (Lk.6:27-30). The New Covenant was designed to include the Gentiles, and opened its invitation to 'whosoever would' desire to be part of the work of the Cross and the power of the Kingdom of God.

The Law had always and only been given as a divine code of moral conduct which pledged the promise of eternal life - through the coming of the Messiah - to its obedient followers. Although obedience continues to hold weight in matters of blessing in the New Testament - as it had in the Old Testament - it was never meant to be the means of salvation.

For all practical purposes, salvation and the reclassification of 'the just' were part of this new dispensation of grace. The question of obedience to the Law, however, still gave opportunity for controversy, as was seen in the heated discussions between Jesus and the religious leaders of His day. Unfortunately, differing ideas as to Who this Messiah would be caused confusion and division in the people, which created an obstacle in their acceptance of Jesus Christ.

Ultimately, Christ came as a demonstration of God's mercy, to both satisfy the Law, and complete the requirements of justice. The epistles describe Christ as the 'fulfilling of the Law', which has left 'religion-ists' and 'list keepers' and 'doers of the Law' baffled. How could behavior be monitored, or justice and right- eousness maintained, if the 'teeth' were taken out of the Law, they reasoned? How would they continue to garner public interest in the merit of keeping the Law, if the divine threats were gone, replaced by mercy and forgiveness?

Never mind the fact that, in spite of their best efforts, no one had ever been able to keep the Law without offending in at least 'one point', though all seemed driven to keep trying. The fear of throwing out the Law, and standing on the promises of God through the finished work of Jesus Christ alone, became too great a step of faith. Rather, faith in the Promises of God became a stumbling stone and a rock of offense for those who followed the Law who were now invited to follow Jesus.

Keeping the Law as an active part of Christian doctrine and theology has continued to work to the disadvantage of the believer and to the great advantage of the Accuser. He could now use it to divide the followers of Christ and send them down a multitude of paths in search for righteousness and salvation. Confusing the tenants of the Gospel of Good News by mixing them with the old mandates of legalism was a brilliant move on the part of Satan. Would they venture into freedom and answer the call to the Law of Liberty, (Ja.125; Ja.2:12, Gal.5:1 & 13) or would they choose to remain gripped by the familiar? Would they stand with Guilt, or would they embrace the Grace of God as the foundation of their righteousness and their relationship with Him?

The words of Isaiah, "Make the heart of this people dull, and their ears heavy, and shut their eyes;" (Is. 6:10) had come to pass in the words of Jesus (see Matt. 13: 14-15). They have eyes, but they do not see; and ears, but they do not hear. Romans 11: 5-10 clearly describes this stupor and the hardness of heart that comes upon those who mix works and grace. "Even so then, at this present time there is a remnant according to the election of grace. And if by grace, then it is no longer works; otherwise grace is no longer grace. But if it is of works, it is no longer grace; otherwise work is no longer work. What then? Israel has not obtained what it seeks; but the elect have obtained it and the rest were hardened." (Ro. 11:6-7)

The debate over religion and grace has continued since the beginning. It has become the 'perfect storm' for mixing truth with error in Satan's attempt to divide the house with Controversy, and conquer the hearts with Confusion. Deception and Divination have run rampant in our midst in the attempt to destroy the church's power. To this present hour, the disputes over Law and grace fuel powerful and fatal arguments with those who could be classified as the 'blind leading the blind' (Lk. 6:39).

This dispute about the shifting status of the Law was originated and promoted by the Evil One to bring a real 'bone of contention' between some of the early church fathers who held onto the old line of religious legalism, and the new Gentile converts (Acts 15). To this day, the controversy between Law and Grace has remained a point of confusion in the Church of Jesus Christ, and for the Blood-bought sons and daughters of God.

For the New Testament believer, the difference is that now the Law is no longer written on tablets of stone, but upon the tablets of our hearts. And though we are 'saved by grace', and the word of our testimony both is, and is in, the finished work of the Cross of Christ; the need for knowing the truth and understanding the agenda of the Enemy remains remarkably important to our well-being. God has set forth in His Word a very clear declaration. The Law "cannot save or justify us" (Gal. 2:16). Nevertheless, the

Enemy still uses the Law millions of times every day in order to convince the saved that they are not saved, and the lost that they are beyond God's love and salvation.

Despite our complete deliverance from the wages of sin, the Law remains one of the main features of almost every believer's life. The church, with its promotion of religion, has not distinguished its many religions from the Gospel of Jesus Christ. Rather, mixing the Law with Grace is presented as part of the true Gospel of Good News, when, indeed, it is NOT.

Though the demands of the Law were fully and completely satisfied by the sacrifice of Calvary, that truth seems to remain hidden from most of us. Satan continues to use the Law - and our failure to keep it - as his principal means of justifying his continuing destruction of our spiritual and physical freedom. The mixing and mingling of truth and error holds us in a rut and keeps us stuck, vacillating between trying to walk in the Spirt and avoid fulfilling the lusts of the flesh. We are caught in the middle of condemnation - even when the Word tells us "there is now, therefore, no condemnation to those who are in Christ Jesus" who do not walk not according to the flesh, but according to the Spirit." (Rom. 8:1)

IN THE MATTER OF FREE WILL

God will not force us to do anything against our free will, and Satan can not make us do anything, without our consent. Our agreement, in choosing whose report we believe, therefore, becomes the deciding factor in determining who will win the war and settle the dispute in the contest for our souls. The one and only rule in the war between God and Satan for the souls of mankind is the law of consent. Simply stated, it says, "You are that one's slaves whom you obey, whether of sin to death, or of obedience to righteousness". (Rom. 6: 16) Obedience to God becomes the key to freedom and blessing; whereas disobedience opens the door to destruction.

In His dealings with us, God has demonstrated both His love and His justice. We could not expect Him to deny one to serve the other, any more than we could expect Him to compromise His righteousness to promote sin or wrongdoing. His repeated pleas with the people in the Old Testament to obey Him were not the promptings that came out of His own self-absorbed narcissism. He understood the consequences of disobedience, and the danger it brought to those who rebelled. He knew how the Enemy, the Accuser of the Brethren, would examine us to find fault with us and demand to test us.

The First Commandment says, "I am the LORD your God, who brought you out of the land of Egypt, out of the house of bondage. You shall have no other gods before Me." (Ex. 20:5) In the Old Testament, idolatry was the sin of misplaced worship. To worship idols is - and always has been - the worshipping of the demons behind them. Seeking to form a benevolent relationship with and follow after other gods was both idolatry and - to God, Who had entered into covenant relationship with Israel - an act of adultery. (I Cor. 10:14-21), (Jer. 2:20-25).

Putting other gods before Him empowers those gods to act in the primary place of our affection; which is, in essence, the same as committing adultery in our relationship with God. God knew that His people were submitting themselves to the power of evil spirits and setting themselves up for capture. The sticks and stones and the golden calves they worshipped were only fronts for the thousands of demons who promoted alienation from God. They disseminated a false narrative about the One True God of creation, and His benevolence, by stirring up the imaginations of the people against His goodness and the truth.

God knew what the humans could only suspect: that Satan would twist any circumstance to separate His Children from Him. He knew the Devil would intimidate humans and get them to worship The Liar, even as he was deceiving them into believing that he (the Evil One) was the source of their blessings. Everything the Devil did was for the express purpose of concealing his diabolical intentions to kill God's children and discredit God.

Every story he told; every enticement; every seduction; every amusement; every event; the satisfying of every appetite; every lust; every waking moment to their dying breath; Satan would be there as their savior, their provider and their benefactor. He would block out the light of God's Son for one purpose: to deceive and destroy them forever, cutting them off from all hope or knowledge of the love of God. He would convince them that it was foolish to believe they could be loved by Him. Satan would shadow them, control them and draw them, until he was sure they had moved beyond the grace of God and the voice of the Good Shepherd. Then he would gather them up, one at a time, into the valley of the shadow of death, to reveal the terror his true identity, who he really was all along, and kill them.

Before Jesus came and saved us, God knew that the only way jurisprudence would allow Him to bless and protect His children, was if they would willingly choose to obey Him rather than the Devil. He set forth those instructions in the form of the Law and commanded the people to obey Him. When they walked with Him in obedience, their obedience would permit Him the legal recourse He needed to bless and keep them from the Evil One.

In the New Testament, as in the Old, idolatry is the sin of misplaced affection. God demonstrated His love for us by giving His Son. He rescued us, while we were as yet sinners and unconvinced of His love. Therefore, seeking any source for life and salvation - other than the One True God - is a rejection of His love. When we fail to believe God and question His Love for us it is the same as rejecting the love of God. Rejecting the Love of God only adds proof to the Devil's argument that no one will reciprocate God's love and that God was a fool for making us in the first place.

In the New Testament, all the Law is fulfilled in this: Thou shalt love the Lord your God with all your heart, soul, mind, and strength. The Ten Commandments never forced us to love one another. Love cannot be demanded or commanded. Love cannot be legislated. Love is only love when it is freely given, whether or not it receives a response of love in return. In the New Testament, God continues to demonstrate His integrity and intention to be in relationship with us. He acted in our behalf, despite our utter failure to keep the commandments or even believe He really loved us.

Giving us the Law was simply the first part of God's redemption initiative - even though He already knew that we would not be able to keep it. In the end, the whole point of the Law was not to save us, nor provide a means for salvation through it. The Law was given to provide a means of identification and protection for His people until the fullness of time would come, and the Savior would be sent. The Law could not save us. That was never God's intention in giving us the Law. The Law was given to prove to all of us that we need a Savior.

The Law could not legislate the requirements of love. It could only prove to us that we could not 'be good' or 'good enough' to earn our own righteousness, or love in our own strength. Through the Law, God settled any arguments that we, or the Enemy, could make that we could save ourselves. Our failure to keep the Law only confirmed our desperate need for the Salvation that came through faith in the Son of God, and for His deliverance from the Snake Pit of life we had come to believe was our home.

Sending His Own Son to die in our place became the only remedy for sin, and the only right response to the demands of death. "For what the law could not do in that it was weak through the flesh, God did by sending His own Son…" (Rom. 8:3) The Law is like an umbrella. Its protection was only a temporary shield from the elements of the storm of sin; and only as effective as the strength of the hands that held it. It was only as effective in its ability to protect the people as they were in their willingness to stand under it.

Salvation was an eternally-established covering for 'whosoever will'. It had to be given as a free gift that it might be available as an option, given to 'whosoever will'. The Law, however, as a mechanism for salvation, could ultimately only produce failure in those who sought to use it. Salvation could not come by the Law or be mixed with it. The Love of God had to be an unconditional gift in order to carry the clear message of God's love through His gift of grace and eternal life.

GRACE ABUSE

On the opposite side of the spectrum, although some have chosen to ignore the gift of grace, others tend to abuse it. The gift of salvation given to us by means of grace is not a 'carte blanche' (blank check) where one is given complete freedom to act as one wishes or thinks best, to do whatever they want. 'Greasy grace' and 'sloppy agape' and 'cheap grace' are not grace at all. Real grace is not cheap. It is priceless!

Grace is essential in God the Father's desire to regather us unto Himself since we are no match for the wiles of the Wicked One. Grace and Faith form the dual core of our salvation. God gave salvation through Grace; and we demonstrate the desire for that salvation through our faith in believing Him for it. Obedience follows, as the demonstration of our faith in believing the promises of God that "whosoever will call upon the Name of the Lord will be saved." (Rom. 10:13)

Grace and Faith are integrated in such a way that both are necessary to mutually activate our salvation. Together they form the dynamic culmination of the 'whosoever will' invitation made by God, which permits Him to come back into our lives to redeem us. Grace can only be given to "whosoever will call upon the Name of the Lord" (Rom. 10:13). Those who do not 'call' or 'ask' do not meet the one qualification for the bestowing of salvation and the grace to receive it - that is, to ask for it.

Grace is the pivotal point for both our salvation, and the final justification of our soul. Without grace and forgiveness, there is no final justification for sin or salvation, but only a fearful, helpless anticipation of judgment. And if that be the case, what profit is there in so foolishly rejecting grace by "continuing in sin, that grace may abound"? (Rom. 6:1) The only point to that 'madness' would be in proving our own ignorance in refusing to choose love and the goodness of God. No point is worth proving that sends its followers to hell.

Why would we prefer to strive to 'perfect ourselves', with endless lists of religious duties, false humility, and self-improvement that only cry 'never enough'? (Col. 2:18-23) Could it be that we have failed to realize that the Enemy has used our very desire to get rid of our sins as bait to catch us on the hooks of Hell by taking the matters of sin and righteousness into our own hands?

My attempt to get rid of 'my sin' still makes my life 'all about me' - which essentially distorts the whole concept of Grace. God makes salvation all about 'the Son'. Sin - and the religious activities we practice to get rid of it - essentially constructs a monument to 'self', and makes me responsible for my own salvation. This makes the death of Jesus Christ unnecessary, and God a debtor - who owes me something for what I have done or tried to do - to earn my own salvation, based upon my behavior.

Our religious efforts and man-made forms of godliness only work to undermine true fellowship with the Father and keep us strangers to true love and goodness of God. They perpetuate independence and deception that are so 'second nature' to all of us. Provoked by Pride, the need to be right, and the search for peace, we are deceived into 'biting the hook and taking the bait' set up by the spirits of Religion, Self-deception, and Error to take control over our own destiny, including salvation.

We fail to recognize the obvious, and the ongoing, severity of the insidious subtlety of the battle for truth which rages within us. Captured by the schemes and seduced by his counterfeits, few really seem to "come to their senses and escape the snare of the devil." (II Tim. 2:24-26) We remain set up "in opposition to ourselves," (II Tim. 2:24-26 KJV), even as we promote our own self-righteousness in our pursuit of God.

6

THE PLACE OF DIVINE BLESSING

THE COVENANT

God's relationship with us is established as a Covenant, as written and revealed in the Old and New Testaments. God has made all things and sustains them through specific, well-ordered laws. The code which God uses to manage the harmony of the universe in its relationships within itself is called, by some, The Universal Code of Justice. The Universal Code of Justice forms the basis for both Justice and Harmony in providing each creature in God's creation with the things it needs for sustenance and participation as a valid, functioning member of creation. Therefore, the Universal Code of Justice both is, and undergirds, the Law of Love which it is called to protect.

In the Old Testament, that Law established a set of rules and statutes that basically forbade the people to kill each other; and to restore whatever they had taken. The code of Justice in the Old Testament simply says that - if we are unable to find enough grace to do unto others that which we would have them do to us - we are at least expected to do them no harm.

Before Jesus Christ came as the Word of God made flesh, and

descended to the earth as a man, God had encapsulated His justice into a simple live-and-let-live formula of "an eye for an eye, and a tooth for a tooth." (Ex. 21:24) In order to protect each of His creatures from ongoing harm, and the threat of offense and injustice, His justice demanded that "If any lasting harm follows, then you shall give life for life, eye for eye, tooth for tooth, hand for hand, foot for foot, burn for burn, wound for wound, stripe for stripe." (Ex. 21:23-25)

Satan uses this literal interpretation of the Word of God as the basis from which he formed his own system of justice. Those tempted to get justice for themselves by using this Demonic Law of Reciprocity - which is an "eye for an eye, blood for blood" - will not only fail to settle an offense; but will, in fact, end up breaking a greater law, which is the Law of Love. According to the Law of Reciprocity, if someone pokes out your eye, you get to poke out theirs, right? But how does this kind of justice allow us to keep the precepts of the Law of Love and Forgiveness, written and adopted as the complete fulfilling of the Law?

Galatians 5:14 tells us, "For all the law is fulfilled in one word, even in this: "You shall love your neighbor as yourself." How does poking out your enemy's eye get your own eye back, or make you guiltless in failing to fulfill the Law of love yourself? "A new commandment I give unto you," Jesus said, "that you love one another; as I have loved you, that you also love one another." (Jn. 13:34) The ultimate and final rendering of the Law of Reciprocity which most concerns us is the one that has to do with forgiveness. "For if you forgive men their trespasses, your heavenly Father will also forgive you. But if you do not forgive men their trespasses, neither will your Father forgive your trespasses." (Mt. 6:14-15)

The death of Christ activated the New (second) Testament, (Covenant) for this very reason. In the dispensation of grace, we now have a second option. We can choose to forgive. We can choose to live - accepting the shed Blood of the Lamb of God slain from the foundation of the world (Rev. 13:8) as full and final payment for our sins under the New Testament - or we can pay for our own sins under the Old Covenant, which still interprets the Law as, "an eye for an eye, a life for a life." (Ex. 21:24) For any who need or will be in need of forgiveness, Grace is by far the better and only option to solving the issues of personal sin and injustice.

THE PROTECTION OF THE COVENANT BLESSING

A curse comes when we step outside the parameters of the Covenant. God's Covenant with us establishes His blessing over us. The dictionary defines a curse as a 'prayer for harm'; 'to call on divine power to send injury upon'; and 'something that comes in response to a curse'. It is not God's desire that His children live under a curse.

Iniquity and injustice, however, have opened the door to the curse. They must be dealt with in order for love to live, the curse to be broken, and blessings restored. God's commitment to the Covenant is maintained through His justice. God has obligated Himself to advocate on our behalf, within the limits of our free will, even despite our rejection of Him. Because of the Rule of Consent, His justice must permit a curse to come upon those who violate the Covenant of His blessing through disobedience.

The choice is ours - although the Deceiver is ever working to influence and intimidate us in the exercise of our free will by manipulating us to disobey - so that he can claim his right to bring a curse upon us. "Behold, I set before you this day a blessing and a curse: a blessing, if you obey the commandments of the Lord your God, which I command you this day; and a curse, if you will not obey the commandments of the Lord your God, but turn aside out of the way which I command you this day, to go after other gods, which you have not known." (Deut. 11:26-28)

It is not lawful for one to take from another that which God has rightfully given them. Although God knew that greed and offense would be perpetrated upon the human race by the Evil One through fear and lack; He offered Himself as the Provider and Source of provision for those who would put their trust in Him. Both vengeance - and perfect love which casts out fear - belong to the Lord. Mercy and vengeance are the double-edged sword of God's justice, and the promise of hope to all who wait upon Him for the restoration of that justice.

At the end of the age, all things will be brought back into full alignment with God's perfect will and justice. His perfect will is love, and all of our actions and words will be judged by the Law of Love. His justice will restore everything back to its original nature and divine order. His justice is the proclaimed remedy for every infraction and violation. All inequity will be judged. The curse and Chaos will be removed. Anarchy and Apostasy will be defeated. Safety will be re-established in the earth. The Law will be fulfilled and satisfied in its alignment to, and its agreement with, love.

'FAIR' AND 'MINE'

As already mentioned in our earlier discussion on fairness, the Universal Code of Justice is an innate recognition of the divine standard of equity and 'fairness'. Similar to the concept of 'fair and not fair', the concept of 'mine' is quickly grasped without even needing to be taught.

Rooted in fear and insecurity, 'mine' and the need to 'take care of myself' both encompass our innate need to survive in a world filled with danger, injustice, and offense. Injustice challenges love, in the fair distribution of the goods and services necessary to sustain life. The conflict between Faith and Fear is desperate, and designed to challenge our trust in God to make things right.

To believe in the love of God in the midst of ugly favoritism and cruel injustice draws us into an unseen battle which drives us to take matters of justice into our own hands. We are tempted to do that which is right in our own eyes, believing that God does not see or care what has happened or is happening to us. We move in our own strength to recover what was lost. We respond buy feeling hurt. The helplessness and the humiliation it generates creates a renewed determination to hold onto bitterness until justice can be served. We dedicate our lives to holding onto anger, and keeping the offense alive until we are vindicated. We control fear with anger; and protect ourselves from getting hurt again, by 'fueling the flames' of getting even. Hatred and unforgiveness rule until some semblance of justice can be regained.

For many, this means holding onto unforgiveness and bitterness until the matter has been settled. Carried away by hurt and offense, we risk holding onto anger and unforgiveness as a way of maintaining control. We feed off the energy which anger stirs up in an effort to justify ourselves and preserve the scene of the crime until justice arrives. We spend our lives in the futility of taking matters into our own hands as we take a stand against injustice - at the extreme risk of breaking every tenant of the law of love - including loving our enemy and forgiving others - if we ourselves want to be forgiven. Spiritual blindness and hardness of heart overtake us in our effort to prove ourselves right. We take a stand even at the expense of losing our own lives (souls) and our physical health, simply to regain justice.

Until we are introduced to a higher concept of God's love and His commitment to justice, we are tempted to operate in such a way as to establish our own justice in order to preserve our own life. Even as 'fair' becomes synonymous with doing what is right in our own eyes, the pursuit of it often jeopardizes not only our righteousness, but also destroys every hope of justice.

The pursuit of 'fair-ness', and the desire to 'right a wrong' often collide with mercy and righteousness. If - in our hot pursuit of justice, we find ourselves justifying unrighteousness as the means by which to obtain justice - we are promoting injustice. If we are committed to do 'whatever it takes' to settle the score, then we do well to acknowledge that we have gone too far. We have gotten caught in a trap - an irresolvable conflict, a 'Catch twenty-two' - of attempting to bring justice in our own strength and according to our own intentions.

The injustice manifested in that entanglement is anger. Anger is defined as being sensitive to injustice, and the motivation or desire and energy to fix it. Anger, and our determination to restore justice, mix and mingle 'mine' with fair'. We are caught in the trap set by the Enemy designed to alienate us from one another, bring agitation and division into our relationships - and cause an endless battle of judging each other in order to right the wrong and make life fair.

ANGER AND FIXING UNFAIRNESS

The Law, defined as an "eye for an eye", pushes justice even further from our reach. Anger becomes normal, and the law of Lawlessness begins to rule. Anger is energy, and a sensitivity to injustice. We attempt to right wrongs and make things fair. We try to restore the balance and bring back the safety of justice that has fallen under the 'heavy hand' of offense, injustice, hurt, fear, greed, hardness of heart and unloving spirits. We get angry and offended. We are tempted to take matters into our own hands in order to procure justice for ourselves.

The attempt to procure justice for ourselves ultimately demonstrates a doubt or an unwillingness to trust God or wait for His justice. Some may doubt that His justice even exists. Failed attempts to secure justice ourselves give way to bitterness. Bitterness is swallowed anger. Tucked away inside, kept alive by the fires of hurt and offense, anger bursts into flame and burns inside of us as inflammation, fevers, rashes, heartburn, and a myriad of manifestations of a broken heart.

Living with injustice, and loss of hope for restoration, creates pain and suffering. If we commit that injustice and the resultant suffering that comes with it to the LORD, we can look forward to that final day of reckoning when God - the righteous Judge of all the Earth - will make all things right. Trusting God to make things right also allows God to intervene in our present conditions and relationships to bring restoration and healing. Our faith in God's Goodness and Justice allows us to rest our case, knowing that God hears every grievance and establishes equity and truth in every matter.

Faith waits for God to act, and permits every allegation and every crime to be addressed by the Court of Heaven. "For the LORD is a God of justice; blessed are all those who wait for Him." (Is. 30:18) If we will not, or cannot wait, anger will provoke us to act in our own strength and on our own behalf. Acting in our own behalf out of anger sets us up to make rash and hasty judgments. Satan uses these judgments to 'dump' on our own heads the very thing we judge another person for doing. We fail to believe God's promise to make things right. The Enemy uses the vows we make to get even as the permission he needs to hold us to our ill-spoken words and return judgment back on our own heads.

Using - or, more correctly, misusing God's own Word to justify his demonic judgment of us - the Enemy uses unforgiveness, resentments, and bitterness to keep a record of wrongs against us, as we keep those same record of wrongs against each other. Unforgiveness opens the door to Hatred and Guilt, and perpetuates the flow of demonic activity down through our own lives and generational bloodlines.

The Word clearly tells us we will be forgiven as we forgive one another. "And forgive us our debts (trespasses) as we forgive our debtors, those who trespass against us" (Mt. 6:12). Basically what the prayer is saying is, "God, use my forgiveness of those who have trespassed against me as the template for Your forgiveness of me." The use of the word 'debts' reflects the fact that Jesus paid a debt, the debt of sin, which called for death. We have no means or resources with which to pay it ourselves.

The Lord, the Righteous Judge, invites us to trust Him and relinquish the crimes committed against us over to God. Forgiveness allows the justice of God, and the Court of heaven, to make the final determinations of acquittal or guilt. Forgiveness simply means that we 'turn the crimes committed against us over to God', and let Him be the Judge. Because He is a Righteous Judge and can do no wrong - there is no concern that the issues will not be resolved in favor of truth and justice, vindication and restoration, for the innocent - and wrath and judgment for the wicked.

Judging others for what they have done to us ultimately makes us the judge in our own case. Judging our own case will never bring a final end to a dispute. It cannot be considered a genuine and lawful settlement of a crime. Acting as the judge and the plaintiff in the same case can never clear the charges or bring a righteous settlement to an injustice. Settling a matter ourselves cannot bring us a legitimate and unequivocal vindication any more than being our own judge will be seen as a lawful or binding resolution of a judicial matter. (See Ja. 4:12)

As justice and truth move further and further from their rightful place at the center of our interactions with each other, hatred and callous indifference set in. We lose our human connection with each other, and become vulnerable to becoming less human. Love grows cold as the gods of war builds their case in turning us against one another, both in our minds and in our world. Truth diminishes, and strife increases in direct proportion to our failure to forgive one another. We get caught up in the snare of Satan's own hatred. His contempt for God intensifies and pushes forward his plan to purge the earth of the creatures made in the image of God.

As the world moves closer and closer to its final day of reckoning, the distance between justice and injustice widens. Injustice invites

Anarchy and Terrorism to rule in the lives of men. Pain and iniquity intensify their oppression in, and between, one another. The 'avalanche' of iniquity buries us under mountains of madness. Justice stumbles in the streets. Violence rules. "Righteousness stands afar off, for truth is fallen in the street and equity cannot enter. So truth fails, and he who departs from evil makes himself a prey." (Is. 59:14-15)

INIQUITY EQUALS INJUSTICE

Sin and iniquity separate us from God (Is. 59:2). That separation causes Him to hide His face from us. Our hands are covered with blood, and our lips speak lies. We have not chosen to walk in alignment with the truth and justice of God's commandments. Truth is viewed as debatable, and has become a favorite topic for discussion among many modern church leaders. It is especially popular among seeker-friendly churches, where conflicts are resolved with a decision to tolerate opinions; "You have your truth, I have mine". Any who would speak on behalf of there being One source of absolute truth contained in the person of Jesus Christ are considered narrow-minded and biased. Any who reject the multifaceted, pragmatic renditions of 'truth' are held in contempt for their ignorance, and labeled intolerant.

When God's truth is not honored as absolute, law and order becomes arbitrary; and eventually, the people cast off restraint. Safety is lost. Anarchy rules. Where there is no justice, Anxiety and Fear grip the human heart. More laws are passed, but to no avail. When Truth is no longer the established standard of behavior for a moral code of conduct, justice, peace, and divine freedoms are lost. Justice becomes 'each man for himself'. Stability and dependability disappear, as everyone "does what seems right in his own eyes" (Deut. 12:7-9).

Relationships shift from deep and genuine; to shallow, selfish and deadly. Each one is looking for his or her own way to survive. The collision of personal interests with those of others sets up a conflict for control, with each seeking their own advantage at the expense of others. The resulting injustices and deprivation of love and kindness make the world a mean, dangerous, and violent place to live.

Trust and safety are exchanged for freedom to pursue one's self-initiated directives. Isolation and loneliness offer little consolation to those who face bullying and abuse from others. To live means coping with fear, and surviving without the hope of justice. Without justice and the goodness it brings, we are left to our own devices, as helpless to maintain justice as we are in desperate need of it.

REDEMPTION

"Then the LORD saw it, and it displeased Him that there was no justice. He saw that there was no man and wondered that there was no intercessor; therefore His own arm brought salvation for Him and His own righteousness, it sustained Him."(Is. 59:15b-16) Understanding God's intended purposes in redemption - and its all-encompassing power to ransom the human race - is essential if we are to partake in and partner with God in the process of the restoration of our generational blessings. God's rescue of His creation intends for the redemptive work of Christ to transcend time and embrace all generations, including those past and any yet to come.

His intention to save us from sin's debt by paying the price of sin Himself is accomplished. It is done. The price demanded for our release was satisfied when Jesus cried out triumphantly, "It is finished" and died. Our debt to Satan was 'paid in full'. God had won the right to utter the final word! And in that divine utterance, we were free. As His Son drew in His last breath on the Cross, death's demands on the human race were thrown out of Court! Mercy and Justice were satisfied. The Law was fulfilled. We were forgiven and forever free of sin's obligations. Everything that needed to be done for the will of God to be accomplished in the earth, and in us, was complete. We no longer owe the Devil anything.

And, even as the battle for our soul has just begun, it is already won. Just as everything was 'finished' at Calvary, it is still being appropriated for us who live 2000 years later. As Hebrews teaches, "For by one offering He has perfected forever those who are being sanctified." (Heb. 10:14) Notice that that which has been done is still being done (worked out)! The work of Calvary is still valid, and being used to save and sanctify us to this very day.

Salvation involves our will, and is to be the beginning of the conversion experience. Whosoever will accept Christ's payment for their sins is saved. The acceptance of Christ's death and resurrection as the full atonement for our sins begins the process of conversion - which is the transformation of our mind, will and emotion - to the purposes of God. We come into agreement with the truth, as spoken and declared by the Holy Spirit. The work of reclaiming our lives begins at the moment of redemption (salvation). Truth begins to restore and renew our souls; our lives are beginning to be transformed and changed into something beautiful again.

WE ARE BOUGHT BACK

Some of us live, never realizing how precious or priceless we are; while others are caught on a 'narcissistic hook' of entitlement and vanity. Both give way to sin: one to false piety and unworthiness, the other to selfishness and arrogance. If Satan can keep us from knowing who we are, we will live without a revelation of God or the understanding of our value. (See Hos. 4:6 & Is. 5:13) We move far from the place of God's blessing and miss the power of His redemption.

We are redeemed with the "precious blood of Christ." (I Pet. 1:22)

That redemption includes not only our souls and assurance of 'reserved seating' in heaven, but the buying back of all that pertains to us. Everything that was lost in the 'Fall' - including our life's purpose and its fulfillment - is restored through the revelation of Jesus Christ. Even the most dedicated followers of Jesus Christ often fail to recognize the connection between the negative things that are still happening in their lives, and the sins of their ancestors. We have been conditioned to expect difficulties and 'lump' all the hard things into the chastening of the Lord and the refining of our faith. We never suspect that many of the things we suffer from are coming from the crimes Satan has committed against us and our ancestors. These crimes and injustices are the very things God wants to judge and make right in His desire to deliver us from evil.

Salvation is the first act of redemption, as we are grafted into the Vine. We continue to be nourished in that relationship through hearing His Word. We are abiding in Christ, even as we are admonished to "work out our own salvation, with fear and trembling, for it is God Who works in us both to will and do of His good pleasure." (Phil. 2: 12-13) The wonder and mystery of that finished and final work, is that we continue to grow even as we are exposed to adversity. We are part of the expression of the ongoing work of Calvary that expands in an ever increasing, life giving stream of healing and restoration, even to this present day.

And even as redemption flows forward, its work is a part of the mystery that was foreordained by God before the foundation of the world. (I Pet. 1:20-21) It "pleased the Father that in Him all the fullness should dwell, and by Him to reconcile all things to Himself, by Him, whether things on earth or things in heaven, having made peace through the blood of His cross." (Col.1:19-20) We who "once were alienated and enemies...yet now has He reconciled," (Col. 1: 21) that He might present us as "holy, and blameless, and irreproachable in His sight." (Col. 1:22)

Sanctification is a process that begins at the moment of salvation.

It is the application of the righteousness of Jesus Christ and His Blood to our lives, in order to restore them to holiness. We experience the redemption - the buying back of our lives, our souls, our health, our relationships, the successful completion of our destinies, and our legacy - through the sacrificial death of Jesus Christ. In Jesus we are complete. He is our life. "For in Him we live, and move, and have our being..." (Acts 17:28)

Many are under the misconception that salvation means I must now no longer sin; and if I do, my salvation is in jeopardy. How is this impossible expectation any different from those who tried to keep the Law in the Old Testament? None were able to do that, any more than those who would try to be perfectly sinless in the New Testament. The very point of the Cross and the failure of the Law is that the Law could not make anyone perfect or keep them from temptation or sinning.

Sanctification is that process of reclaiming the soul from the inward control and entanglements of sin that hold our second nature, the old man, in place. The Devil uses our ignorance of spiritual warfare, and our eagerness to be good, to bring us to one of two ends; there is nothing I can do, or it is all up to me. Believing that everything has been done and dealt with at the Cross may cause the unsuspecting follower of Jesus to look no further in their attempt to rout out the vestiges of evil still lurking in their bodies and souls. The operation of the body-of death-software program (still running in the background of their souls) causes others to believe it is all 'under the Blood', and their days of deliverance have been accomplished.

This 'all or nothing' position on sin and salvation, leads those who continue to sin after they have been born again to doubt the validity of their salvation. It is true that everything that needed to be done to accomplish our deliverance was finished at the Cross. Although it was finished, however, there are specific things that still need to be brought to completion as they pertain to each of us individually.

This type of 'magical' thinking leads us to believe there is nothing left for us to do but to sit back and enjoy an un-conflicted life of bliss, and experience an uninterrupted flow of God's goodness in our lives. When things do not go as we expected, Doubt and Confusion present themselves. Because the Biblical understanding of what is going on in the spiritual world is not accurately taught, the poor or partial explanation as to what to expect after we are saved eventually leads us into deeper confusion and error.

We get caught up in feeling disappointed and making excuses for ourselves. Ongoing sin that did not 'magically' go away must now be hidden for fear of being judged by others as unsaved. Some give up. Many cover their sin, pretending all is well; while still others are more motivated than ever to try to change their ways and 'get it right'. None of these temptations would persuade us if we realized that our sanctification and deliverance are the work of the Holy Spirit, who has been sent to lead us into all truth. Consequently, we deny the need for repentance, putting confession into the category of 'past tense'. We begin to succumb to many harmful and destructive religious habits and self-improvement strategies, without ever gaining real peace or a lasting sense of victory over our Enemy, or deliverance from him.

TRESPASSING ON THE TEMPLE PROPERTY

We are called to the simplicity of the Gospel, and to know that we are the temple of the Holy Spirit. Many of us suffer from loneliness and feel abandoned in this life, because we do not comprehend that God dwells in us by the power of the Holy Spirit. His presence abides within us, that He might live His life through us, in order that we might know the power of what it means "to live is Christ" (Phil. 1:21). In Him "we live and move and have our being." (Acts 17:28).

Without this revelation, we will only see ourselves as isolated individuals. Our influence and the extension of our lives will be limited to our own personal and physical expressions. We will live as islands unto ourselves, or drift alone in the sea of life, deprived of true communion with God and meaningful relationships with one another. God not only sees each of us as individuals, but He has also put us into His family. Together we make up the body of Christ and the habitation of God. We are the temple He has chosen to dwell in, a temple not made with hands. The temple must be sanctified and the people must be holy; then the blessings will be restored.

To Satan, our ignorance is his opportunity. He continues to use past agreements with fear and lies to operate his strongholds inside of us - even after we are saved. His objective is to operate his activities in our life as much as he can, even though we are the temple property of the Lord God. Even though Satan knows that salvation makes what he is doing to us technically illegal; being saved does not prevent him from pursuing his ruthless attempts to invade our lives, build strongholds in us, oppress us, and steal anything he can from us.

Once we are saved, everything the Enemy continues to do in us to lay claim to our life, is trespassing. We are bought and paid for by Jesus Christ. Our life is hid with Christ in God (Col. 3:3), and our sins are all under the blood. We must not be deceived or live in denial. We must walk in the power of the Holy Spirit. If the Enemy can get us to sanction the illegal claims he is making against us - by getting us to agree with him that we are guilty and deserve to be punished - he will be able to continue to steal, kill, and destroy regardless of our salvation.

Satan does not stop tempting us in his efforts to manipulate or deceive us into sinning, nor does he stop accusing or condemning us just because we are now saved. The battle for truth and freedom has only just begun. For some, the war actually intensifies after salvation. They are confused and filled with doubts about the blessing of salvation; and the power of the Gospel to change them, to forgive their sins, or give rest to their souls.

Salvation sets up a beachhead of righteousness, and a pavilion of safety for the believer. Freedom, and the restoration of blessings, requires that we come back into agreement with God. Our agreement with God's truth removes the authority from the Devil's hand and puts the power back into ours. Our cooperation with God facilitates the eviction of the Trespasser from our lives and assures the eradication his strongholds, including the "body of death" programing that runs those strongholds.

7

CAN A BELIEVER BE CURSED?

ES THEY CAN!

The question as to whether or not a Christian can have a curse is complicated by an explosive mixing of concepts. Some say we are new creatures and it's all under the Blood; old things, including the curses, have passed away. Others point to the long list of physical health issues, poverty, relational breakdowns, pain, and circumstantial difficulties which continue to operate as frequently in some believers' lives as they do in non-believers, and ask, 'Are divorce, diabetes, and car accidents not curses'? And, if they are, it appears that being a Christian does not automatically exempt us from experiencing the negative effects of the curses. Why not?

To answer the question we must first sort out the categories in order to define and isolate the group of people we are examining. We have the Old Testament, which calls for obedience to the Law. We have the New Testament, which calls for obedience to the Law of Love and the Holy Spirit.

We have the Curse of Original Sin which gives the Devil and his 'body of death' software program (See Rom. 7:24) general operating privileges within the human race to bring a curse upon all human beings. We also have the specific curses that come upon specific individuals and families, which we will examine more in depth later.

We have disobedient people, both believers and nonbelievers, struggling under curses. We have godly and obedient people who suffer from sickness and loss. We have those persecuted for right-eousness' sake. We also have innocent people suffering as a result of sins that have been committed against them, all struggling under curses of pain and injustice. We have all been the victims of other peoples' sins, including individually; as part of our genera-tional and familial bloodlines; and as citizens of our particular nations.

In sorting out the question of curses, we recognize that we have believers and unbelievers. Unbelievers have no option for real freedom until they are released from the Devil's kingdom by receiving Jesus. They are still technically the Devil's property and under his control. They remain under the constrictions of the Law, whether they are striving to sort of keep it or completely disre-gard it.

Believers, however, have the ever expanding option of deliverance and freedom. How well they understand these options and take advantage of them will determine the way in which and how much of their lives will be played out for good. If we understand the depth of God's love and goodness in our lives and respond to His commands obediently, we can live beyond the curse. There are two covenants: one based upon the works of the Law, the other based upon the promise of God; one on the fruit basket of good works, the other on the blood of the Lamb.

It is well to mention here that, just as we assume that God blesses us, we must know that the Devil also has the prerogative to bless his subjects. His temporary blessings are designed either to bribe or boycott, for the express purpose of manipulation as a tool by which to keep the lost blind to their dangerous condition. Their blessings keep them content not to search beyond their good fortune for the truth. Demonic blessings move like a silent killer among those who refuse the love of the truth, to cause them to assume they are fine. (See Jer. 7:17-18 and Jer. 44:15-18 and Thess. 2:9-12 for a biblical example of this kind of deception.)

LAW AND GRACE

The confusion between Law and Grace inside the church has allowed the Enemy to set up a third option for deception in the mixing of Law and Grace. When we 'cross' legalism, in the pursuit of our own righteousness - with grace, in the pursuit of God's righteousness - it creates a hybridized modification of salvation that God does not recognize as legitimate.

"Lord, Lord, have we not done many mighty works in Your Name?" (Mt. 7:22) illustrates this well enough. The Enemy's ability to confuse and counterfeit the Gospel of Jesus Christ at its core has set up the contest in the Devil's favor and made it possible for him to bring his star players, Fear, Doubt, Confusion, Guilt, and Shame, onto the field.

Mixing works and Law with grace and the Spirit creates hardness of heart, a stupor, and a spiritual vulnerability which increases spiritual sterility, anxiety, and apathy in our service to our King. Confusion and Doubt about what is required of us creates an opportunity for Guilt and Condemnation to misuse the scripture and consume our zeal for God and His truth. Not understanding or being able to separate the true Gospel of Jesus Christ from the counterfeits weakens the power of the Good News and makes us an easy target to the ongoing accusations of the Evil One.

Though obedience is the required position for both the Old and New Testament believer to receive blessings, obedience does not exempt the obedient believer from being tested. And though some believers are walking in the understanding of the freedom they have in Christ, many New Testament believers are still walking in their 'old soul software'. Even though they are saved, they are under the condemnation that comes to those who are walking in the "flesh," (Rom. 8:1-2) and not in the Spirit.

They have not understood their new position in Christ and still seek to satisfy the Law of religious expectations through works in order to stay saved. The Bible tells us that "as many as are of the works of the law are under the curse; for it is written, Cursed is everyone who does not continue in all things which are written in the book of the law, to do them...But the just shall live by faith." (Gal. 3:10-11). It seems clear to those who have ears to hear.

From this it is evident that justification does not come through the Law, but through faith. Many Christians are saved, yet they continue to live and strive under the requirements of the Law, invested in a rigorous religious program of good works. Good works will flow supernaturally from one who is nourished by and abiding in the Vine. Those who are still walking in the old mind-sets of the carnal nature are still trying to do what only God can do and has already done in the Spirit.

Not understanding that all the Law and its demands have been satisfied in the death and shed blood of Jesus Christ, many have unwittingly turned back to the keeping of the Law to obtain and maintain their own righteousness. They become driven by the spirits of Religion and Performance in an attempt to keep the Law and be perfect. This was the whole debate and discussion in Acts 15 between the new Jewish believers and the Gentile converts.

This kind of rote legalism is not the relationship God seeks to have with us now, nor is the compliance of 'going through the motions' anything He ever wanted. Compliance is not love. Love is and comes out of devotion, not duty. The Law has been fulfilled and completed through the work of Jesus Christ on the Cross. The 'wiles' of the Devil have used our desire to obey God to actually tear us apart and set us up in opposition to both Him and ourselves. This makes us vulnerable to the spirit of Condemnation and sets us up in opposition to ourselves, while putting us at odds with God's grace.

Those who still believe keeping the Law is the key to righteousness are set up for Condemnation, just as disobedience in not keeping the Law allows the Enemy to bring in his demonic judgments and patterns of destruction. Disobedience to the Law gives Guilt, Hell's lead attorney for the Prosecution, ample opportunity to press charges of blame and failed responsibility. The Enemy uses breaking the Law as his strong argument in the Court of Heaven, to build his case to disqualify a person from God's blessings and justify his request to punish them with his demonic judgments.

BLESS THOSE WHO CURSE YOU

Our Lord instructs His followers to "Love your enemies, and bless those who curse you." (Mt. 5:44). From this passage, it is apparent that a believer can be the target of someone's curse - i.e. that someone can pray for evil to come upon a believer's life. We are instructed to deal with those who curse us by forgiving and blessing them. These deliberate acts of love and forgiveness remove any justification the Enemy might use in claiming a right to bring a judgment of harm upon the righteous one he seeks to curse.

Believers can also bring curses on themselves. If obedience brings a blessing, then disobedience can bring a curse. As believers, we still have a free will and can still be tempted to disobey. If we, as believers, disobey the Law of Love, then, yes, it is possible to come under the shadow of a curse even after being saved.

Is that what God wants? Absolutely not! God has established obedience as the prerequisite for blessing. If obedience is a prerequisite to blessing, it is also a protection against the curse. Obedience, along with God's remedy for restoration - repentance and confession of sin are also critical in breaking the curses and the demonic patterns of judgment the Enemy wants to bring against us.

If the curse without a cause does not come, then for the curse to come, there must be a cause! (Pr. 26:2 NKJV). If it is true there must be a cause, then a disobedient believer will suffer the consequences of his sin just as an unbeliever will, and maybe more so, as the Enemy often does not punish his sleeping subjects immediately. The converse is also true. If the Accuser can find "nothing on me" as Jesus declared of Himself in going to the Cross, then for the Enemy to attack a believer, he must get special permission, as in the case with Job.

Because God declared Job to be a righteous man before Satan started his petition to "sift Job as wheat", and he could find no cause or fault in Job from which to start his case against him, the Accuser had to make up an accusation and then seek special permission to "test him". We see the same to be true many centuries later when Jesus told Peter that Satan had desired to "sift" him. Jesus assured Peter, however, that He had prayed for him and that he would be converted and when he was, to strengthen his brethren.

Satan was building his request to test Job on the premise that God's goodness toward Job was undeserved and he did not believe Job's love for God was genuine. The Enemy challenged God to prove to him that Job's righteous behavior was not a dishonest manipulation just to get and keep His blessings, and that God was not merely bribing Job to buy His affections.

Satan's challenge to God's love for His children, and The Enemy' accusation of us are the mainstay and sum total of Satan's activity on earth. Therefore, since we are still easily deceived and confused, influenced by lies and uncertain of God's goodness and unfailing love for us, it is not difficult for Satan to provoke us to become discouraged and find fault with God. Our response to

God's actions - even the ones we do not understand, including how we keep His Word and His admonition for us to obey Him, becomes the critical determinant of the outcome of these testings.

Grace feels awkward and undeserved in a world where everything must be earned. Guilt feels normal and warrented. It is easy for the Devil to convince us we are bad and guilty of making God mad. We have been programmed to believe we are bad because we have been trained to believe we 'are what we do'.

PERSISTENT SIN IN A BELIEVER'S LIFE

Persistent and willful sin in believers' lives, on the other hand, can create an ongoing string of consequences which keep us tied to the curses Jesus died to free us from. Persistent sin would indicate that we have not yet come to a full revelation of truth of God's love and a true concept of who we are, made in His image.

We are God's workmanship, created in Christ Jesus unto good works. Our sanctification is under the management of the Holy Spirit who lives inside of us. Sanctification is the process in which He cleanses our house and restores it to its original state of holiness. In that process of sanctification, He will not throw anything out, however, without our permission.

Following Jesus is in essence, the process of sanctification. That is why we are to follow Jesus. Following is a willful and voluntary act on our part. We are not forced to do the right thing. And sometimes we find, like the Apostle Paul, that we want to do the right thing, but find that we cannot. Those are the times when we cry out, "Who will deliver me from this body of death?"

Spiritual warfare in the physical and spiritual takeover and destruction of our lives is real. Without putting that knowledge in the mix, there will be no satisfactory resolution of any matter by making better choices and being good. Surrendering to the wisdom of the Holy Spirit, though not mandatory, is absolutely essential if we are to be victorious in overcoming the evil of this present world. Many people never consider the need to fight the spiritual battles or the need to go to this deep to resolve their issues of guilt and pain and regret.

Following Christ is not a journey for the cowardly or for the faint hearted. We are, and can only be, victorious in the Enemy's onslaughts against us if we recognize the depths of the treachery in the spiritual war being fought for our souls. Even as this war is going on all around us all the time, the first revelation we must have is that in and of ourselves, we are no match for the enemy. Only in surrendering the struggle to Jesus Christ will we have power over the things that have had power over us, including persistent sin.

The root of that persistent sin is trying to quit what we cannot stop. The Enemy is strong-arming us to do what we do not want to do, (Rom.7:20) and then condemns us for doing it! The Righteous Judge is not unjust or unfair in judging us for doing something we did NOT want to do and have tried to quit and get free from. The Evil One baits us into thinking what we are doing is our fault and that we must overcome what we cannot overcome in order to be okay. This becomes an irresolvable conflict and he delights in snaring us in his "sin traps" of condemnation. He baits the hooks with the very things we are hungry for in order to get us to give up the good fight of faith and receive his judgment.

As long as he can get us to sin, he can condemn us for sinning. Guilt and Condemnation become our constant companions. "There is therefore now NO condemnation to those who are in Christ Jesus who do not walk after the flesh but according to the Spirit." (Rom.8:1) How can that be if I still see myself sinning? Freedom from condemnation requires that we walk according to the Spirit, that we stop using the 'old soul' software – which has been activated by the agreements that have been made in our soul, - also known as our flesh. The Bible admonishes us to -

"Walk in the spirit and you will not fulfill the lusts of the flesh." (Gal. 5:16).

In matters of addiction and bondage and life-controlling habits, Paul tells us very clearly that we need deliverance (Rom. 7:24). The Enemy tells us we need to 'try harder' to quit. If we do not understand the truth, we will stay bound in the Enemy's judgments of us for those sins, even after we have - in truth - already been set free from them through the death of Christ and His resurrection.

Many very devout and godly people still seem to struggle under the weight of a curse even after they are saved and are being obedient. These are the ones mentioned in Hebrews chapter 11, the Hall of Faith, of whom the world was not worthy. These are those who are persecuted for righteousness sake, and not for a fault of their own, although the Enemy would orchestrate his patterns of attack and illegal judgments against them as much as he can, as in the case with Job. God is always aware that we are being tested, and watches over us to keep us - even if we do not feel like we are being protected.

HOW FREE AM I?

Not fully understanding the power of God's grace and forgiveness makes us vulnerable to condemnation. Believers who continue to work to please God in their own strength - or feel they must be under the directives of some other religious holy-man, or guru, or man-made traditions or doctrines, in order to enter into the rest of God - miss the whole point of having a relationship of their own with God.

Trying to be good binds us to the Law, which keeps us hooked into works and striving. The failure to be good enough makes us feel guilty. Guilt and failure persuade us to believe we are no good and deserve to be punished. This kind of thinking opens us up to the attack of the Enemy and persuades us to believe, not that we are the son or daughter of the Most High God, but that we are undeserving and unworthy.

The better question with regard to the desire to be good would be, 'Why would I want to be bad?' when being bad is not who I am! Sinning undermines both our identity in Christ, and the rest and peace Jesus Christ died to give us. It binds us to a life of anxiety and reflects fear rather than the knowledge that we are loved. We become filled with religious obsessions and compulsions, neurosis, panic, and condemnation.

This kind of thinking greatly diminishes the value of the blessings God so lavishly bestowed upon us, making them a matter of works and rewards earned rather than gifts freely given to us by the grace and goodness of God. Putting love and the accumulation of good things (blessings) into a context of works and earning exalts self-effort and redefines love as conditional.

Pursuing the Law and good works as a means of salvation keeps us from knowing that it is through the gracious goodness of God that we are FREE from the curses, and not because our own merit. For those so inclined to earn their own salvation, "Whom the Son sets free is free indeed" (Jn. 8:36) becomes merely a nice thought, but not a serious spiritual reality.

If we are free and do not know it, however, then really how free are we? If we do not know that we are free, how might the Enemy use our ignorance of that freedom in order to promote the lie that perpetuates his bondage? How clever and helpful of him to use our desire to 'be free' to deceive us into believing his intentions to 'assist us' in getting free are genuine?

And if we do not know that we know the truth about the Gospel of Grace and Good News; or if we are still uncertain in our hearts about who God is; or if we are still basing our self-concept on what we do; then how free are we? How can we rise up and insist upon our new identity, inheritance, position and authority as bona fide members of the Kingdom of God unless we know the truth?

And, ultimately, how can we resist the Devil or conduct business on behalf of the Kingdom of God if we are still controlled by the Devil's definitions of truth, which, in actuality, are lies?

OBEDIENCE BRINGS BLESSING

The original covenant blessings were promises made to Abraham, the father of the nation of Israel. Those blessings were obtained through Abraham's faith. Faith is trusting in God to fulfill His Promises. Abraham believed God and "it was accounted to him for righteousness." (Rom. 4:19-22).

Our faith in God is demonstrated in the same way, by our obedience to Him. The blessings of God in our lives are contingent upon our obedience. Even though we no longer live under the Law but under grace, obedience is still obedience and obedience is still required for blessing.

Grace does not eliminate the need for obedience after we are saved. Even as Romans 6:1 asks, "Shall we continue in sin that grace may abound? Certainly not!" Faith is not lip service. It must be walked out in the midst of resistance and oppression. We fight the good fight of faith against sin and the temptation to believe the lies that bring forth the sin. "Therefore do not let sin reign in your mortal body, that you should obey it in its lusts. And do not present your members as instruments of unrighteousness to sin but present yourselves to God as being alive from the dead..." (Rom. 6:12-13).

God knew that we can and will still sin, even after being saved. Whenever we permit or allow sin to prevail in our lives, we have already come under the influence of the lie. We may not yet know it is a lie or that the Tempter has 'tricked' us. Nonetheless, sinning allows the consequences of sin and its resulting curses to continue. Therefore, the curses can and will still operate in the life of a New Testament believer if that believer continues to believe lies and disobey. Lies produce sin. Sin brings with it consequences. Those consequences open the door to a curse.

Just as obedience is the prerequisite for blessings, sin and iniquity are precursors to curses. The more we walk in the truth, the less we sin. The less we sin, the less ground the Enemy will have in our lives. Grace does not let the believer 'off the hook', but offers us a place to come for mercy and a place to stand where we can find strength from God's Spirit to repent, to resist the Devil and reject his lies.

Our 'responsibility' before God in the matter of sin is to repent. Repentance means to change our mind - i.e., to stop believing the lies. It is meant to be a part of our daily walk with Jesus. When we change our minds, we come out of agreement with the lie and come into agreement with the truth. We confess our sins to God. Our confession is a declaration of the truth that breaks the power of the lie. We demonstrate our agreement with the truth, the Word of God, by obeying it.

God has done His part to make the blessings of His love available to every believer. Our part is to obey Him and receive them. Obedience opens us up to the blessings and shuts down any claims Satan would make in his desire to shape our lives according to the patterns of bloodguilt that have gone unaddressed and unconfessed by our former generations.

The Bible teaches us that there are reasons for curses. They do not come as random acts of 'bad luck'. Satan uses legal parameters, including the Law of Reciprocity, to inflict specific curses for specific reasons on specific bloodlines. This does NOT mean these people are more wicked than others in their family line. Like the man born blind, they may not have even sinned, but that does not mean no one had sinned and that the Enemy does not have some legal grounds against them in building his case to gain permission to test them.

CHRIST BECAME A CURSE FOR US

Please note that Jesus Christ has redeemed us from the curse of the Law, by becoming a curse for us (Gal. 3:13). He redeemed us from the curse of Original Sin. His death brought in the New Covenant, which purchased for us a new option, life and forgiveness. His sacrifice destroyed the curse of death and opened up the way for "whosoever will" to return to God.

Those who accept His gift of salvation are free from the curse of sin and death. Satan has no more legal right to them. However, like many of the newly emancipated slaves in the Civil War, if we do not claim our new-found freedom we will still live in our old slave mentality, bound by the power of fear to the old system of slavery and oppression.

Because the finished work of Christ in our personal life is contingent upon our receiving it - even in spite of the fact that all the work has been done to accomplish our healing and deliverance - curses can still operate in our life under certain circumstances. The first of these circumstances is ignorance of the truth of God's love and our emancipation from the Hell's plantation.

Though the activity of the Devil in a believer's life is now illegal, he is still permitted to tempt us. If we fail to submit to God and resist the Devil (Ja. 4:7) -either out of ignorance because we do not know our authority, or because we continue to live in our old, carnal mindsets - Satan will be able to continue his work of destruction in our lives as if nothing has happened to change all that.

Remember, salvation is not the same as sanctification. Salvation is like boarding the plane to heaven. The ticket has been purchased and freely given to us. Sanctification is the process that determines the shape we will be in when we arrive there. Life and the lies of the Enemy would still persuade us not to use our ticket or board the plane. And for those who board the plane, the Enemy would persuade them that they can only ride in the cargo bin with the dead weight of all their sins still surrounding them.

The difference between salvation through grace and good works is like the difference that can be seen between being a butterfly and a caterpillar. To become a butterfly we must let go of our own lives and go into the cocoon. Only through the transformation by death will there be a new birth. Through the Resurrection, we can experience metamorphosis, much like changing from an ugly crawling brown caterpillar into a beautiful butterfly. We no longer have to pull ourselves along in an ever-increasing exertion of self-effort; but like the majestic monarch butterfly, we can fly thousands of miles in our migration without getting lost or disorientated. This is the power of the Cross and the change it makes in the lives of 'whosoever believes'.

If we continue to embrace the lies and believe that all the thoughts we think are our own, we will be deceived. As long as we are deceived, we sin. God cannot bless disobedience on either side of the Cross. If sin and disobedience continue after we are saved, so will the curses. Curses are the result of the agreements we make with the lie or lies that produce sin. Sin is the result of believing lies. That is why Paul urges us to "be transformed, by the renewing of our minds." (Rom. 12:1).

Some are content to be saved and 'hold on' until Jesus comes to take them home. They live a sub-standard version of the abundant life and never know the power of their new life in Christ or the wonderful blessings of peace and assurance He died to give them. The mercy and revelation of those blessings go unclaimed because of lack of understanding as to the depth or the power of the Blood of Christ - not only to cleanse us from sin but purge from us its power and consequence.

When we invite the Lord Jesus Christ to come and reign in our lives, He begins to heal our hearts and rebuild our houses. Our hearts have been broken by disappointments, failure, rejection and shattered dreams. The blessings of love and family have turned into pain and rejection. The blessings of health and hope have been stolen our children from us.

As a result, we live in sickness and despair. The house that was intended to be a home has become an inferno of hatred and hurt. We have learned to live without the blessings of God's love and care by learning to cope with life and live in anxiety and exist by barely surviving when Jesus died that we might have more than enough.

Many, if not all, of the deep things of God appear as foolishness to our carnal minds (See I Cor. 2:1-16). Human reasoning and logic cannot serve us in the place where only the mind of Christ is able to keep us. Using our human mind and emotions as a spiritual compass to understand the things of God is like using a tweezers to pick a star out of the sky. It cannot be done.

Only through the indwelling of the Holy Spirit are we able to see the Light of His truth and understand the mysteries of the Kingdom of God. We are called to be "servants of Christ and stewards of the mysteries of God," (I Cor. 4:1). God is not looking for orators and scholars or technicians and theologians. The power of the Gospel of Grace does not come through excellency of speech, but in power and demonstration, as we bring forth the Gospel of Jesus Christ and Him crucified. (I Cor. 2:1-4).

In the mysteries of God many things cannot literally be sorted out into piles of 'either/or', as so many of us would like to do. God is not a politician or merely one in an assortment of religious figures. God is infinitely more marvelous, existing beyond anything we can describe or have defined Him to be. He does not consult with us on the daily order of earth's operations, although He calls us His friends and includes us among the most priceless and precious of all He has.

He is not persuaded by our demands to explain His omniscience, nor is He obligated to abide by our theologies. He is not contained in the doctrinal discussions of the Emergent, the Armenians, or the Calvinist. He is not the personal property of any specific sect or denomination. He is not contained in our paradigms, nor impressed with our discussion of Truth.

We have not called Him; but rather, He has chosen us and appointed us to "go and bear fruit." (Jo. 15:16). We are called to believe that Jesus Christ is Who He said He is and that He came down here from Heaven as the Son of God incarnate to die on the Cross, to break Satan's stranglehold on creation and save us. He died that we could be brought back into our original family, as the sons and daughters of the Most High God.

This is the Gospel message of our salvation. Through His Word, God bids us to both "rightly divide the word of truth" and "shun profane and vain babblings." (II Tim. 2:15-16) Paul tells his young prodigy Timothy to "Remind them of these things, charging them before the Lord not to strive about words to no profit, to the ruin of the hearers." (II Tim. 2:14). But rather, God calls us to believe Him and rise up and take back that which has been stolen from us of our blessings and the destiny to which He has called us.

PART II

UNDERSTANDING THE WAR WITHIN

8

TAKING BACK THE LAND

*S*TRONGHOLDS IN OUR SOULS

Many of us live in a land of spiritual giants, bound in strongholds of destructive habits and life-controlling problems we cannot seem to escape. As we consider the task of taking back our souls, we are much like Joshua and the children of Israel preparing to re-enter the Promised Land. Though they were the legal descendants of Abraham, and rightful heirs to the land given to Abraham by God, their 430 year absence had allowed the 'termites' of paganism and idolatry to infest the fertile soil and fruitful hills of the land God had promised their Father. The Promised Land had been 'trashed'- over run and occupied by people who were the enemy of God.

The land had been taken over by followers of Baal and an assortment of evil-spirited gods and deities that animated the sticks and stones worshipped by its inhabitants. In spite of Canaan being the rightful property of the Israelites, God did not offer to hand it back to His Children on a silver platter. He would not meddle in the affairs of men and risk being accused of playing favorites. Rather, God would let them decide. If they chose to obey and follow Him, He would help them come up against the giants and get their land back. Through Him, they would be victorious.

God told Joshua, "'Every place that the sole of your foot will tread upon I have given to you', as I said to Moses." (Josh. 1:3). In that command, God instructed them to "load their weapons" (the literal translation of that verse) and remove the occupants by legal contest. God gave them the strategy for taking back that which was rightfully theirs. He now directs us to do the same. The parallel drawn here between our souls and the territory known as the Promised Land is based on what Jesus describes as the kingdom of God being within us in Luke 17:21. His Kingdom is incarnate within us, making our souls and bodies the real battlefield on which the War of Kingdoms is fought.

The Kingdom of Darkness uses lies to bring us under the control of fear and bind us in desolation. When we pray, "Thy Kingdom come, Thy will be done", we are agreeing with the invasion of The Kingdom of Darkness by the Light of God's Truth, the revelation of Jesus Christ, Who is the Light of the World. We agree with The Kingdom of Light invade and over throw the invasion of the Kingdom of Darkness that has held our souls captive and stripped us of what is rightfully ours for many generations.

Wherever the Light comes, it drives back the darkness. We are coming as the Children of Light to drive back the penetration of Darkness and to take back our lives, our identities, and our rights as the Blood-bought Children of God. Whom the Son sets free is free indeed, Jn. 8:36). We are free, bought and paid for in full by Jesus Christ. We do not owe the Devil anything. He no longer has any rightful claim to our lives. We are the Redeemed come back to take back what the Kingdom of Darkness has stolen from us and defeat the lies of the god of this world.

As believers, freedom is our spiritual legacy. As Freedom Fighters we are faced with a similar situation as Joshua. We have come to recover, not only the restoration of truth and freedom to our own lost souls, but to reclaim our spiritual legacies and the divine mandates given to our generations that had been lost to years of despair and desperation created by Enemy occupation. We are the Redeemed, the Children of the Light who have been trampled down by the invasion of enemy forces and evil spirits who feast on our blessings in order to destroy our legacy of freedom and spiritual identity. It is time for us to reclaim our inheritance and the Promises God gave us through the Light of His Truth. (Is. 61:4-5).

We are directed, as was Joshua, to "take back our souls," and reclaim the territory lost to sin. We have been held hostage by the Kingdom of Darkness under the persuasion of the wicked one for too long. Just as God directed Joshua and the Israelites to recover the land He had rightfully given to Abraham and his descendants, God wants us to take back that which has rightfully been given to us by God. It is time to clear the record and "wipe out the hand-writing of requirements that was against us which was contrary to us" - because it was nailed to the Cross of Jesus Christ, (Col.2:14).

God is glorified when we are vindicated. We are vindicated and He is victorious when we believe what God says about who we are and not what the Enemy has tried to get us to believe. Victory is to understand the war and boldly reclaim our true identity as the redeemed of the Lord. It is knowing that His truth has defeated our Accuser and overthrown the charges he has made against us. The indictments of sin and shame have been thrown out of Court through the Death and victorious Resurrection of Jesus Christ.

The battle to take back the land and recover all that has been given to us by God begins with salvation. Salvation refers to ownership and buying the house back through redemption. It restores the 'Title deed' of our 'house' back to us and opens the door to freedom from the slavery of sin. Salvation, however, does not automatically halt the Enemy's activities in our life. He continues to operate from the strongholds he had set up in us by using the 'open accounts' he had obtained through the agreements he made with our ancestors. This allows him to resist our new life in Christ and hinder our growth and development as he tries to retain or regain his power to hold us captive.

Sanctification, on the other hand, is the process of cleaning the house and clearing out the 'giants', the 'squatters' that have taken over our lives. Sanctification becomes the process of transformation through the renewing of the mind by sweeping out the lies and picking up the garbage that has been left lying around by sin. Sanctification under the direction of the Holy Spirit drives back the darkness and gives us control of the areas of our lives that have been controlling us.

Sanctification means declaring war on the powers of darkness that have detained us in the prison camps of Hell and held us hostage in their attempt to brainwash and annihilate us. It means tearing down the strongholds of sin that have been built by agreements with the lies that shape and undergird the fortresses of darkness, and replacing them with the revelation of Jesus Christ. It means rebuilding and healing the places that have been destroyed by generations of idolatry including the false gospels that have separated us from the love of God, in order that we might discover again the true purposes for which we were created. It means having our health and our freedom restored to freedom to love God and use our gifts for the glory of God.

After salvation anything and everything the Enemy does in our lives becomes 'trespassing'. In the places he once rightfully occupied, however, specific strongholds and areas of human vulnerability will still exist, as will our susceptibility to his ongoing attempts to deceive us. We must remember that the body is weak. We are vulnerable to the need for many things to sustain our life. This vulnerability permitted by God does not come as a flaw or fault of our own and is not in itself sinful. It does, however, make us an easy prey for the Devil who would 'help us' solve our problems and get our needs met by using his solutions. Embracing the

Evil One's answers to our needs only creates additional problems and enslaves us to his demands at yet another level.

Although these 'pockets' of sin and resistance are still operating under the control of the familiar spirits, even in in our life after we are saved, they do not invalidate our salvation or God's rightful ownership of our house. Our salvation is secured by our agreement with the Provision for our redemption made through the Blood of Jesus Christ given in our place. Salvation transfers the true and rightful ownership of our souls back to us and the Lord. That battle was fought and won on the Cross. And though the battle seems to be far from over, it is - at the same time - already finished!

The truth of our liberation does not stop the Liar from lying or making his now unlawful claims in our lives. He will continue to occupy the strongholds and carry on his illegal activities in our lives even though they are technically not legal any more. Our agreement with salvation and our cooperation with the work of the Holy Spirit through sanctification are crucial in allowing the Lord to reclaim for us what He had rightfully given to us. We are able to take back our city-souls, which have been overgrown by sin and occupied by giants. In coming against the generational strongholds, we are re-establishing the rule of God's Kingdom within us, on earth, even as His kingdom comes and His will is done in heaven (Mt. 6:10).

LOST CITY SOUL

As human beings, we are three part beings made up of body, soul, and spirit. The 'flesh' is the word used to describe the connection between two of those three parts, the body and the soul. To be alive, the body and the soul must be connected. The body is the vessel, the hardware that carries the soul. The soul is the 'operating software' the body uses to navigate through life. The soul has been programmed by the experiences of the Pit, and uses those experiences to evaluate the next set of decisions. In essence, the soul is the place out of which the 'carnal man', also known as the 'old man', operates. It is the place from which the Enemy conducts his operations to tempt and pervert the counsel of God. The Enemy sets up a debate between the soul and the spirit - the spirit man being that which has been activated through salvation to receive the download of the revelation of God's Holy Spirit.

The Tempter can tempt and influence both our mind (thinking) and our heart (feelings and emotions). When we are persuaded to yield to those temptations, it becomes sin. Accepting Satan's solution to the problems he set up in our lives gives him permission to solve the problems and the irresolvable conflicts he has generated in our lives. Believing his lies feeds the desires and promotes the inclinations of the carnal man. Need opens the door to seeking a solution. When need and Satan's solutions conceive they bring forth sin, and create the ongoing iniquity that opens the door for the curses to come down into our lives. (See Ja. 1:13-15)

God's instructions for the sanctification and recovery of our lost city-souls are clear: "For this commandment which I command you today, it is not too mysterious for you, nor is it far off... See, I have set before you today life and good, death and evil, in that I command you today to love the LORD your God, to walk in His ways, and to keep His commandments, His statutes, and His judgments, that you may live and multiply; and the LORD your God will bless you in the land which you go to possess."(Deut. 30:11 & 15).

"I call heaven and earth as witnesses today against you, that I have set before you, life and death, blessing and cursing; therefore choose life, that both you and your descendants may live." (Deut.30:19). All of us have already been predisposed to accept and live with the prearranged agreements set up by our ancestors. Many of us, however, have chosen to sign a contract with the Devil ourselves, and in so doing have obligated our children to serve the same cruel master who rules over us.

SIGNING A CONTRACT

Sin engages, or 'signs', a contract with the Devil. Every time we sin, we enter into an agreement with the Tempter. We come into this world as servants under the old contracts and agreements put into place through the sins of our ancestors. We unknowingly suffer many things under the longstanding, though hidden deals our ancestors made with the Evil One. Buried beneath years of forgotten generations and left hidden in the closets of shame are the deeds and documents the Enemy has used to claim his right to continuing his harassment and destruction in our own lives.

The land lawfully given to us has been invaded and overrun by the familiar spirits that have lived with us for many generations. Coming in through the gates that have been left hanging open, the Wicked One slips in almost unnoticed, like a familiar 'friend', using the back doors of sin and disobedience to make his 'legitimate' entrance to come in and pay us a visit. If those sins are left unresolved from one generation to the next, the door stays open and the destruction is carried down. This allows the Enemy to continue to exert his rights and claims over our lives, to visit the "sins of the fathers" onto the next generation. (Ex. 20:5).

FRIENDS OF THE FAMILY - OR NOT

"Company is here!" These visitors from Hell have come to bring the sins and their negative effects down from the fathers onto their children. They first came to our ancestors and made their home among them. Now they make themselves ready to take up residence in our house. They are on standby, ready to begin their work of corrupting and confusing our body and soul as soon as the agreement with fear has been transacted. Their presence as illegal trespassers is not meant to be permanent, even though they have set up their fortresses and strongholds as mindsets which operate inside of our souls as an everyday extension of the Kingdom of Darkness.

The Bible clearly says, "the iniquities, (patterns of sin) of the fathers are 'visited' on the children to the third and fourth generations of those who hate Me." (Ex. 20:5). Though we might debate the exact nature and method of this demonic invasion or the transmission of information that is used to control us - whether it is environmental, biological, or spiritual, or a combination thereof - the curses do, nevertheless, come. And, though God never meant for them to become a permanent part of our lives, the effects of the curses brought on as demonic judgments are, nonetheless, real and deadly.

The transmission of evil, brought down through these 'visitors', carries the curse from one generation to the next, to become Satan's masterpiece in the destruction of the family. The family holds within it the essential building blocks of human life and love. It forms the foundation for society and is the classroom for the training and instruction of the next generation. As individual and family relationships erode through offense and injustice, the basic concepts of love and justice are cast off. The defiling influence of sin begins to reprogram us to promote the concept of 'doing' in order to secure the spirituality of our 'being'.

The reduction of the Gospel to that of law and performance in order to achieve the desired answers to life's problems is called 'transactionalism'. The Enemy uses pain, confusion and need to push his agenda of 'do it yourself', leading the desperate and disillusioned to believe the basic lie behind witchcraft, 'It is up to me". Failed expectations obscures the 'rest' Christ offers to those who abide in Him and creates a new level of fear and anxiety that drives the believer into unbelief. It diminishes our social interactions to conditional love, failure, dysfunction, and pain.

The Devil uses these 'visitors' to strike deals, make agreements, create conflict, make war; and, ultimately, bait the hooks of destruction in every conceivable way to market his counterfeit promises of immortality and reincarnation packages. He offers the unsuspecting masses who are ignorant of his intentions and his incessant contempt for God, a growing number of alternative immortality life plans as 'trade in' options in lieu death. Hoping we will not notice that - in making the deal - we have traded the promises of eternal life given to us by the Author of life, for the short lived pleasures of sin for a season. Satan is blinded by his own brilliance by assuming the 'joke' will be on us.

FAMILIAR SPIRITS AND IMPERSONATORS

Included in the diabolical intentions of the Evil One and his demons, is the innate desire to control the world and crush the human spirit. Through the judgment for their rebellion, these evil spirits lost access to their own bodies. This left these disembodied-spirits drooling over our bodies. They must have a body to be able to satisfy their own lustful appetites. They see our bodies as fitting and suitable extensions for themselves, and seek to inhabit them to continue their own fitful, tormented existence. Knowing he has no automatic or unauthorized entrance into a human life does not stop him from taking up residence inside of humans if he can secure an invitation. This is the catch. Someone on the inside must be persuaded to open the door and invite him to come in.

And though the lies have already been planted like seeds by those who had worked that field many generations earlier, they can only grow if they germinated. As with seeds, the lies are lying dormant, merely waiting for the right conditions for them to sprout. When we believe the lie, the lie is activated (germinated). Believing the lie activates the lie. Activation of the lie extends the invitation to the familiar spirits waiting outside the door. They come to us as old friends of the family. Believing the lies opens the door and gives them the invitation, the right of access they need to enter in and begin to block and hinder the rightful occupant of the house.

The 'Visitors' from hell must receive an invitation to come into our life. This is standard operating procedure for the Devil. When we choose to believe the lie (though many times we do not understand the "legalese" of Hell and failed to read the 'fine print'), he is permitted to enter our house. Even though we have no clue that we have made any such agreement, these destroyers come in and begin to compromise our biological systems and weaken our will. They eat away at our intention to follow God by confusing us. They influence our decisions by distorting the truth. These malicious 'guests' specialize in demonic oppression, mental and spiritual attacks and internal control of human bio-systems. Their assignment and insatiable appetite for power render us vulnerable to the spirits of Fear and Perversion, making us both a prey and their prize.

These visitors build their strongholds within our minds and hearts, setting up filters of offense and weaving a web of lies around our thoughts and feelings. Using the old family patterns, these familiar spirits slip in as tempters who disguise their temptations as our own thoughts and feelings by convincing us to believe that the thoughts and feelings we are having in our minds and hearts are our own. Once the temptation/thought has passed the vetting process, the temptation is accepted as 'my own' genuine thought. It is no longer questioned as part of an alien invasion but is awarded the status of unrestricted access to the mental activities of my mind. Remember, not every thought you think YOU thought are thoughts YOU thought. If the Enemy can convince you they are your thoughts, however, you will automatically accept them without question.

The familiar spirits are demons assigned to our particular bloodline. They are not strangers to our dispositions or our family disputes. The secrets held by Shame and the skeletons hidden in our family's closet are not a secret to them. Though they cannot 'read' our thoughts, the question is irrelevant, since they are the writers who have scripted most of those thoughts and directed the story behind our family's tragedies in the first place. Though they themselves remain hidden and uncharged, the crimes they have committed are blatant and appalling. The huge, yet undiscerned influence they have had upon our ancestors down through the centuries is only now becoming manifested in our lives as real and relevant.

Our ancestors have either knowingly or unknowingly granted these spirits permission to conduct their operations in their lives. They have worshipped idols and payed them homage. They have curried the favor and invited the assistance of these familiars, who have come in as false benefactors and protector demons, playing the same old 'Trick or Treat" negotiations on us as they did to our ancestors. The fearful used witchcraft and demonic powers as a way to stay safe and succeed. To gain favor and power and the promise of protection for themselves, many gave Fear a place of control in their world through superstition and pagan practices. Fear permitted the evil designs of the Enemy to operate freely in the lives of his subjects.

Some knowingly 'sold' their future generations to the Devil in order to win the promise of protection in the present. Others, bound by Fear and Superstition, worked out deals with the Devil unknowingly. They exchanged the truth for the lie and came under bondage of sin without even suspecting a deal had been struck. The familiar spirits used the sins of one generation to separate and alienate and lay claim to the next. Those sins gave them permission to penetrate into the lives of the descendants, breaking down their relationships and assaulting their health in ways very similar to those of their parents. Through those agreements the familiar spirits were able to draft patterns, forge ruts, re-route neurological pathways, and open the doors for the transference of evil from one generation into the next.

Generational sins and the perpetuation of evil do not just go away on their own or decrease over time, however. Things left undone do not fix themselves or get better. Neglect and Denial do not solve the problem. Though sin and iniquity and the injustice they bring do not go unnoticed by the Lord God, our refusal to address the issues only promotes the ongoing degeneration of our bloodlines.

If each generation would have understood what was going on in the spirit world they could have taken responsibility for cleaning up their own generational junk through confession and repentance. God would not have had to use such drastic measures to rid the temporal world of the mounting threats to its own survival. It is not God's will or desire for the curse or the familiar spirits that carry them to continue to flow in an uninterrupted avalanche through the lives of His children. He does not want these 'visitors' to be allowed to take up permanent residence in our souls or corrupt our legacy.

THE HUMAN DEFAULT TO SIN

Rebellion and iniquity bring judgment and the curse. "All have sinned and fall short of the glory of God," (Rom. 3:23) points us back to the idea of Original Sin as the new default setting in every human being. However, please note, what we call the Original Sin is NOT the original sin, though Satan wants us to think we were the first ones to sin and rebel against God. The genesis of every man, woman, and child built by God did not begin in a state of alienation from God, but in intimate union with Him, as reflected in His intentions to make us in His own image. Just because we are all born lost - facing in the wrong direction, and in need of a Savior - does not mean we are bad or depraved although some very bad things did happen to all of us.

Psalm 51:5 confirms the matter. "Behold, I was brought forth in iniquity, and in sin my mother conceived me." This does not mean that the act of conception is sinful, though the act of conception can occur under less than ideal circumstances. Neither do the circumstances surrounding my birth determine my worth and value or define me as BAD! The verse merely recognizes that, even in the best of circumstances, sin provides the context into which we are born, with iniquity being the mark of our fallen nature. Sin and iniquity set the temperature and regulate the environmental conditions of the Snake Pit, the place into which every one of God's sons and daughters are born.

The 'Fall' has made sin and Fear the common disposition of the natural man. The natural, carnal man is prone to believe that what presents itself in reality is the truth. Because our experiences truly, really happened, we believe they are the truth. This makes the lie based in reality easier to believe than the truth (Rom. 1:21-23). The credibility of the lie flourishes in this evil world system where we live by appearances and feelings to determine the merit and truth of something. Making judgments based on what something looks like sets us up to tumble more readily into personal sin and makes sinning easier than not sinning (Rom. 3:10-12). Despair and negativity and bondage flow more freely from our lives and lips, than does hope, justice, praise and love (Rom. 3:13-14).

This natural bent toward darkness is referred to by theologians as our "sinful human nature" and by preachers as "living in the flesh" (Rom. 7:18). Living in the flesh, in response to the dictates of this second nature allows for the division of our house and the reign of sin in our mortal body to continue. We are doubleminded and divided, torn between our new man and the old carnal man. Romans 6:12 tells us to "reckon ourselves dead indeed to sin, but alive to God in Christ Jesus our Lord. Therefore do not let sin reign in your mortal body, that you should obey it in ITS lusts, (evil passions and cravings)". (NKJV Rom.6:12) Division between sin and sonship was not God's original intention for Adam and Eve, nor did He declare our resistance to the 'flesh' to be the remedy for sin or the requirement for salvation. Obedience to the truth undergirds both freedom and the sanctification process.

All of our hearts, though fashioned by God and knit together in our mother's womb by His care, are tainted with sin. We are all born into spiritual darkness, in the middle of a spiritual war. We have been set up to be deceived. We are lost and directionless, navigating with a broken moral compass. How could we think it would be any other way since Satan is the god of this world?

The outcome in the contest between God and Satan for the souls of men is determined by our consent. Jesus said in John 8:34, "... whoever commits sin is the slave of sin." Like the scent of blood to a hungry shark, being unaware of the power of our consent makes us a prey to whatever seeks to devour us. Absorbed by the world around us, we are easily influenced and deceived. We are no match for the wiles of the Devil, who makes it his business to sedate and stupefy us as he circles closer, moving in for the kill.

Cooperating with the grace of God is only one part of the plan. Without making an effort to resist the Devil, our submission to God is only half a remedy. New life in Christ requires that we turn from evil ourselves and resist the Devil and the lies he tells us. We must fight the good fight of faith and lay hold of our inheritance lest the consequences of sin end up shaping us into looking more like the Pit (or our parents) than Jesus.

ENVIRONMENTAL BOXES

No one can deny the strong influence parents have on their children for good or evil. The environment provided by the parent(s) becomes a powerful persuasion in shaping the soft holy clay of a child's soul. Abuse, neglect, silence, negative words, and angry actions make indelible impressions on little minds and soft hearts and growing bones. Even as a good report and pleasant words are health to the bones, an evil report makes them weak and unhealthy. (Pr. 15:30 & Pr. 16:24).

Inability to discern the truth from lies makes it impossible for children to sort out the messages they receive while growing up though it is impossible to escape the effects of those messages. The corruption of their innocence, through the treachery of the lessons learned in the Snake Pit turns their young minds out to wander in the inevitable wilderness of sin. Their trust, along with their innocence, are replaced by the survival mindsets and fear-based behavior. They live according to what they have been taught to believe is true, even though their 'reality' may be far from the truth: "As a man thinks in his heart, so he is" (Pr. 23:7) though the Word of God admonishes us to 'walk in the Spirit'.

In Ezekiel, Chapter 18, however, God shows us the way He desires to address the parental 'pre-set to sin' problem and the consequences generated through it. "What does this mean, He asks?" 'The fathers have eaten sour grapes, and the children's teeth are set on edge?'" The proverb which connects the behavior of the fathers and their dispositions to their children's reaction to the parent's action has drawn God's attention.

And even as the father's bitterness was provoking their children to adopt bad attitudes, God declares, "'As I live,' says the Lord God, 'you shall no longer use this proverb in Israel.' " No longer shall the father's disobedient behavior lock their children into the loss of a godly inheritance or a belligerent disposition if they choose to act righteously. God reminds us that all souls are His, "the soul of the father as well as the soul of the son is Mine; the soul who sins shall die. But if a man is just and does what is lawful and right; ...He shall surely live!" (Ez. 18:4-5).

God is giving us an option to the human default to sin. He declares that there be a solution for the "visitation of evil" that has come coursing down the line from one generation to the next, as recorded in Exodus. No longer are we doomed by the choices of those who have gone before us to live a life predestined to destruction. We can choose to break the curse of sin and restore the blessing by choosing to live lawfully and righteously.

The inevitable patterns of sin and destruction set in motion by our ancestors can be broken by those who choose to confess the evil of their father's ways and walk in righteousness. We are not choosing to place blame our parents and grandparents. It is not a question of blame; but, rather, each one doing business on behalf of all members of their family to get back what the Devil has stolen from each particular family bloodline.

FIGHTING THE GOOD FIGHT OF FAITH

God's entrance into our soul through salvation does not automatically evict the Enemy or dissolve his entrenchments any more than Joshua's arrival in Canaan drove out the Canaanites. The vast holdings gained by the Enemy through years of assault and alienation because of disobedience, are now threatened by Jesus Christ, Who comes into our lives to set up a beach-head of righteousness. However, the battle for salvation in no way signals the end of the war.

God's life in us and the renewing of our souls is by no means a done deal as far as the Devil is concerned. And, though his activity is now illegal in the believer's life, there is no reason to believe that he will evacuate his strongholds or let us go without a fight simply because Jesus has come in. The Enemy will continue to press and oppress us until and unless we stand up and declare the truth of God in our life.

This is what Paul meant when he talked about "fighting the good fight of faith" and laying hold of eternal life (II Tim. 4:7). Though we are now eligible for the release of blessings into our lives and the reversal of the curses, nothing changes until the lies are exchanged for the truth. That exchange is accomplished through repentance and confession of sin. The process of sanctification is a process of bringing our minds and hearts back into a right relationship between God and ourselves.

Repentance (changing our minds) and confession initiate the process of reprogramming our soul by re-establishing our relationship with the truth. As we come into agreement with the Word of God (Rom. 12:1-2) and recognize the truth, the lies and the bondages they bring are broken. Confessing our sins and rejecting the lies are essential in the sanctification process and critical to breaking the curses.

As long as the lies are in place, the generational curses - including the generational trauma marked on the DNA - are still active. The devastation of the trauma, along with its 'switches and triggers', can be re-lived and used by the Enemy to bring the consequences of sin down into the next generation. This is now verified in scientific research (see the cherry blossom/mice studies, 2013), with even the finer unlearned details of the original event being re-enacted in the life of the offspring. As the descendants of those who participated in or were victims of the original offense/crime, unless the power of the trauma is broken through confession and forgiveness, the lives of the offspring can still be subject to the power of those events. The injustices and the agreements made with them, along with the pain and affliction, are set up to be repeated in the experiences of the next generation.

The difficulties, setbacks, and diseases experienced by believers are the result of believing lies. Believing the lie activates it and allows it to operate as truth. Lies that act as truth bring forth deception. Deception leads to sin. Many times the deception goes unnoticed and uncorrected. The chaos and dysfunction begins to feel normal. Trouble is explained as coincidence. If left unchallenged, it becomes part of the accepted patterns we learn to live with. Agreement with those accepted patterns allows the sin it generates to build up into iniquity. Iniquity opens the door to the curse and permits the Enemy to bring his demonic judgments upon the heirs of the original signers of the agreement with the Kingdom of Darkness.

Disguised as familiar friends of the family, the trouble these spirits bring become commonplace. The expectation of bad things happening begins to operate at a subconscious level, leaving the curse free to operate although unidentified. These curses continue to eat away, like a cancer, at the very core of our soul, taking away our joy and removing our peace. Because we see them as 'normal' or explain them as 'accidents' or 'fate' or 'bad luck', we allow them to continue without resistance. We begin to feel like we deserve the bad things that are happening to us. Our agreement with 'it is what it is' comes full circle, or we become weary and disgruntled and lose heart in God's faithfulness.

The bitter roots of unfulfilled expectations take root in our minds and begin to grow, bringing forth fruit of Regret and Self-condemnation. We begin to spiral downward, pulled into a vortex of pain and guilt. We feel angry and bitter against God, ourselves, or others. The injustices and offenses tear our soul apart. The negative consequences - including the side-effects of Satan's second round of solutions - begin to operate. Drugs, addictions, divorces, mental health problems, perfectionism, obsessions, religion, and striving all line up to 'help us' deal with Rejection and Fear and Loneliness, as Pain and Frustration start the next round of damage on the torture racks of Hell.

The lie begets the sin. The sin brings forth guilt. Guilt justifies the demonic judgment which the Enemy brings forth as a penalty and punishment for that guilt. The demonic judgment becomes the expected and accepted pattern of what will happen next as we identify with the curse. The curses generate wave after wave of destruction and depletion of life's energies and resources. The Enemy washes away all hope of restoration or remedy as he moves in to take more holy ground for his unholy purposes.

The undiscerned source of the difficulties opens the door to the continuation of confusion and discouragement. We fail to understand why these things are happening and are tempted to become bitter against God or blame ourselves or others. We begin, like Job, to question the reason for divine displeasure and feel estranged from His goodness. The Enemy uses that confusion to separate us from God and promotes an internalized system of self-reliance.

9

TRIALS AND BLESSINGS

GOD'S UNFAILING LOVE

Although God's *love* for us never fails, we need to know that God's *blessings* over us are contingent upon obedience. Many believers are confused about the difference between God's blessing and God's love. They are not the same thing. God's love for us is unconditional. It cannot be earned or destroyed. It covers and carries us at all times. He longs for us, and is jealous over us for our good. "For the Lord, whose name is Jealous, is a jealous God". (Ex. 34:14) Like any good parent, He is eager for us to succeed, be fulfilled, and do well.

Regardless of our mistakes and bad behavior, or sin, God's love never fails. God loves us because we are His; we are of Him. We are His offspring! Just like you love your children because they are of you; they are yours. Nothing we can do, or have done, or that has been done to us, can ever change that. The place of our origin defines our identity. Therefore - because we cannot change the place or fact that we are begotten by the Father - our identity is stable and settled, no matter what happens to us or what we do. Although what happens to us and what we do can readily change our perception of who we are! Our God is our Father. He is there for us, no matter what happens. He is there, operating on our behalf to protect, and redeem, and deliver us from whatever circumstances the Enemy has tried to arrange so as to destroy us.

Our blessings, however, are conditional - based upon our obedience - and thus disputable and vulnerable to the Enemy's opposition. Because they are linked with our behavior, and because God does not force us to walk in truth, and because He cannot bless disobedience, the Accuser finds any number of reasons to present objections to God's patience with us, to provoke Him to withdraw His hand of blessing and protection from us. God is not bound by the Devil's evil whims, nor is He at his mercy, nor must God get the Enemy's permission to bless us. God is just and fights this war for the recovery of His children by the rules.

That means that God's divine justice must also permit the Devil to exercise his free will, just as He permits us to exercise our free will. Because of divine justice, the Lord God permits the Devil to have what is his and allows him to do what he can to keep it. The Devil is Evil. He is a Liar and a murderer from the beginning. There is nothing redeemable about him, to his very core. God is letting the Devil do what he does in order for him to be exposed for who he really is. God is revealing the truth about who he is by permitting the Devil to do all he can do. Therefore, on Judgment Day there will be no doubt or dispute or diabolical objection the Devil can use to accuse God of playing favorites; or fault Him for using His 'I am God - the final and Righteous Judge' card.

We must know, however, that in any given situation, God and Satan are both working in the same place, at the same time, to accomplish opposite purposes - diametrically opposite purposes. We see this clearly in the story of Job. The Enemy was jealous of Job's steadfast trust in God and eager to find fault in him. He was searching for a way to test him and make God look bad at the same time. Satan knows we are God's "workmanship created in

Christ Jesus for good works which God has prepared beforehand that we should walk in them." (Eph. 2:10) Satan is determined to find fault with God by 'trying' the strength and stability and quality of God's workmanship in us by testing us!

Satan set up the test by using the very thing Job desired the most, which was divine protection for his children. Rendering the devastating blow to his family, Satan was hoping Job would feel abandoned and betrayed by God. However, Job did not take the bait - because <u>he knew Who God was</u> , and that He was honorable and trustworthy in every situation. <u>He also knew who he was.</u> His foundation and firm footing held him fast to that truth and caused Job to stand strong under the ruthless interrogation of his three friends, who were sure he had sinned and made God angry, and that his calamity was the result of divine judgment.

Job's patient and faith-filled responses were anchored in his knowledge that God is just. Although he did not even know what was going on, he was able to confess his faith in God's faithfulness in the midst of his trials, by boldly declaring his position of faith. "Though He slay me, yet will I trust Him", Job proclaimed, (Job 13:15) because he knew that his "Redeemer lives". (Job 19:25)

In every situation where there seems to be a withholding or a withdrawal of God's blessings, we must rest in knowing that God is good and God is 'for me'; and, as Job said, "that you may know there is a judgment". (Job 19:29) Justice is coming. Truth will bring to light what is really going on. Condemnation and Confusion will be called to give an account of themselves. And, though we know that God hates sinful behavior and weeps over the separation that it causes between Him and us, He does not hate us. He longs for us to be all that we were created to be. He hurts when we hurt. He is in pain when we are in pain. He comforts us to know that we are never alone, or on our own in any of our trials.

"In all their affliction He was afflicted, and the Angel of His

Presence saved them; in His love and in His pity He redeemed them; and He bore them and carried them all the days of old." (Is. 63:9)

"O you afflicted one, tossed with tempest and not comforted, behold, I will lay your stones with colorful gems, and lay your foundations with sapphires."

(Is. 54:11)

"In righteousness you shall be established; You shall be far from oppression, for you shall not fear; and from terror, for it shall not come near you."

"No weapon formed against you shall prosper, and every tongue which rises against you in judgment you shall condemn. This is the heritage of the servants of the Lord and their righteousness is from Me, says the LORD." (Is. 54:14, 17)

God is committed to our eternal destiny and wellbeing more than to our temporal, transient comforts. He will not bless us in our rebellion, nor reward us for disobedience - although His love for us is unwavering. Just as it the sacred duty of every earthly parent to train their child to learn; to grow up; to make wise decisions; to become a healthy, productive member of the human community; God is committed to raising sons and daughters destined to rule and reign with Him in the Kingdom of Heaven. As with any parent, He must do this at the risk of being judged as uncaring and misunderstood for what He does - because we know the constraints He is under, in that God cannot bless disobedience or misbehavior.

How many times have we misunderstood the chastening of the Lord and become tempted to become discouraged by it? (See Heb. 12: 5-11) We become confused and ask 'Why'? 'If God loves me, why did He let all these bad things happen to me?' 'Where was He? 'How can I trust Him?' The possible list of questions that lead to confusion about the goodness and faithfulness of God are as disheartening as they are endless. The other reason the Enemy uses to explain the troubles in our lives directs the fault and blame at ourselves. 'It must be me', 'God is mad at me', 'It is because I '_____.' Here the Accuser will help you fill in the blank with any number of reasons to bring the blame, shame, and guilt back onto yourself for something you did or did not do.

The Enemy uses that confusion and condemnation to cause discouragement and bring woundedness and alienation. If he can divide us against ourselves and set up misunderstanding and brokenness in our relationship with our Heavenly Father, we will be at risk of becoming bitter and discouraged. If we fail to understand the chastening of the Lord and its purpose, the Enemy gains access to our thoughts and begins to construct a stronghold of bitterness in our life. "Do not despise the chastening of the LORD, nor be discouraged when you are rebuked by Him: for whom the LORD loves He chastens." (Heb.12:5)

Additionally, he uses every opportunity to bring discord in our relationships with ourselves and with others. Lack of understanding as to the chastening of the Lord and the process necessary for the refining of our faith makes us vulnerable to offense, self-judgment, and every form of rejection and mistrust. Anger and unforgiveness toward God cause us to lose hope in the restoration of justice. We become offended. This provokes us to take matters of justice into our own hands, which opens the doors for Satan's lying spirits to come and pay us a 'visit' on the premise of offering 'sympathy'. Hell sends its false benefactors to offer us solutions to the injustice. They tempt us to take the matters of justice up in our own hearts; to hate the offender and plot revenge, or cause us to remain mad at God until He does something to right the wrong suffered.

To understand suffering and affliction in the life of a believer, we must not make assumptions. Both Job's friends, and the Pharisees who questioned Jesus as to the reason for the affliction of the man born blind, assumed that the afflictions were a judgment because of the personal sin of the one suffering the affliction. In response to that assumption - in His defense of the man born blind - Jesus pointed to the fact that "Neither this man or his parents sinned." (John 9:3) Make note that the 'sins' we suffer from are not always our own, nor are we always the ones 'guilty' of committing the crimes we are suffering for.

Secondly, it would be presumptuous for us to assume that, because Jesus absolved this man and his parents, He cleared their entire generation from sin and wrongdoing. He would not contradict one of the primary themes of the entire Old Testament - sin, the curses, and judgment - only to address the issue differently than the truth to which the Scriptures already bore witness. Jesus' answer elaborated on the subject of sin and judgment, and expounded upon what God was saying to us in the book of Job: we are not always suffering for something we did wrong.

He did not say that 'no one' had sinned. Rather, He clarified that the purpose of this man's blindness was to bring glory to God. And, with that, Jesus took the demon of blindness by the scruff of the neck and cast it out for hurting one of His children. Is this not truly the express purpose of God in all of our trials and tribulations, to deliver us from the Evil One? Is it not to give Him the opportunity to show His goodness to us - in the midst of our affliction - so that we can pass the test of faith in trusting Him, and bring glory to His Name as He vindicates us through His faithfulness to us?

WHAT ABOUT TRIALS?

Trials and testings can be confusing. Are they from God? Are they from the Evil One? If they are from God, how can God be good? If they are God's will, how do I have a right to pray for healing or deliverance? Are they punishments because of a wrong committed? 'It must have been my fault that I am suffering because I made a bad choice'. If these valid questions about suffering are left unanswered, the confusion will keep us from using our God given authority to address the situation. God wants us to understand and explain the negative things that happen in our lives to keep us from error and discouragement.

First of all, let us not waste time 'splitting spiritual hairs' over defining the difference between 'trials' and 'testing'. They are, for all practical purposes, the same. Both, by design, serve to refine our faith and reveal the quality of the fruit in our lives. The Tempter uses them to test our motives and challenge the durability of God's workmanship in us; God uses them to prove that He is faithful to keep us in the midst of the fiery trial.

Trials can come as a result of being righteous and doing good. They can also come as consequences from unconfessed sin. "For what credit is it if, when you are beaten for your faults, you take it patiently? But when you do good and suffer for it, if you take it patiently, this is commendable before God. For to this you were called, because Christ also suffered for us, leaving us an example, that you should follow His steps;". (I Pet. 2:20-21)

From this passage, it is clear that we can suffer a fiery trial either for doing good or for doing bad. We can easily be confused as to why these things are happening and search for the cause. Is this the consequence of sin, and justified as such; or is this the result of a hidden curse, something for which I am the victim? Is it the result of my actions, or is this the chastening of the Lord allowed to test my faith and prove God's faithfulness?

So is it a consequence, a curse, or a chastening? Is it from God or the Devil? Is it because of my sin, or that God is testing my faith? Because they can all look and feel the same, we must have the wisdom of the Holy Spirit to know how to "glory in tribulations, knowing that tribulation produces perseverance, character, hope, and reveals the love of God in our hearts." (Rom. 5:3-5) The purpose of tribulation is for the perfecting of the saints - even those temporarily caught in sin, "that patience might have its perfect work." (Ja.1:4)

The scriptures tell us to "take the prophets, who spoke in the name of the Lord, as an example of suffering and patience to count them blessed who endure. You have heard of the patience of Job..." (Ja.5:10-11); and how Paul's imprisonment "actually turned out for the furtherance of the gospel". (Phil. 1:12) We know that Job was "patient" in all his tribulations and the Lord restored to him everything that had been stolen from him during the Devil's examination of his faith. Paul's suffering in chains was for Christ's sake, not as a judgment for sin. We know that Paul's imprisonment made his brethren more confident and "much more bold to speak the word without fear." (Phil. 1:13-14) We know that "all things work together for good to those who love God and are called according to His purpose." (Rom.8:28)

Understanding the reason for difficulties is imperative in order to know whether it is the result of a curse, a chastening, or a conse-quence of sin. As with Job, the Enemy can send those well-inten-tioned folks, who are operating out of their souls and reasoning, to 'help us' examine our life to find fault and discover the sin where there is no sin. Like Job and Paul, some are actually suffering for righteousness' sake. Making judgments based upon appearance and assumption, however, will cause confusion and even persuade some to believe or accept the idea that it was their fault when it was not. They reason that they must have done something to deserve it, not realizing that neither God nor Satan work from the premise of 'karma' - where bad things only happen to bad people and good things only happen to good people. Karma is a concept which was invented by Satan himself. It provides no place for forgiveness or repentance in the life of its followers. Karma is another ploy of the Deceiver to further confuse the issues of love and justice and who's to blame.

Others may believe that they are suffering for righteousness sake, when, in actuality, they are suffering - not for love's sake, but for religion's sake - which is actually suffering for sinning against the Law of Love. The real danger in not discerning the correct origin of the ongoing difficulty lies in misunderstanding God's intentions and being unaware of our own vulnerability to the schemes of the Devil. Is the trial to be rendered as a punishment for wrongdoing, or as a privilege to wrongfully suffer for Christ's sake? This is the 'slippery slope' every believer faces in seeking to rightly understand the chastening of the Lord. (Heb. 12:7) The purpose of the chastening of the Lord is designed to bring forth "the peaceable fruit of righteousness in those who have been trained by it." (Heb.12:11)

With every trial, an appropriate measure of grace is given for us to pass the test and escape the condemnation of the Devil. God tells us, "No temptation has overtaken you except such as is common to man, but God is faithful, who will not allow you to be tempted beyond what you are able, but with the temptation will also make the way of escape, that you may be able to bear it". (I Cor. 10:13) For many, however, the trial brings with it the temptation to become bitter. Bitterness, discouragement, and a weakened resolve to "pursue peace with all men", come when we refuse the grace God gives us to experience victory through the trial. (Heb.12:14)

This is why our attitude is essential in determining the outcome of the test. We must not only discern the origin and cause of the curse, but the purpose for which God allows it. Both are imperative to understanding how to walk through the trial in victory. God does not want us to assume the guilt for which He died to set us free. He does not want us to continue to suffer for the iniquities of our generations past. God does not want us, His blood-bought children, to suffer the loss of our spiritual legacy due to the curses that continue to pour down through our bloodline, whose purpose it is to steal our blessings and the reason for which we were created.

God does not want us to accept His Enemy's explanations for the trouble and believe that God is the one causing it because He is mad at us or we 'had it coming' because we sinned. On the other hand, God does not want us to live in ignorance of the Enemy's devices or denial of wrongdoing.

God has called us to live in victory. Ignorance and fear are not excuses for believers to continue to live under the curse, nor will reliance on them enable the believer to fulfill the heavenly mandate laid upon the Church. "To the intent that now the manifold wisdom of God might be made known by the church to the principalities and powers in the heavenly places... in whom we have boldness and access with confidence through faith in Him." (Eph. 3:10-12) We are called to enforce the defeat that Jesus put upon the Devil at the Cross and through His Resurrection.

As believers, we may be needlessly suffering from a curse - a demonic judgment that Satan was able to inflict on us because of the agreements made between him and those of our bloodline many generations ago. Because we are misled into believing 'it is what it is'; a punishment for wrongdoing; or something I can do nothing about; we take on the role of a helpless spectator in this cosmic war between God and the Devil - a war we're not always so sure God is winning.

THE DIFFERENCE BETWEEN SUFFERING AND PUNISHMENT

Another area in which the Enemy brings confusion is in misunderstanding the difference between suffering and punishment in a believer's life. Suffering, an innate part of love, is common to every trial. Suffering, however, is not synonymous with punishment. Suffering and punishment may appear to be similar on the surface, although the presence of suffering does not necessarily mean we are being punished for doing something wrong.

Clearly, not all suffering can be interpreted as punishment for what seems to be a consequence of sin - although there are those who do suffer as a result of their sin. Think of the righteous men and women who suffered for their faith, "of whom the world was not worthy". (Heb. 11:38) "For it is better, if it is the will of God, to suffer for doing good than for doing evil." (I Pet. 3:17)

Because sin and generational iniquity make us an easy target for the Enemy's wrath, God wants us to understand the origin and purpose of suffering. Suffering is unavoidable on this planet. When we suffer, God does not want us to suffer because we have sinned, nor does He want us to think the chastening of the Lord means we did something wrong and, hence, 'deserve it'.

We know that both God and Satan are always working in the same place at the same time for antithetical purposes. That is why it is important to discern the spiritual source and purpose of the trial, lest we become overwhelmed by it. To better understand the spiritual roots and reason for our trials, let us look at the trials of three different godly men: Job, David, and Peter.

Notice that each one of these men entered their test from a different vantage point. Job had already been declared righteous by God. David, after serving God faithfully for many years, fell into the sin of adultery and murder. Peter had walked with Jesus and declared Him to be the Son of God, when Satan petitioned to sift him as wheat, just prior to the crucifixion of Jesus. Job had done nothing wrong; David had sinned; and Peter was about to be tested prior to his promotion to a more notable position of leadership among the Apostles.

In all three cases, Satan took advantage of the opportunities to find fault with God. He challenged God regarding the purity of Job's motives for serving Him. With David, he sought to hold God to His Word, demanding that God punish David for his blatant violation of the commandments in committing adultery and murder. With Peter, the Accuser questioned God about Peter's qualifications and ability to carry on the mission of Jesus after He departed, pointing to his instability in leadership and his failure to endorse Jesus' mission of going to the Cross.

In the cases of both Job and Peter, Satan had to petition for the right to test them, because he found no open door of sin which would have allowed him to enter the 'back door' of their lives. With David, the door was wide open, so Satan did not have to make a petition to test him. The permission had already been given through the decision David made to sin with Bathsheba. The Enemy took advantage of the opportunity to request the destruction of both the man and his child.

This forced God to step in and take action to deal with the situation Himself, lest the Devil take full advantage of the circumstances and destroy David completely. Nathan explains to David, "Because by this deed you have given great occasion to the enemies of the LORD to blaspheme, the child also who is born to you shall surely die." (II Sam. 12:14)

We can also see the after-effects of the curse coming down into David's family line when David was told, "Now, therefore the sword shall never depart from your house... I will raise up adversity against you from your own house." (II Sam. 12:10) From this Bible passage, we can see there was both an immediate consequence to the sin, and a generational curse that got activated.

This is the same thing that happened in the Garden when God puts a curse on the Serpent, who was caught intentionally deceiving the woman, who in turn deceived the man. In both the Garden and with King David, we see God handing out the curses in order to stop Satan from doing so. This served to silence His adversary, and caused him to lose his opportunity to annihilate his victims through the application of the death sentence before God could intervene. Satan had no choice but to accept the temporary discipline handed out by God.

Confusion and misunderstanding regarding sin and testing leave us vulnerable to the temptation to become bitter and discouraged, which brings with it condemnation which the Lord never intended. This is why God wants us to understand the true nature of the spiritual world, and the spiritual war that goes on in us. It is in us, around us, between us, and against all of us who are held under the persuasion of the Evil One.

This is not to say that all suffering will cease once we stop sinning, or that the curses will automatically be broken as we become obedient. Suffering is not a 'heads or tails' theological issue. Suffering has a valid place in God's Kingdom economy. Suffering is essential to our personal growth and maturation in our relationship with God. "All those who live godly in Christ Jesus will suffer persecution." (II Tim. 3:12) But let persecution and the tribulation have their perfect work, developing the character and image of Christ in us.

And let us remember that in all our suffering - whether for our own sin, as a result of the sin of others, or as persecution for righteousness - God grieves with us. He goes with us; and in all our afflictions, He is afflicted. He suffers with us, just as a parent suffers with their child when the child is in pain. "In all their affliction He was afflicted, and the Angel of His Presence saved them. In His love and in His pity He redeemed them; And He bore them and carried them all the days of old." (Is. 63:9)

No matter how difficult or unfair it may seem, we know that this trial of our faith, being much more precious than gold that perishes (I Pet. 1:7), will bring forth "the peaceable fruit of righteousness in those who are trained up by it." (Heb. 12:11)

In every trial, surrender to the Lord God is the key to victory. Jesus chose that surrender Himself, as He prepared to go to the Cross saying, "For the ruler of this world is coming, and he has nothing in me." (Jn. 14:30) Satan had desired to have Him, to sift Him as wheat, to grind Him to powder, to find some weakness in His love for the Father, some flaw in their love and dedication to one another in rescuing the human race.

Jesus knew that Satan would scrutinize Him in an attempt to find something with which to charge Him that would permit him to disqualify and reject the Atonement. But Jesus knew there had been no evidence of sin or wrongdoing. He knew Satan had nothing on Him! He had no accusations, no agreements with sin, no fault that could be found. Jesus was about to suffer for being good, and pure, and holy, and obedient, and faultless. Satan's only way to stop Jesus was to kill Him outright, an innocent man!

In anticipation of this ordeal, Jesus said something which is critical to the outcome and validity of the Sacrifice He was about to make. He revealed the terms of the substitution of His life for ours. A human had sinned; a human would have to die. To offset any attempt the Enemy would make to disqualify the act of substitution and atonement, there had to be a sinless offering, a lamb without spot or blemish. In this moment Jesus was both the Shepherd seeking His lost sheep, and the sinless lamb Who would be sacrificed to make the final atonement for His flock.

Jesus offered to die in our place. He agreed to suffer the most unimaginable humiliation, a trial of cruel mockery and false accusations, with all the gruesome bloodshed as the human sacrifice He was destined to be. By consenting to His crucifixion, He proved that He was willing to die as the final sacrifice for our redemption, knowing that He would be raised from the dead for our justification. In essence, He knew He would be turned over to the will of His cruel tormentors who were given unrestricted access to every part of His body and soul.

Jesus suffered in all points like unto us, including abandonment and devastation, as He cried out "My God, My God, why have You forsaken Me?" (Ps. 22:1) Yet, in all points He remained sinless, although he had been tested like us, "For in that He Himself has suffered, being tempted, He is able to aid those who are tempted." (Heb. 2:18) In all points He learned obedience and He proved His obedience to be perfect, by the things He suffered for our freedom. (Heb. 5:8)

And in His complete innocence, He suffered the effects of every curse, in becoming a curse for us. He suffered for us - to set us free from the curse - by choosing to take on the curses for us! (Gal. 3:13) He willingly took the death penalty for us, in order to redeem us from the power of sin and reestablish our lives in God so that our lost blessings could be recovered.

God wants us to know that He gets no pleasure or glory in permitting what He permits, although He has agreed to allow suffering for purposes of training and character development in His children. Trusting God to bring justice gives us courage to prevail against the enemies of Fear and Doubt until the already-finished-work of Christ has accomplished its work in us and we are fully delivered. God knows all of this is necessary in qualifying us to be "joint heirs with Jesus Christ".

For this reason, He allows us to endure life's tests and trials. Just like those who go through military training, we must be tested before we can become part of the Special Forces. Like those who must pass various licensing exams in order to work in their field of knowledge, we must also be trained and declared to be 'qualified' and deemed faithful to work in the harvest field of souls. It is not appropriate for soldiers or students to become offended or strike out in anger at their drill sergeants or professors who write the tests. They realize that this is part of the prerequisite for their promotion. Spiritual tests - including the trial of our faith - are also required in order to qualify us for much greater things than any earthly kingdom. We are called to nothing short of the privilege to rule and reign with Christ in His heavenly Kingdom.

THE WAR ON THE WORD – THE LETTER OF THE LAW

Trying to stuff all the different scenarios of suffering, and testing, and sin, and punishment, and generational curses, and demonic judgments, and bad things happening to good people, into 'one-size-fits-all' does not work. Neither does reciting rhetorical or religious 'pat answers' to the questions generated by trials and skeptics. We are learning to "submit to God and resist the Devil", to "stand" and "having done all, to stand!" (Ja. 4:7 & Eph. 6:13)

The one and only rule in the war between God and Satan for the souls of men is set up on the principle of 'whose report do you believe'? Scoffing and skepticism do not prepare the ground for planting the seeds of faith. Abraham believed in the promises of God and it was counted to him for righteousness. All of the trials and tests of the saints are tests of obedience. Our response to those trials becomes a demonstration of our faith and confirms the surety of whose report we believe, God's or the Devil's.

God has bound Himself to us and to the Universal Code of Justice which we know as the Law. Jesus told us the "Spirit gives life, the flesh profits nothing" (Jn. 6:63). Paul clarifies this statement by telling us we are "ministers of the new covenant; not of the letter, but of the Spirit: for the letter kills, but the Spirit gives life." (II Cor. 3:6) The letter of the Law kills, but the Spirit gives life.

The Devil is not 'into' life; hence, he interprets the Law according to the letter. To him, the letter of the Law reads, "an eye must be given for an eye taken". The Enemy is meticulous in his search to discover violations of that Law. When violations are found, fault must be ascribed to someone. According to him, only punishment and correction of the violator will bring a restoration of the Law. This is the Enemy's premise, but does he really love the Law? Absolutely not! He hates God and His Law! However, the Enemy has found a way to use God's Law (the means by which He identified and protected His people) against God and His people.

Whenever the Enemy finds unconfessed sins and crimes left standing in the bloodlines, he calls for reactivation of the case in order to pursue a judgment against the descendants of the one who committed the crime. This is how he uses the sin and iniquity of the fathers (Lev. 26:31) to add to his arsenal of accusation in his attempt to destroy and discredit the children. In being able to bring the sins down onto the children, the Enemy gains a distinct advantage by leveraging the ignorance of each successive generation; this is the mechanism by which he ensnares them in the same patterns of sin and shame, which binds them in the same legacy of death that enslaved their fathers.

These are the demonic judgments that pulverize each new generation with confusion. Confusion generates trouble for the believer, making it difficult for him to believe and trust that God is good. It alienates those in need of mercy from the concept of God's forgiveness by 'persuading' them to judge themselves or blame/judge others. Adding our own personal agreements with the Enemy's accusations allows the Accuser to justify calling for our judgment - citing unbelief, doubt and feelings of guilt, bitterness and agreement with him - as his reasons for punishing us.

If we do not resist his accusations by declaring that we are both forgiven and bought-and-paid-for by the blood of Jesus, the Enemy can catch us on a technicality, declaring that we have 'refused' God's pardon. Failing to believe that God has forgiven us, by indirectly embracing guilt or the feelings of guilt dumped upon us by the Enemy, allows him to immediately turn around and use our agreement that we have sinned as evidence to prove that we are guilty. Satan uses our agreement with guilt to charge us with not believing in God's forgiveness; and therefore, still agreeing with his conclusion that we deserve to be punished.

Both God and Satan are bound by the same rule: whom we yield ourselves servant to obey, his slave we become. (Rom.6:16) This makes our agreement in the matter of faith, obedience, judgment, and receiving God's forgiveness, critical to the completion of God's mission to rescue us from Satan's plan to press his false or inflammatory charges against us.

GOD KNOWS

God, as the author and finisher of our faith, is committed to complete the work of His Holy Spirit in us. He knows the disdain and full-blown hatred Satan has for us. He knows the Enemy will do everything within his restricted 'rights' to prove that God is wrong for loving us, and we are wrong for believing in God's goodness.

God does not take pleasure in, or need to, teach us a lesson or 'put us through the paces' to prove our loyalty to Him. He already knew from the foundation of the world what the Enemy would do to set us up in an attempt to undermine our trust in God. God already knew how He would avenge us to deliver us from the grip of the Evil One. He already knew that He would be at risk of being judged by those who are under the pressure of the trial. He knew their tongues would curse, and their hearts would be tempted to become bitter against Him. He knew their lips would speak lies that would promote more pain and potential separation from Him. He already knew that we would be tempted to make premature judgments against Him for not being there and for letting all those terrible things happen to us in the first place.

God gets no glory in being blamed for what the Devil does, although He permits those things in order to allow the Enemy his right to scrutinize His workmanship in us. God's work in us is complete when we understand and acknowledge that He can be trusted in the midst of our trials; and we know that He is working all things together for our good. God wants us to understand how the Devil seeks to find fault with us directly for sinning and with God indirectly for letting us suffer.

The Enemy builds his case against us by using our own sin and disobedience, along with the generational iniquity and unresolved bloodguilt that is still present within our bloodline. He calls for the right to test our affections and try our faith. Our agreements with Fear and the lies Fear tells, become his justification before the

Court of Heaven to call for his right to bring his demonic judgments upon us.

In his 'eye for an eye' rendition of law and justice, the Evil One considers his judgments to be the rightful consequence for our sin. Sin becomes the evidence he uses to pressure God to give him permission to sift us. In the sifting, the Enemy uses our human vulnerabilities (needs) and situations to his advantage. The ultimate purpose of these tests is to determine our character and our reliance upon the strength of God to keep us. Whose report will we believe? Fear would push us to take control of the situation ourselves, to panic and become anxious; whereas trust calls us to rely upon God and His faithfulness to complete the work He has begun in us, to protect and provide for us.

Many of us get trapped in the persuasive arguments of sin and guilt as the Accuser sets forth his treacherous and seemingly 'airtight' case against us. He uses our own feelings of guilt, or being caught in the very act of sin, to cross-examine us in his insidious treachery to flip the guilt coin back on us, thereby slipping his noose around our neck. Assuming the blame and owning the accusation made against us by Guilt - a.k.a. 'we had it coming', allows the Prosecution to wrap up his argument against us by using our own admission of guilt to cinch the deal with a verdict of 'guilty as charged'. God provides a way of escape from the judgments of sin - through repentance, confession, forgiveness and receiving God's forgiveness - although He cannot force us to use any of His remedies.

God does not get glory in our being an easy target for the Devil's revenge. He gets no glory in our being tricked into believing our feelings of guilt, or that the Accuser's accusations against us paints a truthful picture as to what happened and who we are. He does not want us to be ignorant of the Enemy's devices, or give place to the Devil in giving him an opportunity to justify his demonic assault against us. It is for our very justification that God chose to die in the first place: to clear the record of wrongs and expose what the Devil was doing to His children as illegal. However, God must have our agreement in order to enforce the victory and pardon of Calvary.

God does not get glory when we get into trouble for sinning, or struggle under the burden of suffering for sins He already paid for. Nor does He get glory by getting blamed for all the bad things that happen to us when, in actuality it was the Enemy who deliberately took advantage of us in an effort to get us to exercise our free will in order to manipulate us into sinning the first place.

God does not get glory from those who do not understand the chastening of the Lord, or when fists of anger are lifted upward by those who take the matters of justice or sanctification into their own hands. God is not glorified by our ignorance, or in the deception that translates into 'railing' against Him when things are not fair or do not go our way.

God does not want us to live under the Law of demonic justice and retribution. When we embrace the guilt that could easily have been taken care of by repentance and confession, we are, in essence, rejecting God's forgiveness. Embracing guilt gives power and consent to the Enemy, who uses our hesitation in receiving forgiveness to stake a claim to his right to judge us.

Job did not capitulate to bitterness against God, nor did he make a false confession of guilt under pressure from his 'comforters'. In patiently standing his ground, Job maintained God's original declaration of righteousness over him. The Devil had nothing on Job, nothing to work with in his objection to the declaration of righteousness God had already pronounced over Job.

As far as God is concerned the charges made against us are no longer valid because the penalty has been paid. That makes the concept of penance and punishment in suffering for our own sins to a completely useless exercise in the pursuit of God's forgiveness, and unnecessary in the Holy Spirit's work of sanctification. The divinely prescribed measures for partaking in the finished work of Christ and His victory over sin and the grave are repentance and confession. (I Jn. 1:9)

The Enemy's assignment of punishment and penance for sin - brought on by Guilt and Pain - has been the cause of much needless suffering in the Body of Christ. Pain and suffering do not absolve us from the condemnation of sin, nor do they bring God glory. Suffering for our sins is not the remedy for sin. God does not get glory when we mess up any more than we as parents get glory when our kids mess up. When the child has learned something wrong and acts on it, the lie must first be corrected before the behavior (sin) will stop.

The parent cannot fully defend their child or protect them from the consequence of their sin, which jeopardizes the child's future well-being, if the parent fails to address the root issue. If they 'bail them out' time and again, they will enable their behavior to continue to lead the child down the path of destruction and lies. The real issues of fear and lies believed must be addressed before we can be released from the consequences of sin and know the power of restoration and freedom.

OUR FATHER OR OUR JUDGE?

If we are God's workmanship Created in Christ Jesus, then God's workmanship in us must be tested. If the Enemy would ever find fault with God or His workmanship, his only hope of finding it would be in us. That makes us the greatest target of the Enemy's relentless attack, and the sharpest point of his bitter disdain. His deep contempt for God is manifested in his violent hatred of us. He is ever so delighted when he hears the contempt he has for God being expressed by and coming out of our very mouths - especially when we believe it is our own words and feelings that are being expressed.

Would God become an enemy to His own children? Would we, in our inability to believe that God loves us, rebel against the love of

God and allow hardness in our heart to find fault with Him? Would He set us up 'between a rock and a hard place' to act as our Judge rather than as our Father? What could really grieve His Father's heart more than to have to watch the destruction of His children? What gives the Devil more pleasure than to use our agreements with the unloving spirits of Fear and the actions that come from it to 'checkmate' God through our disobedience? Would the Enemy use our suffering to make our Father suffer? Would he hold us hostage to demand a ransom for our soul?

Is God helpless to save us? Absolutely not! However, love - in any relationship - must be the consent of two mutual parties who want to enjoy each other's company. Needless to say, love is only love when it is given freely -without coercion, bribery, or black-mail - by all those involved. True love suffers to promote the good of another, even at the cost of suffering and bringing hurt to oneself.

Is not our faithful and steadfast clinging to God as our refuge the best evidence God has in refuting His Enemy's charges of folly against Him for making us in the first place? Is not our response to the love and loyalty of Father the only means God has in justi-fying Himself for acting so unselfishly in our behalf? The revela-tion of His Love and generosity lead us to believe that our personal trials and tests not only give God an opportunity to show Himself strong on behalf of those who trust in Him, but also give us the opportunity to declare the strength and beauty of His work in us. This elevates the experience of suffering by trials and testing to the place of necessity for the maturation of our faith.

"In all their affliction He was afflicted, and the Angel of His Pres-ence saved them; in His love and in His pity He redeemed them; and He bore them and carried them all the days of old; but they rebelled and grieved His Holy Spirit; so He turned Himself against them as an enemy, and He fought against them." (Is. 63:9-10)

Our faith in the faithfulness of God is the evidence of God's faithfulness to us! Without His faithfulness to us, we would very presently cease to exist. God's 'keeping' us is a demonstration of His love for us. As His children we are the source of both His greatest suffering, and His purest delight.

CONNECTING THE DOTS

*D*ECIPHERING BLOODLINE CURSES

The Devil justifies his activities in our lives based upon what he perceives to be a legalistic, blow-for-blow, blood-for-blood, interpretation of justice. Understanding his rigid, 'black and white' rendition of justice in dotting the 'i's' and crossing the 't's' gives us a better understanding of how he tallies up the score for justice. He intends to use the Law to settle our accounts with sin at the same time he challenges our position as heirs of God. He is rigid and legalistic in his interpretation of the Law in matters of sin and justice. He is a stickler for detail. 'The Devil is in the details' may be more true than we think. When we color outside of the lines of the Law, the Accuser feels justified in making his accusations against us, even though he himself is the most lawless being in the universe.

This meticulous insistence upon rigid justice also gives us a better understanding in how to trace his steps, so as to identify the cords of iniquity which he uses to call for the activation of the curses in our lives. Iniquity is the accumulation of generational sins. If those iniquities are not dealt with, they will bring forth trouble in the next generation. Iniquities are the result of deception and disobedience, as reflected in the sins and the spiritual deterioration of the bloodlines they represent. The Enemy deceived our ancestors into believing lies, and tempted them to act contrary to God's Word. Their agreements with those lies brought forth the sin and iniquity which the Enemy continues to use to bring his patterns of destruction upon us even today.

The agreements made with the lies are the root. The shameful behavior, (sins) are the fruit. The original agreements have been buried underneath decades of secrets, and lost beneath layers of silence for many generations. Without confession, the truth has never been told or permitted to come into the light. The crimes have been covered up and forgotten, or changed, to keep the Enemy from being incriminated. And, although the integrity and anointing for the family's calling has been 'derailed', the work of the familiars has stayed the course of tearing down the family's generational history from "antiquity through iniquity'.

Covering up the past as to what really happened, and concealing the discovery of the demonic patterns of iniquity, make it possible for the Enemy to continue using the same old strategies and agreements he has used since the beginning. Using these patterns to judge the unfinished business of the past, Satan has had great success in calling for the destruction of each new member of a particular bloodline.

Covering up and concealing the truth keeps us from discovering the truth freedom brings. The only real remedy for sin is repentance and confession. "Confess your faults (sins), one to another and pray for one another that you may be healed." (James 5:16) Confession and repentance bring the sin into the light. The light of God makes manifest the hidden works of darkness. Shame and Silence would keep it hidden in order to prevent healing and deliverance. Restoration of the human life can only come from confession and repentance and forgiveness.

THE WARNING

God's warnings were not meant to be curses, but to keep us safe from the curses. He knew the Enemy would demand that judgment be made against any he found breaking the Law. Until the fulfillment of the Law was accomplished in Jesus Christ, God's instructions for obedience to the Law were invaluable in keeping His people safe. <u>Obedience demonstrates our agreement with God's commandments</u>. God's first commandments form the foundations of life and blessing and deliverance to keep us safe from the curses.

Disobedience, and the injustice that comes from it, must be judged. God will eventually be obligated to bring justice and restoration for the damage the Enemy has inflicted on His creation. Deuteronomy describes a specific list of warnings from God for specific sins, and the corresponding judgments disobedience would bring. The consequences of sin are the demonic judgments we describe as curses, which are most often wrongfully ascribed to God.

<u>Ascribing the consequences of our sin as judgments from God makes it very hard for us to be reconciled to Him or feel forgiven by Him in the aftermath of sinning.</u> If we do not put the Enemy into the spiritual equation in explaining how things happen and who is doing what, it is very easy to question God's goodness. We get confused about His intentions in parenting us. This decreases our hope of being reconciled with Him.

All sin and iniquity are, ultimately, crimes committed against the Law of Love. The Laws God wrote on the tablets of stone could not force anyone to love another. You cannot force anyone to love you! Love must be freely given, and can only exist when the Law of Love is inscribed upon the table of our hearts. The Law was given by God as a temporary protection for His people. The Devil perceived it as his grand opportunity to hold them accountable and justify his petitions to destroy the people of God.

Sin and the crimes generated by it deprive their victims of hope, dignity, and the right to complete their lives in satisfaction. Fear and the Unloving Spirit perpetuate the injustices which promote loss and pain on every level of human experience and relationship. God has the prescribed remedy for sin. It is the Blood of His Son. This is the only prescription for restoration. We will either accept and apply that remedy through repentance and confession of our sin, or we will perish.

Like any good Parent, the Father stood to warn His children about the deadly intentions of the Evil god of this world who was waiting to catch one of them off-guard and sweep them up into destruction. He knew that the Wicked One had temporary jurisdiction over the places they would live. The Snake Pit prepared for them by the god of this world. He knew Satan would try to seduce them into the pagan religions of idolatry with which he surrounded them. God gave His children a clear, strong warning about the consequences of disobedience and the curses that disobedience would bring. He knew the Devil would grasp every opportunity he could to snatch them up, rip them apart, and scatter them in the wilderness of sin.

The consequences of sin are the demonic judgments the Enemy puts upon us as punishment for disobeying God's Laws. The Enemy twists our perceptions to believe that those consequences of sin are a punishment from God. This creates great confusion in our relationship with God, especially if the consequences of those sins linger and seem to become a permanent part of negative circumstances in our lives. When the consequences of sin linger, we begin to accept the life problems and physical illnesses as 'normal'. We become disheartened and feel hopeless. We fail to identify the suffering we are going through as anything that needs to be resisted. Rather, we perceive them to be deserved, the result of our sin; and as a judgment from God.

God understands the Devil's strategy and how he would use generational iniquity to blind us to the revelation of truth. He knows that the only way to effectively deal with the sins of our bloodline is through the Blood of the Lamb of God Who takes away the sins of the world. God knows this truth would be lost in the typical pious rhetoric of self-condemnation and self-discipline. He knows that the Devil would produce as many counterfeit religions as needed in his approach to solve the 'problem' of sin. He knew there would be a deadly diabolic mixing of Law and grace intended to pervert the truth and prevent of the good news of the Gospel of Jesus Christ from reaching Hell's prisoners. Therefore, it behooves us to understand that - it is not through law-keeping, but through the Atoning Blood of Christ - that the power and intention of grace to erase the stain of sin from our souls is accomplished.

THE LIST

The curses that first appeared in Genesis 3 reappear as an expanded list of specific maladies in Deuteronomy 27 and 28. The calamities and diseases described read like the daily newspaper or a like a copy of the Physician's Desk Reference for Diseases.

In Deuteronomy 27 God gets specific about the behavior He calls sin and what will happen to those who practice it.

"Cursed is the one who makes any carved or molded image, an abomination to the LORD...

Cursed is the one who treats his father or mother with contempt...

Cursed is the one who moves his neighbor's land mark...

Cursed is the man who makes the blind to wander off the road ...

Cursed is the one who perverts the justice due the stranger, the fatherless, and the widow ...

Cursed is the one who lies with his father's wife...

Cursed is the one who lies with any kind of animal...

Cursed is the one who lies with his sister...

Cursed is the one who lies with his mother-in-law ...

Cursed is the one who attacks his neighbor secretly...

Cursed is the one who takes a bribe to slay an innocent person...

Cursed is the one who does not confirm all the words of this law. And all the people shall say, 'Amen.'" (Deut. 27:15-26)

The rules were set. The boundaries for safety and the identification of God's people were established within the parameters of obedience to the Law. Within those guidelines, the obedient could enjoy God's covering of protection from the roving eye of the Accuser.

Their obedience would afford the Enemy nothing with which to build his case against them. Their continued blessing and protection were assured. Transgressing outside those lines, however, opened them up to the troubles and the curses the Enemy eagerly desired to put upon them.

"Cursed shall you be in the city, and ...in the country. Cursed shall be your basket and your kneading bowl"... (your personal affairs and finances).

"...The Lord will send on you cursing, confusion, and rebuke in all that you set your hand to do, until you are destroyed and until you perish quickly, because of the wickedness of your doings in which you have forsaken Me. Your efforts to get ahead will fail and your hard work will not profit. Nothing will work out right and setbacks will be common. You will not be able to find a place to settle down, or a purpose. Your life will be hard."

"The LORD will make the plague cling to you until He has consumed you from the land. The LORD will strike you with consumption, with fever, with inflammation, with severe burning fever, with the sword, with

scorching, and with mildew; they shall pursue you until you perish."
(Deut. 28: 21 & 22)

In modern language these verses describe specific curses, including medical problems, sickness and disease, that will cling to us. Auto-immune system disorders, anemia, anorexia, infections, brain damage, cancer, candida, yeast infections, and all manner of physical maladies will overtake us.

> *"The LORD will strike you with the boils of Egypt, with tumors, with the scab, and with the itch, from which you cannot be healed. The LORD will strike you with madness and blindness and confusion of heart."*
> *"...And you shall be only oppressed and plundered continually, and no one shall save you."*

> *"You shall betroth a wife but another man shall lie with her; .... "Your sons and your daughters shall be given to another people, and your eyes shall look and fail with longing for them all day long; and there shall be no strength in your hand."*

> *"The LORD will strike you in the knees and on the legs with severe boils which cannot be healed, from the soles of your foot to the top of your head. ..." "Then the LORD will bring upon you and your descendants extraordinary plagues – great and prolonged plagues – and serious and prolonged sicknesses." (Deut. 28: 27-30 & 32, 35, & 59)*

In Deuteronomy 28 the LORD describes very particular curses that followed the transgressions listed in Deuteronomy 27. These are also very specific. And though the LORD takes full responsibility for the curses, He is not the One Who issued or initiated or executed them. The curses were the permissions granted to the Enemy according to the Rule of Consent. "To whom we yield ourselves servant to obey, that one's slave we will become." (Rom. 6:16)

When we disobey, we are using our free will to override God's perfect will. God is then forced to allow His permissive will to operate because He had obligated Himself to abide by the rules in giving us a free will. Giving His children a free will also requires that He allow the Devil his free will to have, and work to keep that which he had technically won. And because his gain was by means of deceit, his hold will someday be reversed.

"IT WAS MY CHOICE"

We are no match for the wiles of the Devil. He pits our hatred of sin and injustice against a false sense of responsibility, and then accuses us of making bad choices. He justifies our suffering as being the result of our own sins and bad decisions. God did not respond to Adam and Eve's sin by accusing them of being irre-sponsible. We hear no conversation between Him and them about being disobedient, despite the fact that it was their choice to eat of the forbidden fruit which had initially provoked this crisis.

When the LORD God called to Adam and Eve and they heard the sound of His footsteps they hid. When He questioned them, the Woman explained what had happened. When He asked them if they had eaten from the Tree of Knowledge, she said, "the Serpent deceived me". She did not deny her own wrongdoing. She simply pointed to the instigator. God did not correct or blame her for listening to the Serpent. He did not demand that she admit she had sinned. He did not use the situation to castigate her further by letting her figure out her mess on her own.

Unlike God, we, as parents, are quick to punish our children and let them lie in the 'beds' they made for themselves in the hope of teaching them a lesson. Most of them succumb to discouragement and shame long before they ever learn anything positive from the bad behavior (the sin) they had been deceived into doing. God was not trying to teach His children a lesson by shaming them with words or making them feel responsible for fixing what He knew they could not fix. He did not refuse them mercy or justify Himself in letting them live with the consequences of their sin by withholding from them the remedy for sin. Obviously, hiding and fixing their nakedness with a bunch of fig leaves was not a suitable remedy for sin, or the shame that had so immediately accompanied it. Their self-remedy would not work to satisfy sin's demand for the death penalty. Only God could do that. Only God knew that.

His final rendering of the situation did not put any requirements on the couple to fix, pay for, or respond in a certain way to do penance for their sin. His only requirement was that they accept the remedy He gave them. They did not have to prove that their repentance was genuine before He helped them. At that point they did not even understand the grave ramifications of their actions. He took on the matter of sin and the setback it had caused His Children, including the removal of peace and goodness Himself!

It was, and is, the Enemy who uses the argument, "You made the choice!" It is part of his official and final justification for placing his demonic judgments on the gullible, thereby transferring guilt to the guiltless. Jesus said it best, "But if you had known what this means, 'I desire mercy and not sacrifice,' you would not have condemned the guiltless." (Mt. 12:7) Satan captures the moment of our sin to bind us and lock us up in the 'prison houses of despair' and detain us in the 'concentration camps of hell'.

Sin doubly deceives us. We first believe our problem is a consequence of our own choice and action. Then we believe the lie that we are bad and must fix our sin by being good. Choosing to use the Deceiver's solution to sin to solve the problem of sin does not make the problem of sin go away.

The truth is, we were set up. We bit the hook and now we 'feel' bad and guilty and obligated to 'fix it'. The 'catch twenty-two' is that we were tricked into taking the bait and sinned, only to be snared a second time into thinking we can get ourselves off the hook by using the Enemy's solutions to solve the problem. These solutions are especially appealing, since we are built by God to hate sin and are eager to get rid of it ourselves. The most diabolical trick of all comes from believing that the thoughts we think and the feelings we feel are our own personal, private thoughts and feelings, which they are not!

'It's my fault, my sin, my choice, so now I must fix it by trying harder to be good, trying not to sin, doing penance to atone for my sin, and taking responsibility for my sin'. This puts me on the demonic 'torture rack' of trying to resolve the irresolvable conflict that 'I must be good, but I'm never good enough'. This is how the Devil ensnares us, and reaches out to kill us.

We resolve to be perfect in an attempt to justify ourselves by never making that mistake again. We are convinced that what we did was our fault because we did it. We ignore or do not understand the Apostle Paul's admonition that "if I am doing that which I will not to do, it is not me doing it." (Rom. 7:20) Satan has many different ways he can put the 'spin' of shame and self-blame on us for sinning.

Yes, we did DO it. But why did we do the sin? We did it because we believed a lie, much like the hungry little fish. We bit the hook in search for lunch. Any of the Deceiver's suggested approaches to deal with the problem of sin, however clever or appealing they may appear, will only lead to the same deadly assumption in the end: 'It is and was my fault and I'm cut off from God'. Remember, Jesus told us we would know the true nature of something by its fruit. The fruit testifies to the genuine nature of the thing being tested.

Feelings are not a true test of the genuine nature of anything. Feelings of love may be a case of infatuation. Feelings only last for a time. True endurance comes from the inner determination in knowing the truth. Guilt or taking on the feelings of guilt ultimately reduces the issue down to condemnation and believing that we are bad, and we deserve to be punished. The biggest mistake believers make is in navigating through the maze of spiritual warfare using our feeling instead of our spirit software.

If we deny our sin or become defensive and attempt to get vengeance for ourselves, we fall into the grip yet another set of traps, those of anger and blame; or self-blame and shame. We spend precious time and energy seeking to make things fair or divest ourselves of the charges made against us - only to get trapped in the snare of confusion in attempting to figure out whose fault it is. We become bitter and get swallowed up by unforgiveness and 'go around the mountain' yet again.

We get caught up in the 'cascade' of the consequences and begin to try and alter our mood or feelings, taking measures in an attempt ease the pain. The Enemy offers us yet another solution which only serves to heighten the torment. The torment of the pain elevates as we intensify our desperate attempts to stop the bad behavior by 'being good'. The trap is set. Like an avalanche of snow, once this 'avalanche' begins, it becomes impossible to stop its' momentum, the force of its' power.

Evil passions and cravings (Rom.6:12 Amp.) will not be placated or replaced by self-control and will power. "Discipline is not a substitute for deliverance, and deliverance is not a substitute for discipline." (Derek Prince). Trying to 'white knuckle' it in order to control or stop the sinful behavior without seeing any victory only leads to frustration. Our life becomes all about our sin and getting rid of it. The cycle has begun. Believing it will happen again, we desperately try to take responsibility to take the measures to stop it. We fail. We are caught in the 'try harder/never enough' cycle of frustration and failure.

Failure and exhaustion (depression is exhaustion that comes from trying to solve irresolvable conflicts related to a life situation) cause some to resign themselves to the consequences of sin and learn to coexist with it. There is a measure of belief that the suffering we live with is deserved. We continue to live out this perpetual injustice, accepting it as our 'cross to bear'. Whether we take full responsibility for our sin, or succumb to it, makes little difference to the Accuser. Neither passive acceptance nor profuse denial are the friends of truth and justice. Nor are they found on the road to forgiveness, freedom and peace.

Some are suffering for things they have done themselves and often live their whole lives in the confusion and condemnation, viewing themselves as ruined and bad because of choices they have made. There are just as many who feel 'less than' and disgusted with themselves, victims of something that was done to them. One of the main issues with both sinning and being sinned against is dealing with the residual pain, injustice, loss, sorrow, and guilt that lingers.

Knowing that we do not benefit by seeking mercy from the Enemy - nor do we benefit from assuming the role of a victim in Satan's treacherous plots against us - we do well in this matter of sin, only if we know the truth! Let us not see ourselves as victims of the Enemy's perverted justice and assume the guilt of his wrong doing. Rather, let us see ourselves as victorious warriors and Satan's enemy in this spiritual war for the souls of men!

Failure to see his plot will blind us to the second part of his attack, that of taking the blame and feeling guilty and responsible for the terrible things we did or that were done to us. When we agree with his vehement accusation against us, it allows him to confirm his claim against us that it was our fault. This allows him to afflict us with his demonic judgments. This provokes us to seek a solution (the fig leaves, Gen. 3:7) to try and fix the problems that have come into our lives. The Enemy's solutions to sin only provoke the initiation of a more insidious, aggressive, and ongoing cycle of destruction.

For example, a child who is sexually abused will readily believe that it was their fault. Now, as an adult, they suffer the emotional pain of seeing themselves as ruined. In an attempt to ease the pain of their loss and the burden of hopelessness, they begin to drink, or do drugs, or live in a fantasy world to cope with the pain. They drink too much and are in danger of losing everything. The first lie has never been corrected; as a result, the lie grows larger and diversifies. More sorrow, and strife, and loss, plague them until they feel crazy or create a pseudo-self and pretend to be someone else in order to function.

Then they go to treatment and fail to work the program. Now they are labeled an addict and miss yet another 'rung' on the ladder of expectation and self-actualization (a psychology term indicative of ascending to superiority and the 'arrival' to independence, being one step closer to winning the mental health 'award', deemed to be self-sufficient and mentally sound). So on and on goes the devastation of the lies and the consequence of believing them.

The Evil One sets us up to feel guilty, and then leads us to try to reverse the effects of sin - by using our desire for truth and vindication - as his bait to snare us again. He twists the truth to get us to believe and accept that we are the ones responsible and need to make things right. We feel devastated, compelled to fix the mistakes or correct the identified imperfections through self-effort, self-discipline, self-help, performance, or penance - which, in the end, makes us victims of our own desire for goodness.

Taking the matter of righteousness into our own hands by trying to make things right in our own strength is, in truth and reality, rejection of the Cross! The Blood of the sacrificed Lamb of God is God's ONLY provision for our sin and the recovery of our righteousness. (This does not minimize the need for restitution or deny the need for asking forgiveness or apology for things we have done to or stolen from others; nor does it cancel the need for repentance and confession). This does not justify rejection of the Holy Spirit's conviction of sin, like the harlot in Proverbs: "This is the way of an adulterous woman; She eats and wipes her mouth, And says, I have done no wickedness." (Pr. 30:20)

This is to say that <u>none</u> of our efforts - no matter how sacrificial, or unselfish, or religiously impressive - can set us free from the grip of sin or its stain. Nothing can resolve the matter of our innocence except the Blood of Jesus, given as a ransom for us. Only by receiving and accepting God's forgiveness for believing and acting on the lies, can we be set free us from the Enemy's accusations of guilt. Only knowing the truth can set us free.

With the Devil, no one is innocent, ever! He is the 'king' of shifting the blame, defensiveness, and excuse making! Because we naturally see ourselves as guilty of sinning or breaking the law, it is easy for him to lead us to conclude that we deserve to be judged and that the consequences we suffer are justified. Quite often, even our Christian brethren 'chime in' to help him convince us we are bad. We rarely suspect that we are the victims of the Devil's lies when he speaks them from the pulpit. For the Accuser, guilt and blame are in the 'flip of the coin'. However, whichever side of the sin coin surfaces, he will call us guilty.

Even as it is common for some to ascribe sin to themselves, others have fallen prey to modern theology, pop-psychology and a pragmatic sociology, including self-styled religion which teaches us to believe that there are no spiritual and moral absolutes. The Word of God is viewed as a useless collection of antiquated stories which has nothing relevant to say about anything we experience in the twenty-first century. This is another demonic strategy for covering our shame, much like the fig leaves of old, with the 'fabric' of religion. These self-styled religious options strip all the moral underpinnings that undergird the notion of right and wrong from the conscience of mankind. The moral code of ethics has vanished, having been replaced by a strong spirit of self-reliance, self-will, self-deification and the free expression of self-interests.

In the context of Hell's massive effort to deceive and capture the souls of men and women, is it any wonder why many have come to deny the Devil's very existence?! In his effort to rid the world of the message of Hope and Good News, the Enemy has multiplied the number and complexity of the 'counterfeit gospels of sin', which has added catastrophic numbers to the casualty list of those dead and dying in this spiritual war.

Satan's agenda has never changed. It is still to lie and deceive, to steal and kill and destroy whosoever and whatever he can. His thrust has never changed direction nor abated from his original vendetta for even a moment. We must KNOW that the relentless cold-heartedness of our Enemy is only equaled and surpassed by the goodness and compassion of our God in 'clearing the fog' over the battlefields of our souls. The revelation of His love and mercy causes us to embrace His grace and hope in the matchless forgiveness of the One Who died that we might live. No law or tradition or personal sacrifice can replace the freedom or procure the forgiveness He so kindly bestows upon those who seek the truth.

THE PLACEMENT OF GUILT

The Enemy uses our disobedience, and the practice of idolatry come down from our bloodline, to build his case against us. He objected to God's protective covering over His people, citing their violation of the Law as justification for his right to punish them. He still uses the Law to bring the consequence of disobedience upon us as prescribed in Exodus, Leviticus and Deuteronomy. That is why we see the curses listed there still active today in the lives of both believers and non-believers. PLEASE NOTE: the Devil has NOT YET acknowledged his defeat in the Death and Resurrection of Jesus Christ, or His Atonement for our sins. Satan has NEVER moved any of his grounds for accusation over to the New Testament, because it offers him no legal footing upon which to stand. He has no case where the Lord declares salvation and justice through the Blood of Jesus for 'whosoever will'. He must tenaciously, stubbornly cling to the legal parameters and definitions of the Law in the Old Testament in order to wage his war for 'justice'!

It is, therefore, IMPERATIVE that we know the power of the Cross - as given in the New Testament - to set us free. Mixing the two Covenants will set a snare, and bring with it stupor, anxiety, and hardness of heart. (Rom. 11:1-10) There is a time for everything under heaven, a time for law and a time for grace. But remember, in this time for Grace, God has covered our iniquity with the Blood of His Son. Grace is not cheap; it is not to be abused or received flippantly. We need to know Whose we are, and understand what He really did for us!

Thus, we become prey to Evil's assault against us through our own disobedience, which comes from being deceived by the lie. When we choose the Enemy's solution to our problem, we sin. When we believe his lies, we sin. All sin reduces down to and begins with one thing: believing the lie. When we sin, we disobey God and we feel guilty. Guilt sets us up for judgment, condemnation and punishment. When we agree with the Enemy's argument that we did something bad and deserve to be punished, we agree that he is justified in punishing us.

Because we are sensitive to sin, and designed by God to despise it, we are quick to accept the charges brought against us by Guilt and Condemnation when we sin. In accepting the guilt, we are, in essence, agreeing with the spirit of Guilt that we ARE guilty and deserve to be punished. Our agreement with Guilt and Condemnation obstructs God's remedy of repentance and forgiveness. Our agreement with the counsel of Hell delivers us over to the tormentors who claim the right to punish us - because we gave in to his argument that we are guilty of not believing the Lord's promise that we can be forgiven.

The cycle of pain and destruction has begun. The way out of sin for the believer is very simple and straightforward. When we sin, God tells us to confess our sin. He wants us to repent, change our mind, and believe the truth. He wants us to know that "He is faithful and just to forgive us our sin and cleanse us from all unrighteousness." (I Jn. 1:9) He tells us to "Confess [our] trespasses to one another and pray for one another, that [we] may be healed." (Ja.5:16) This is God's New Testament strategy and solution for all who are deceived and believe the Enemy's lie and get caught in the bondage and cycle of sin.

Feeling guilty or not feel guilty is not the remedy for getting rid of sin. Neither is it the way to settle the issue of our innocence or get set free from the curse. Satan is the Accuser of the Brethren. Accusation is what he does. In using his argument that we are guilty because it was our choice, the Accuser completely omits the fact that he is the one who lied to set us up in the first place. Blaming us for making a bad choice obscures the fact that we were deliberately and maliciously deceived into disobedience. We were set up by the one who has premeditated our demise through a systematic and strategic indoctrination program since before we were born.

The Enemy uses our response to situations as his platform for initiating his charges against us. He solidifies his claims in a concerted effort to prove that we were fully aware of our actions, and therefore, fully responsible for them. When we agree that we are freely doing what we do or did, the Enemy sees himself as justified in petitioning the Court for the right to punish us because we did it to ourselves in full volition of what our actions meant.

Even though the Bible in Romans 7:20 expressly says, "Now if I do what I will not to do, it is no longer I who do it, but sin that dwells in me", we opt to believe - not that it is the sin that dwells in me - but that IT IS ME who willingly attached myself to the hook and caused myself to be cast into the frying pan. If our agreement with Guilt and Blame is not followed by true repentance (a change our mind and cessation of belief in the lie), including the acceptance of God's forgiveness, the Prosecution is allowed to skip past the Court's pardon to continue to bring the curse down not only on us, but our children.

TRACING THE CURSES BACK TO THEIR ORIGIN

Understanding the Enemy's legalistic interpretation of God's Word, and his method of translating the justice of the Law to fit his own ends, helps us recognize what's going on in our lives and why. To resolve the curse we must get to the source of the problem. To get to the source of the problem, we must understand the initial agreements made with Darkness that are creating the patterns of demonic judgment. If we can recognize the precipitating events and connect the targeted individual's agreement with the event, we can unravel the mysteries of the curse and address it.

For example, based on Satan's frequent, but misapplied, use of the scripture - including his reference to the letter of the Law with its reciprocal justice (he interprets an eye for an eye) - here is how the Devil would argue his case for inflicting someone with a neck injury or back pain. His argument for stiffness in the neck or back pain would go something like this: The Bible admonished God's people to learn from the mistakes of their fathers; "Now do not be stiff-necked, (rebellious), as your fathers were, but yield yourselves to the LORD...". (II Ch. 30:8) Notice the connection between those practicing witchcraft who also refuse to bow their heads in worship to the One True God. Their necks are stiff and their wills are stubborn. (This does NOT mean the one at the end of the spiritual chain is necessarily practicing rebellion against God, but it is buried in their bloodline and it behooves them to deal with it.)

The Bible also compares witchcraft to rebellion and idolatry. (I Sam. 15:23) Idolatry and rebellion are characterized by a stiff neck and an uncircumcised (hard) heart. (Acts 7:51) Stiffness of neck is a chiropractic description that connects pain with the subluxation of the 6th vertebra. It is not surprising to find those practicing witchcraft often suffer from an injury to the sixth vertebra and as a result, have neck and back problems. The Enemy initiates many of those injuries through Accidents, Assaults and Injury. Car accidents and falls are two of the favorite precipitating events used in setting up the physical effects of witchcraft already found in the injured ones bloodline.

Frequently, Satan uses a car accident, or some type of accident, as the 'springboard' from which to create or continue the neck injury or back pain. Technically, there is no such thing as an accidents because the Bible says nothing is the result of a chance happening, a random event or an 'accident'. The Enemy disguises his mischief as an 'accident', even though the Word of God expressly says, the "Curse without a cause does not come." (Pr. 26:2)

The Devil is meticulous in making the punishment fit the crime. The Israelites' idolatry and their stiff-necked refusal to worship God could be legally interpreted as rebellion. Their spiritual condition was physically applied to their bodies which manifested as difficulty in bending the neck. Under the law of demonic reciprocity, the Enemy finds it a fit rendering of justice that those guilty of practicing idolatry and rebellion, as demonstrated in the practice of witchcraft, should be punished with stiffness of neck and back pain.

Back injuries and back pain are often attached to the act of rebellion and control. Thus, a stiff and sore back will often afflict those who take matters into their own hands and do it themselves rather than surrendering the burdens and challenges of life to God. The Devil regards our fear of letting go of control as witchcraft. He cites distrust of God and idolatry as justification for initiating the judgment against us - even though the sin may have been committed many generations ago by someone you have never met.

Witchcraft, rebellion, idolatry and control bind together to create a hardness of heart which manifests in the physical body. Back pain, especially chronic back problems, are spiritually related to rebellion against divine authority and provision that run in the bloodline of the afflicted one. Fear drives us to take control of the situation ourselves. The idea that 'it is up to me' replaces trust in God and His divine goodness to provide for us.

The Enemy is wily and hides himself and his intentions from us by convincing us to believe the calamity is the result of an 'accident' and 'bad luck'. Not recognizing things for what they really are makes it difficult for us to heed the divine warning, or discern the true nature of the spiritual danger, 'crouching on our doorstep'. Our naiveté and ignorance as to the spiritual war that surrounds us works greatly to his advantage.

Most people are purposely not looking for a demon under every bush because they would not know what to do with one if they encountered it. They prefer to console themselves by considering those who do believe in demons to be paranoid or weird. Those who do see a demon hanging on every doorknob may also be misguided. Jesus warned us to not be deceived. In a war where the main weapon is deception, let us not throw out God's commands in our misdirected pursuit of God. And let us heed His word to cast out demons, one of the most straightforward commands given by the Lord Jesus Christ.

Neither is it wise to ignore or disregard the gift of discerning of spirits. Both ignorance about deliverance, and paranoia about the existence and power of the invisible world of evil spirits, lend themselves well to the hidden agenda of the Evil One. That agenda is, ultimately, to deceive and destroy the whole human race into believing that they are helpless in their ignorance and terrified of encounters with the unseen forces of darkness. That is not the mandate Jesus left His followers.

READING IT BACKWARDS

Uncovering the spiritual mysteries of iniquity is very similar to what archeologists do in their search for and examination of artifacts (evidence of the remains of the past) to understand what was then, and how it relates to the present. Through application of the same strategy that archeologists use, we can discover the etiology (the assignment of cause and origins) of events that happened in our family's deep past to gain a better understanding of both the spiritual and physical mysteries from the past that continue to confront us today.

We will use the <u>principles of Initial First Cause; the Law of Consent; Spiritual Roads; the Cross-Over Effect and the Root-Fruit Test</u> (the ultimate revelation of the root of a tree is in its fruit), to understand more clearly what happened to us in our bloodlines even before we were conceived. We will also use inductive and deductive reasoning to process the known bits of information. Applying the spiritual principles identified above to those known bits of information will allow us to reconstruct the picture in order to better predict and prevent the present mysteries of iniquity that are at work in our individual family line.

First we must define the terms and understand the principles we will be using in our quest to 'connect the dots' in discovery of the hidden works of darkness. This will allow us to be more specific regarding the crimes that have been committed by our family line and against our family line, as we prepare to present our case before the Court of Heaven.

Please note that healing, forgiveness and freedom are already ours whether we understand the details of the devastation or not. The LORD knows what the Enemy has been doing to conspire against us. We have already obtained our freedom through the death and resurrection of Jesus Christ. At the moment we are 'born again', we are seated with Christ in heavenly places and our names are written in the Lamb's Book of Life. These gifts cannot be earned by our good works, nor can they be taken away or purchased with money. All of the above-mentioned gifts are the <u>purchased possession</u> of every believer in Jesus Christ.

However, in order to receive them, benefit from them, and witness the Lord's restoration of the fullness of our godly legacy (which was stolen from us), we are required to know the Word of God and stand upon the promises of God!! Just as Abraham believed God and "it was accounted to him for righteousness," (Rom.4:16-22), so too, we must "fight the good fight of faith" (I Tim. 6:12), "that [we] may lay hold of that, for which Christ Jesus has also laid hold of [us]." (Phil. 3:12) The Good fight calls us back to the foot of the Cross to receive and utilize the gifts Jesus died to give us for His glory.

Understanding the principle of Initial First Cause is based upon the law that all action is first initiated in the spiritual world before it manifests in the natural or physical world. All of our problems first began with the sin that came out of Adam and Eve's agreement, in believing the Lies the Serpent told Eve. The Law of Initial First Cause is verified by the sequence of events as observed in Genesis chapter three. Nothing bad happened in the story or in their daily lives until something changed in the spiritual world first. Sin was that 'something' that changed everything in their natural world - suddenly, immediately, completely, irrevocably.

Eden was gone. All of the destructive things - the curses of death and pain, thorns and thistles, unyielding ground, toiling by the sweat of their brow, abuse and inequality between the man and the woman and snakes crawling on their bellies - all came as a result of that initial shift in the spiritual world. That breakdown came when they made an agreement with the Serpent. Their agreement with him gave him power and jurisdiction over them. The surrender of their authority caused everything which followed, including their exile from the Garden of God's safety into the Snake Pit and Satan's slave labor camps.

That spiritual principle of the Initial First Cause can be applied to our natural, physical world. The world as we know it today is the result and accumulation of what has already been done, permitted, and agreed upon in the spiritual world. The Fall of Man revealed a real and tangible connection between the spiritual and physical worlds. What 'bumped' in the first caused a 'thump' in the second.

This also confirms the Law of Consent. Because our spiritual and physical worlds are connected through laws of agreement, the Enemy must initiate his destructive action against our lives in the spiritual arena first. He must get our consent before any negative influence and interaction can be initiated in our natural lives. The lie comes first. That is why Jesus said "you shall know the truth and the truth will set you free." (Jn. 8:32) The lie binds; it becomes the anchor that obligates us. It is the precursor to sin.

Once the relationship between the lie and sin was established, sin and its consequences became a conduit between our spiritual and our physical worlds. A Spiritual Road was constructed which connects the choices we make and the lies we believe with the events that happen to us. This road, like most roads, (unless otherwise designated as a one way) allows for two-way traffic. Because these roads go both ways, travelers on the Spiritual Road seeking to discover the truth about the ancient agreements their ancestors made can look in the mirror of their own lives and read it backwards to uncover the root of their current troubles.

Because we are permitted to move both ways on this spiritual highway, we can compare what is happening today with what happened back then and find striking similarities - whether the classifications be personal preferences, phenotypes, genotypes, or curses. The lies which provoked our ancestors to sin; the actions and reactions to those injustices; the agreements with the lies; and consequences of sin springing from those agreements; can be now be understood and dealt with in greater clarity. This principle of the Spiritual Road makes the movement of spiritual information even more profound when we realize that we can use the same road to go back to where we came from.

Understanding the concept of this bi-directional movement, and the fact that nothing comes from nowhere, allows us to go backward in time to see more clearly what occurred in the past. Using this information can help us predict more accurately what will happen in the future. Being able to predict the reoccurrence of those malicious patterns and events can make us proactive in breaking those curses before they get started again. For example, how many dread or are 'haunted' by the age their parent died, or the way they died, especially if they see the same age or type of death being passed down several generations in a row?

The laws of agreement with the lie, and the patterns they create with regard to sin, form a fairly stable and predictable relationship. Because the relationship road between the spiritual and natural worlds is a 'constant' (which means it does not move), both the things we observe coming down our bloodline, and the road which permits their bi- directional movement are constant. The road, its origin and end point can be used to predict similar results for the next travelers on that road unless the agreements are broken.

Understanding the principle of the bi-directional road allows us to 'read' the information both forward (to predict) or backward (to uncover) things. We also see that we can start at either end, or even in the middle, of this road to discovery - using either the agreement with the lie, or the manifestation of the problem - to discover pertinent information we need to cancel out the agreements made with death and destruction. These agreements, though hidden, have nonetheless been operating surreptitiously to control and affect our present life. Using the spiritual principles of discovery, we can now begin to make sense out of the senseless and solve the mysteries which lie behind the calamities and the sins committed against the Law of Love and be healed.

Putting these laws all together, we can discover yet another spiritual principle of operation in the unseen realms. Because the Initial First Cause of sin came from believing a lie, we can know that every other first cause or consequence of sin will come from believing a lie. Remember that the connection between believing a lie and consequences coming out of the sin move bi-directionally. Understanding the connection between these principles allows us to understand another principle, which we refer to as the 'Cross-Over-Effect'. The Cross-Over Effect is a corollary (a proposition that follows or is easily proved from another, with little or no further reasoning, as an obvious deduction from something already proven).

The spiritual and the natural worlds are connected (the Law of Initial First Cause). Because the information moves in a bi-directional manner from past to present, or present to past, we can use things observed in the present, natural world to understand what happened in the past spiritual world, or use what happened in the past to predict the future. This causes us to know that whatever has been done in the one is revealed in the other. The Cross-Over Effect tells us that whatever has been done in the spiritual world will find its final expression in the physical world - with our physical bodies often being the ultimate target for very ancient agreements made in the spiritual world.

Again, the Cross-Over Effect defines that, whatever has been done in the spiritual world will find its final expression in the natural world. Whatever is going on in the physical world has already been done and permitted in the spiritual world. Whatever has gone on in the spiritual world is mirrored and replicated in the natural world. Do not be deceived by Denial or Confusion who protest that this is an over-spiritualization of things. Do not 'give place to' Fear, Anxiety, or Panic. Uncovering the mysteries of Iniquity give us great hope that embracing the truth will bring us deliverance and freedom.

The final tool we can use to discern the root of something is to examine the fruit, as Jesus told us to do. The fruit is a litmus test. Love is the desired end in our relationships. Using the tree to illustrate the story of our generations, the roots of our specific generational trees, started in the past, continue to bear fruit to this day. Looking at the fruit will tell you much about the past activities of the Liars and Thieves; Guilt and Fear and Condemnation and Discouragement. We must identify the criminals so they can be rounded up and brought to Court.

DEDUCTIVE AND INDUCTIVE LOGIC

In discovering the origin of the things which bind us, the Word of God is our absolute and constant source of truth and guidance. Many passages give us direct connections and obvious clues in solving the hidden mysteries which plague us and our families. As we observe the general principles that operate in the spiritual world through studying God's Word, we find the means by which we can deduce what is happening in our natural world.

Deductive reasoning means to reach a conclusion without having all of the necessary or relevant information, by using logic; to infer something from a general principle; to reach a conclusion through inference from a general principle to a specific manifestation or occurrence. Deduction is moving from the general to the specific in drawing a conclusion or making a prediction.

Inductive reasoning, on the other hand, means reaching a conclusion based on things which are observed. It means moving from specific observations to form a generalized conclusion or operating principle. (For example, seeing many apples fall from their respective trees, and observing that they all fall down and not up, leads us to form a generalized conclusion called gravity). It is a law or a principle of operation which begins with observable specifics to define a general law that is useful in explaining the specific things that are being observed. Inductive reasoning is used to produce a universal principle from specific, observable instances.

Beginning with the premise of knowing that everything we see has come from something that already is, and that nothing comes from nothing, we know that there is nothing we see in the present which came from nothing or nowhere. We can deduce, therefore, that there has to be a reason for everything, including the specific curses we see or experience manifesting around us. This supports the Biblical statement that "the curse without a cause does not come". (Pr. 26:2) From here we can begin our search for the cause of the curse.

Our generational histories and past agreements have come together to manifest as specific experiences which are bringing the result of past spiritual agreements into our present physical world. Observing that we are similar to our relatives helps in the identification of the laws of heredity and genetics. Genetic transmission of information through the DNA, which describes the traits and aptitudes from one generation to the next, is the process which we first observed and now understand happens through our DNA.

TRAUMA MARKINGS

Understanding the concept of the genetic transmission of information, including trauma markings; and correlating it with the Word of God, which describes the consequences of sin (the curses), gives us a place to begin for discovering the causes for the curses that have come down into our lives. Understanding that none of these things happen without the Law of Agreement, and the Law of Agreement brings forth actions, we can conclude that there must have been agreements made in the past for these specific manifestations to have come.

Because the events are tied to specific agreements, if those agreements were made with lies, those manifestations are the fruit of the lies that will bring problems into our lives. Conversely, we can use what we see and know in the physical world today and read it backward to get a general understanding as to past agreements that may have been made in the spiritual world. These agreements are used to create specific events which are now permitted to operate in the tangible world - despite not having been there to witness the original spiritual agreements. These are the curses Jesus' Death and Resurrection came to break.

A general application of this principle can be seen in the creation of the world itself. We are told that darkness covered the deep and that God spoke the words, "Let there be light" and there was light. (Gen.1:2-3) We now know that His spoken words created vibrations that set everything in motion; and that, to this day, everything is made up of vibrations. The original act can be discovered in observing our present reality, as the present points back to what was done in the beginning.

Once the validity of a pattern is established, inductive reasoning can be used to move us from what we know, see, and observe - i.e., boils on the knee; to what we do not know - i.e., the particular generational sin that the Enemy used to justify his demonic judgment of boils. Checking Deuteronomy 28:27 will lead us back to see that uncleanness, and the sins of idolatry and witchcraft practiced in Egypt were some of the general precursors to boils.

Deductive reasoning, on the other hand, uses logic to reach a conclusion, often without having all the specifics. It starts by using general principles already known to predict a specific outcome. For example, if the Bible tells us gossip causes stomach problems, (Job 20:12-22) and we are seeing gossip in the bloodline, using the principle of deductive reasoning it would be reasonable to ask if the person being interviewed or members of their family has stomach problems.

The reciprocal question is also valid. If they complain of stomach problems, the bi-directional movement of the spiritual world would prompt us to rightly ask if they, or members of their bloodline, have a tendency to gossip or 'back bite'. The sins of gossip, criticism, sowing discord, judging, and backbiting, would then be ones we would specifically identify in addressing the generational sins that cause stomach and digestive problems. Based upon the information gathered, we would then cancel out the lie and ask for forgiveness for crimes of gossip committed in our family line or in our own lives for the healing of stomach conditions and digestive afflictions. The dysfunction of the digestion could also be a result of *being* judged, or criticized, or 'picked on'. If that is the case, the one suffering from the malady will need to forgive their persecutors, those who are bullying and attacking them.

Deductive reasoning is going from the general body of information to a specific conclusion. Inductive reasoning is going from the specific observation to form a generalization. The presence of the pattern provides a reasonable guide which can be used with both inductive and deductive reasoning to form valid conclusions which keep us from making assumptions.

Remember the Cross-Over Effect. Anything the Enemy causes in the spiritual world, can be 'mirrored' in the physical, natural world. For example, injustice and the resulting bitterness (the internalization of the anger that comes from injustice) manifested in the spiritual, non-tangible world, can be replicated as relational friction and pain in the physical world. Arthritic pain in the joints (knees, hips, elbows, and wrists)), for example, is rooted either in self-bitterness, or bitterness and friction in our relationships with each other. Failing to forgive and love and live with one another in grace and peace "causes that which is lame to be dislocated". (See Heb. 12:1-15).

If the deed has already been done in those who lived before us, and there has been no forgiveness or resolution of the injustice, the crime or trauma remains virulent (poisonous) and is still marked on our DNA as a potential point of vulnerability. If the issues are not addressed, the Enemy sets up the pattern to repeat itself. We call these the 'demonic patterns of destruction'. Not understanding spiritual warfare will cause us to casually conclude that arthritis 'runs in our family'. We will let it go at that, without considering a more intentional and diabolical agenda against us (and our joints).

With the old agreement still 'on the books', never having been eradicated, the Enemy can and will seize his opportunity to reactivate it in order to recreate a current event. A car accident for example, will allow the spirit of pain, especially arthritic pain, to once again become an active part of our physical legacy, sourced in our spiritual legacy. (See Heb. 12:11-14) That is why it is beneficial to apply the Blood of Jesus and the gift of forgiveness to any physical, relational, financial or situational 'flare-up' that Satan would use in our lives, or in the lives of family members, to steal, kill or destroy us. (See *Diagnosing Your Family Tree* for more information.)

Please Note: There are three reasons Jesus did not get so involved in the necessity of discovering the spiritual root causes of physical diseases before He could or would heal someone. First, "He Himself took our infirmities and bore our sicknesses." (Mt. 8:17) That settled the matter of payment. Secondly, He did not need to be convinced about the existence of the Devil, or his demons. He knew how they twisted the truth of God's Word, to take advantage of people and tangle them up into believing all kinds of lies. Thirdly, the Devil knew who Jesus was, and that it would be pointless to enter a battle which he knew he could not win. None of these reasons preclude us from moving forward to do what Jesus said to do: heal the sick, cast out demons and preach the Gospel, both by faith, and through obedience to the knowledge of the Holy things of God.

HACKED AND HELD HOSTAGE

The true source of much of the physical pain we suffer in our souls is from the pain of broken relationships. The thoughts generated in our minds, and the feelings that come out of our hearts, become the evidence the Accuser uses to try and convict us in the Court of Heaven. Our thoughts become the thoughts he uses to condemn us. Our feelings become feelings he uses to betray us into the hands of Hurt and Offense. The Enemy does not want us to recognize that he is the one who has set up the attack against us, and that it is he who presents these temptations to us as our own thought in order to conceal their true source and origin as coming from him.

On one hand, when we do not understand the dynamics of the conflict between God and the Devil, Confusion comes into our minds to make us think that God is responsible for permitting all the difficult issues in our lives. On the other hand, we are also tempted to believe that everything we do, or everything that happens to us is our fault. If we leave the Devil out of this equation, the 'riddle' of evil will never be solved and its resolution will not be achieved. Believing that it is our fault that bad things are happening has put us under the 'spell of Hell'!

On the other hand, we might be tempted to think it is everyone else's fault. In the Amplified Bible Paul says it like this, "For though we walk in the flesh, (as mortal men) we are not carrying on our (spiritual) warfare according to the flesh and using the weapons of man. The weapons of our warfare are not physical (weapons of flesh and blood). Our weapons are divinely powerful for the destruction of fortresses." (I Cor. 10:3-4)

These fortresses are the mindsets and belief systems into which we have been born. These are the strongholds that have been built and embraced through decades of exposure to Fear, the 'foreman' of Hell's Construction Crew. These fortresses (strongholds) must be exposed and torn down. In order for us to be set free from the 'body of death' operating software that controls much of what goes on in our souls, we must be reprogrammed by the truth the Holy Spirit relays to us by rightly dividing of the Word of God.

Ours is a 'rescue mission' to set captives free from the slavery of sin and the prison houses of Hell. "But this is a people robbed and plundered; all of them are snared in holes, and they are hidden in prison houses; they are for prey, and no one delivers; for plunder, and no one says, "Restore!"(Is. 42:22) Paul goes on to explain, "We are destroying sophisticated arguments and every exalted and proud thing that sets itself up against the (true) knowledge of God", by "taking every thought and purpose captive to the obedience of Christ." (I Cor. 10:5)

This is what spiritual warfare looks like in battling the war that goes on inside of us, the ones described by Paul in Romans 7:23: "I see another law in my members, warring against the law of my mind, and bringing me into captivity to the law of sin which is in my members." The 'law of my mind' is our original disposition, that we have been created in the image of God, made by God Himself. This is our 'divine identity' which loves the law of goodness and justice and causes us to love the law of God. The law of sin, however, has captured and overtaken our original disposition of righteousness, and has enslaved our members to another law, the law of sin and death.

For us to try and change the degenerated nature of the carnal man by 'trying to be good' is an exercise in futility! We live on a demonic torture rack. We are adapting to sin and accepting it at the same time we are striving against it. We are caught up in an endless quest for spiritual perfection, which ultimately stretches us between 'never enough' and 'try harder'. We are becoming enslaved to and serving a 'counterfeit gospel' based on getting rid of our sin ourselves.

We have come to accept this degeneration as a natural and innate part of who we are. We have been taught to accept a 'sinful human nature', as the accurate description of who we really are, and commonly refer to it and its activities, as "Me". In this swapping out of our divine nature for the sinful human nature, the Enemy has hacked into our lives to pull off the greatest heist in history - the true nature of man's identity!

Our acceptance of this lie allows the imposter who is 'impersonating me to myself' to operate as 'me', in order to undermine the truth of who I am. I find myself doing what is contrary to who I was created to be as the son or daughter of the Most High God. I begin to believe that what I do defines who I am. The truth will always default back to what God says. The truth is, I am who God says I am. The Devil's ploy only works if he can persuade me to disregard the truth and believe the cardinal rule of the Snake Pit: I am what I do or am tempted to do.

The work of sanctification is a work of cleansing, deliverance, healing and restoration. Much of that work, conducted by the Holy Spirit, is not pleasant to the carnal man who has been corrupted and demonically programmed to crave the things of this world, the things that are contrary to our divine nature. Sin is the pursuit of the things of this world that are at enmity with God. (Rom. 8:7) Surrendering to the Holy Spirit – letting go of self-will, and being released from the grip of the Strong Man - is the only way to break the grip of sin and 'walk out' of these demonic fortresses into the righteousness, joy and freedom the Lord died to give us.

RECOVERING LOST BLESSINGS

*T*AKING THE DEVIL TO COURT

Only when we, as the legal representatives of our generational bloodlines, 'take the Devil to court', will agreements with the Devil be broken, his hold over us severed, and justice be restored. Only then will the Devil's claimed rights to enforce the curses already paid for at the Cross be removed. Only then will the freedom Jesus died to give us begin to flow into those areas of our lives that have been negatively affected by the demonic judgments for sin. Only then can the iniquity and trauma marked by pain that targets us for destruction, including those put upon our physical health and current relationships, be erased by the Blood of Jesus.

We are told to come boldly to the Throne of Grace to find help in time of trouble - to present our case before the Righteous Judge of all the earth, Who is ready to hear our plea. He invites us to "bring forth our strong reasons" and "present our case" (Is. 43:26-27; Is. 41:21) without fear. When we approach the Father, our petition is the thing the Devil fears the most. That is why Guilt, and Shame, and Fear desperately try to hold us in their grip. They are determined to keep the demonic judgments and generational crimes the Evil One has committed against us from coming into the light or being brought before the Throne of Justice.

Even in all of the injustice the Enemy commits against us, God does not call us to be victims. The god of this world would want us to identify ourselves as 'victims' and adopt a 'victims' mentality and feel sorry for ourselves. God says we are "more than conquerors". (Rom. 8:37) We are victorious. Faith is the victory that overcomes the world. Coming boldly to the Throne of Grace gives us the opportunity to receive validation and vindication! God wants His Son to get everything He died for including our freedom to live without fear and the oppression of the Enemy.

The Deceiver does everything he can to intimidate us to keep us from coming the High Court for justice. He tries to block us and keep us from confessing or repenting, or even speaking of sin we have done. We are afraid that admission of our sins will somehow implicate us; when, in truth, confession is the only real means for freedom from sin and the demonic judgments it brings. Repentance, and the revelation that we have been tricked, that we did what we really did not want to do - even if, at the time, we may have *believed* that we wanted to do it - is the only way to deliverance and freedom. The truth is, we are no match for the wiles of the Devil. We are not smart enough to out-smart him. Even our good intentions to not sin again are no guarantee that we will not be tempted again. The bottom line is that we were deceived into sinning!

In taking the Devil to Court, we not only resist him (Ja. 4:7) - as the Bible commands - but we are also petitioning the Court of Appeals to reverse the demonic judgments, including the curses he has put on us. We are requesting that the finished work of the Cross and the full payment Jesus, the Son of God, made for our ransom, be applied to our account. Through forgiveness, justice and truth are reinstated, and the purposes of the Kingdom of God are reestablished in our life and legacy.

<u>In order to prevail against the works of Darkness, we must cast off</u> <u>our agreements with Guilt and Condemnation and accept the</u> <u>power of the Blood of Jesus to forgive and restore us.</u> This kind of deliberate and specific action must be taken against the Enemy in order to set the record straight. We are 'calling him out' on what he has been doing to deceive us and destroy our bloodline. We have no desire to be part of anything he is doing. We declare our reliance on, and our allegiance to God; 'Thy will be done, Oh God, on earth, in and through me, even as it is being done and declared in heaven'. We are resolved to love, and remain loyal to God.

As we prepare our case to present to the Judge, the counsel of the Holy Spirit is at our service. Through the impartation of His Wisdom we can "bring forth our strong reasons", based upon faith in the truth of God's Word. He will expose the deliberate intentions of the Accuser, who has come to deceive us - to find us guilty - for doing what he himself tempted us to do.

What blatant hypocrisy and vile misuse of the Word of God on the part of the Enemy! His contempt for God and his disdain for us - in using our sins to make us feel cut off from the love and forgiveness of God - is only a plot to make God appear foolish for declaring His love for us in the first place. *If* God is not requited in His love for us; *if* we do not respond to God's love by loving Him back, and trusting in His love; then Satan is right, and God is a fool for making us and for loving us in the first place!

FORCING SATAN TO DROP THE CHARGES

<u>Confession and repentance replace lies with the truth.</u> <u>Forgiveness</u> <u>releases the crimes committed against us and our ancestors over</u> <u>to the Court of Heaven for a just and fair settlement.</u> Heaven's ruling forces Satan to drop the charges that the spirit of Condemnation has made against us. Guilt and Shame are exposed as false witnesses and accomplices in covering up the crime.

Justice is restored. Reconciliation and peace reassures us of our relationship with God. Our minds and hearts are brought back to hope through the revelation of Jesus Christ and His love for us. The things stolen from us are returned, and our legacy of blessings is recovered. The plot to separate us from the Love of God is nullified and we are brought back into full fellowship with the Heavenly Father.

Until we confess the iniquity of our generations past and the legacy of sin and destruction it has stirred up, the Devil has a right to conduct his operations against us, including the restraint of blessings. Although his charges are founded in the corruption of his own character, and his activities illegally promotes injustice, it makes no difference to the 'Law Breaker'. His only intention is to hold us accountable to the 'letter of the law' and vindicate himself in this matter of sin.

Let us not misunderstand what is going on here. Confessing our iniquity does not save us. Confessing Jesus Christ as our Savior does! Our salvation is secure and requires nothing more from us than that we accept the death of Jesus Christ as the atonement for our sins. Salvation settles the question of ownership. Confessing our iniquity, on the other hand, initiates the process of sanctification in the cleansing of the house. Taking the Devil to Court addresses the matter of 'strongholds' - trespassing and unlawful occupation by those who have come to claim our house for themselves. Sanctification is the process of getting rid of both the garbage, the filth of sin and the rats that feed on the garbage, and making the house holy.

Is it any wonder that there is such blatant disregard for the Law by our Enemy as we examine how he rebelled and came to be in the first place? The contempt he displayed toward his Creator, along with the insidious corruption of his own wickedness, can be seen all around us. With every place he has touched, he has left the marks of pain and destruction. Why should it be any different in the spiritual world? (Meditate on Ps. 49 & 50) His hatred for us is as incessant as his desire for our destruction is insatiable.

Our agreement with Heaven allows the Court to address the injustices committed against us and bring the restoration of justice to our family bloodline. We come into agreement with the One Who testifies to the truth. Jesus is the Faithful Witness. He cancels out the 'slave papers' drafted in Hell which Satan has been illegally holding against us - even after the completion of our emancipation. The Truth sets the captives free. Freeing the captives begins the 'freedom march' for their children.

The original authority God gave us in the administration of the Garden included the management of creation for the purpose of keeping the peace. The administration of justice and equity were easy. God's perfect will was already in place and operating in the pre-sin world of Paradise. When sin entered the world, 'crouching at the door' as it did with Cain, everything changed. Justice was held in contempt, as the kingdom of Goodness was torn apart. The war had begun! Creatures began sorting themselves out and pitting themselves against one another as predator and prey.

Injustice and lies usurped the throne where justice and truth had ruled. All creation began to groan in travail as the horror of bloodshed and death unfolded in their midst. Sin took over and ruled as the first and primary force for reshaping and redefining the character of the sons and daughters of God. Our original, divine nature was obscured by the powerful forces that ruled the Pit.

Those Rulers of Darkness began to control and twist the vulnerable sons and daughters of God - even to the point where the creatures began to define themselves by the standard of the Pit as having a 'sinful human nature'.

All of us have been conceived and born in the confines of sin, and raised in the Snake Pit of Iniquity. The only thing that has changed in this struggle has been the thousands of variables which technology has added to the mix. The clever magic of the 'seduction of mankind through technology' has given the god of this world, the prince of the power of the air, one more amazing weapon in his arsenal to destroy the sons of Adam and the children of God. Through technology and our desire to know more, he has mesmerized us into making an agreement with and bowing to, his indisputable power over us. He works to program and entangle us in an ever-morphing and insidious battle for our souls.

In this world, flooded with injustice and rewritten by sin, God remains true and His standard of Justice sure. We are still called as His ambassadors to declare truth and execute justice, to protect life and preserve a legacy of righteousness for ourselves and our descendants. Exercising our authority and executing justice, in a world system where chaos rules and injustice prevails, has not been easy or straightforward.

We are raised in a world where executing justice often makes us a prey and puts us in the direct line of fire for Satan's retaliation. We are ridiculed and persecuted, presented as weak and mentally unstable, for desiring and pursuing truth. We are victimized by those who lack revelation of the truth and have no desire for it. Reproving the scoffer causes us to be the object of scorn. Correcting the disobedient results in contention and contempt. In resisting evil, we are targeted as troublemakers ourselves. Even for the most willing and worthy among us, anger and bitterness all too often replace righteous indignation.

We find even the simplest matters of justice to be rampant with complications. Equity is ripped out of our hands, and we pursue justice only to find that the Enemy has used even our desire for justice against us. Pulling us into his trap, he uses our very motivation for goodness and the desire to establish it, as bait for luring us into the midst of his 'torture rack' of conflict, torment, and injustice. In the end - except for the Faithfulness of our God - we are no match for the clever schemes of the Evil One - who even uses our pursuit of justice to justify his judgment of us.

THIS DID NOT JUST START WITH YOU

Although everyone lives under the general shadow of the curse of the Original Sin, each one carries the legacy of specific curses that may be different from others. Even within families, individual members may experience things differently, despite the fact that their bloodline comes from the same two parents. This is partially explained by the divine design in each one of us, which appears to be the function of deliberate and purposeful genetic selection. How else do we explain such things as both blue-eyed and brown-eyed children coming from two brown-eyed parents?

If you closely examine any current relationships you are in, you will see patterns, many of which are painful and dysfunctional. Know that what you are going through did not just start with you. Be assured that other people in your family, including past generations, have already suffered or are currently suffering from many of the same things that you are experiencing now. Even within the same family, one member may seem to have all the 'bad luck', while another does well and appears to be blessed. Why is that? If God is no respecter of persons, how can this be?

The curse may rest on the oldest or the youngest. Some curses may be gender related. Some may divide relationships between mothers and daughters, or manifest as addictions. They can twist love, or distort communication. They can create dependencies, or fearless independence. The list and descriptions of curses and the patterns they generate are as endless as they are personalized. Premature and untimely deaths; physical health issues; failures; addictions; obsessions; emotional, verbal and sexual abuse and violence are just a few of the many curses that can manifest in one bloodline and not in the next.

Emotional and physical dependencies, promiscuity, and conflict in relationships may plague one bloodline and not another. Loss of inheritance, poverty, calamities, car accidents, drowning and fires, may be part of one family's legacy and not another. Being falsely accused and blamed, being persecuted and suffering injustice, being ostracized and rejected, being unwanted or treasured, being misperceived, or deemed to be a mistake, are all written and coded in our genetics - which are not only biological in the natural, but spiritual, and powerful in the supernatural.

This information forms the patterns that will be used to shape our initial behavioral responses and dictate our carnal dispositions. And yet, even as the 'head crusher' came, there is hope that those "whom the Son sets free are free indeed" will be restored to their full inheritance as they find their life in Him! It is the Truth that sets us Free and the Truth is the person of Jesus Christ.

FORGIVENESS, THE KEY TO JUSTICE

NOWING WE ARE LOVED

The desire to know who we are and where we come from tugs at us constantly as we journey through life's mandatory corridors of time and space. For some, the journey ends well. For others, the truth remains hidden in the landscape of carnal appetites, spiritual confusion, and failure. The pursuit of immediate and urgent needs serves to push us further away from the truth to a place far from home. The Enemy has desperately worked to obscure the true nature of our divine origin and the passionate love the Father has for each one of us, by distracting us with sin and the preoccupation with self.

Love - and knowing we are loved - becomes the primary issue with regard to regaining our lost blessings including the restoration of peace of mind and health. Knowing that we are neither abandoned nor despised brings us hope. Discovering the purpose for our life comes in <u>knowing we are loved</u>. The revelation of the love God has for us, individually, removes the anxiety of living in this hostile and hateful world alone. We are not alone because God is with us and we are safe. Knowing who we belong to and that we are loved, changes everything!

The beginning of the restoration of all things starts with <u>recognizing and reclaiming the truth which has been inside of us all along</u>, although it has been completely obscured by the Enemy's obstruction and the persistence of his evil intentions against us. The power of the Enemy's narrative, by manipulating our feelings and thoughts, and our inability to discern lies from truth has disarmed us and led us down the path of personal sin and guilt.

The primary antidote for sin begins with repentance, which means to change one's mind. <u>Repentance, confession of sin, and receiving God's forgiveness are His uncomplicated methods for justice. Justice from the High Court is the primary step in recovering the benefits and blessings stolen from us by sin.</u>

Satan deceives us and <u>sets us up</u> to sin. He then <u>catches us</u> in the very act of sin, and complicates our escape from the grip of sin by supplying us with false remedies for our sin. We are caught on his torture rack. He then applies the Law as the plumb line of God's justice to our behavior and pronounces us guilty of sin. The Enemy judges us by the same Law originally given by God - as a means by which to protect His people and identify them as His children - to justify bringing his demonic judgments upon us the punishments for that sin.

Through their obedience to the Law, God was able to shield the Children of Israel from the accusations of the Evil One. When the Evil One demanded they pay the full price required by the Law as retribution for the sins they committed, God stepped in with the Law to protect them and provide a means for atonement. This atonement was only temporary - the annual sacrifice offered by the High Priest. When the Accuser would approach the Throne of God to present his case and find fault with the Children of Israel, God merely had to look down and see if they were still walking within the statutes of the Law. If they were obedient they were innocent and Satan's case against them would be thrown out of Court. If they disobeyed, the Enemy would call for the death penalty. Ironically, the same one Accusing them was also the

Perpetrator of the crime, as he was the one who tempted them to murmur and disobey in the first place.

'But it is YOUR fault,' he says. 'YOU should have resisted the temptation and you would not have sinned.' Does anyone knowingly desire to be misled or go willingly down the path of destruction? The most basic reason we 'fell for' or 'agreed with' the lie is because we didn't know it was a lie. Or, perhaps, we had already given up and been captured by Shame, believing all was lost anyway. Or, perhaps we were deceived by the Enemy's lies and agreed with his solution, because of our desperate need for an answer to the problem we were facing. We sin because we have been deceived, tricked, coerced, or intimidated, to take the bait he offers, believing it will be helpful in relieving the pain or resolving the problem. These are the entrapments waiting at every juncture, like "sin crouching at the door".

FORGIVENESS IS THE KEY TO RECOVERING YOUR LIFE

The Devil did the same thing when he tried to corner Jesus with the Law by throwing the adulterous woman at His feet. Hopeful that Jesus would not be able to find a way to rescue one so obviously caught in the act of sinning, the Enemy stirred up an angry mob of religious zealots as a vehicle for hurling his insults at Jesus. Jesus was aware of his insidious plot from the beginning and easily escaped the trap of those who sought to catch Him with His words.

They may have been astonished when Jesus stooped to write their names in the sand, a custom they may have remembered from Jeremiah, who said, "Those who depart from Me shall be written in the earth, because they have forsaken the LORD, the fountain of living waters." (Jer. 17:13) He made it abundantly clear that the privilege of judging was given only to those who were without sin.

As none were sinless, none were free to throw a stone at her. All of

those who would have judged her were in need of mercy themselves, and were thus unqualified to judge anyone else. In their
attempt to expose Him as a Law breaker, He, in turn, exposed sin
in them. No one was found who was in a place of innocence who
could be justified to stone the adulterous woman.

Judgment was rendered correctly. The Deceiver had been
exposed! The maligned woman was free of her accusers. Jesus
forgave her sin. For the first time in her life, she began to understand the value of her life as seen through the eyes of the One
Who gave her life and died in her place; her hope was restored.
She was free from sin, and free to go and sin no more - because
she knew she was loved and forgiven.

JUDGING OTHERS – EXAMINING OURSELVES

As the little 'I am's', created in the image of the Great I AM - Who
is the Judge of all the earth - we have a natural propensity to
judge both ourselves and others. Like our Father, our sensitivity to
injustice makes us susceptible to making judgments. Our fallen
nature with its natural proclivity to negativity, criticism and fault
finding however, skews those judgments and violates the Law of
Love and true justice. With judgment comes the urge to hold
others in a place of condemnation. In an effort to make things fair,
we often take matters into our own hands, which only serves to
make them worse.

We take things personally. Our feelings are hurt, and we become
offended. Although we perceive most offenses and matters of
injustice to be of a more personal nature, we are only free to judge
them objectively when we do not take the offense personally.
Even when the crimes and injustices are resolved fairly, we have
no power to vindicate ourselves. God is the **only** One who is able
to Judge and make things right.

Vindicating and validating myself is much like bestowing a prize
upon myself for winning a race. To honor myself in a public

competition is not honorable at all. To judge myself as innocent carries no weight. The exoneration must come from due process of Law and from the One who knows all and is not flattered with bribery, nor deceived by the proposition of personal gain. Not only can we not rightfully try our own case; but attempting to bring justice for crimes committed against us, by the very nature of the act of judging it ourselves, corrupts us. "Justice is turned back, and righteousness stands afar off; for truth is fallen in the street, and equity cannot enter. So truth fails, and he who departs from evil makes himself a prey." (Is. 59:14-15)

To judge and bring justice is beyond us, although our hearts long for it. If any justice is to be had, it must be a matter of Divine intervention. Paul warns us in First Corinthians not to judge anything before the time: "until the Lord comes, who will both bring to light the hidden things of darkness and reveal the counsels of the hearts." (I Cor. 4:5) To judge makes us the judge. James reminds us that there is "One Lawgiver, who is able to save and destroy. Who are you to judge another?" (Ja. 4:12)

Even in the natural order of things, we would never think to step into the judge's chambers without his invitation, or take his seat before the Bench. How, then, would we ever think to make ourselves a judge in the affairs of God? "Who are you to judge another's servant? To his own master he stands or falls. Indeed, he will be made to stand, for God is able to make him stand." (Rom. 14:4) As God's servants, we must "all stand before the judgment seat of Christ," where "each of us shall give account of himself to God." (See Ro. 14: 4, 10 & 12)

ON JUDGING AND BEING JUDGED

We are often judged by the world for judging others. The command to "Judge not" is a well-known favorite of the Enemy, who delights in misusing it to suit his own purposes. We will not only be judged, but we will also have to give an account for the attitude we have shown in judging one another. Selfishness and self-righteousness are accusations easy to make and difficult to defend, especially when we are caught in the middle of a situation where a decision must be rendered in the judgment of a matter.

"Judge not, and you shall not be judged." (Mt. 7:1) "Condemn not, and you shall not be condemned. Forgive, and you will be forgiven. Give and it will be given to you... For with the same measure that you use, it will be measured back to you." (Lu. 6:37-38) Judging others makes us vulnerable to being judged ourselves. Judging others makes us a target to the scrutiny of being judged by the Enemy. That which we found offensive and despised in another becomes the very thing the Devil uses to 'measure back to us' our punishment for judging them. How many times do we see ourselves doing the very thing that we hate in another and vowed we would NEVER do ourselves?

God expects His children to love one another, and stand for what is true and just. Any attempt to bring justice that takes matters into our own hands is doomed to fail. Any attempt we make to establish justice for crimes committed against us, push us beyond the boundaries of divine protection and make us a target of Satan's bitter retaliation to bring judgment upon us. He uses our judgment of others as his justification for judging us for breaking the Law.

FORGIVE AND FORGET

The purposes of justice are not served by denying the truth or giving counsel to the plaintiff to forget that a crime took place! Forgiveness does not mean we have to just forget that something bad happened. Forgiving does not mean we must deny that a crime has been committed. To the contrary, forgiveness by its very definition acknowledges that a crime HAS been committed. A transgression against the Law of Love has occurred. For the believer, Jesus redefined the Law recorded in the Ten Commandments as the Law of Love. In any minor or serious violation of the Law, someone's right to love has been violated or disregarded. The purpose of examining the matter is to bring those infractions into the light that the hidden things of darkness can be exposed.

Forgiveness is not forgetting, nor does forgetting prove we have truly forgiven. God does not give us amnesia as a sign that we have truly forgiven someone. However, He does comfort us and remove the pain and anger from our memory, as we receive His testimony to the truth and His promise of divine restoration. Knowing that He knows what happened both calms our heart and gives us peace that He will rule in the matter with complete equity. Forgetting is not the indication of true forgiveness; the peace in our souls is the true indication of forgiveness!

As we trust Him to make things right, and receive the assurance of His righteous judgment, He heals the pain and shame in our memory. The Enemy loses his power to further disturb us by reactivating our feelings of offense or reopening the wound caused by the assault. Forgiveness releases us from the place of confusion and guilt and sets us free from obsessing about the things which have been done to, or spoken against us. Forgiveness moves us from a place of being spiritually attacked by Bitterness to a position of vindication and peace of mind. We are set free from the energy drain that anger puts on us. The emotional pain is turned over to the Righteous Judge. The injustice no longer works against us, but for us.

The Enemy will attempt to confuse us and persuade us to believe that remembering the deed done against us is evidence that we have not yet completely forgiven the other person or ourselves. If he can persuade us to believe we have not truly forgiven - based upon our feelings, or on the fact that we still remember the act committed against us - he can and will continue to accuse us of not having truly forgiven and continue to torment us with Double-mindedness, Guilt, and Self-judgment in order to keep that door open for making further accusations against us.

FORGIVENESS IS NOT CONFIRMED BY FEELINGS

Even as forgiveness is not defined as forgetting, forgiveness is not determined by our feelings. <u>Forgiving is an act of obedience</u>. We do not have to 'feel' sorry or 'feel like' forgiving someone, any more than we have 'feel' like doing the dishes' to get them done. Turning the crimes committed against me over to God is done through <u>an act of my will</u> - just as the dishes are washed, not because I feel like it, but because I chose to wash them!

Forgiveness allows me the freedom to live my life without carrying the burden of injustices, and the bitterness (all the bad things that happened to me) around with me all the rest of my life. Anger and Bitterness are heavy and demanding burdens. By forgiving, they do not <u>get</u> to be my life long traveling companions. The injustices I have suffered do not get to define me, or steal my strength. When I release those who have persecuted me to the Righteous Judge, the Enemy can no longer judge me for judging them, nor am I chained by Resentment, Guilt, Pain, or Anger. The Enemy's manipulation through Anxiety and Pain is broken.

I take captive those thoughts that would lead me to murmur and complain, and submit them to Christ. (II Cor. 10:5-6) I do not permit the Devil's accusations to torment me with the thoughts and feelings of unforgiveness, although it does not stop him from trying. When I stop agreeing with the Tormentor the 'tables are turned' and we are no longer at the mercy of the Evil One. Even when The Tempter attempts to entice us to feel bad, and hurt, and mad, and used and confused, and pressured to pick up the offense again, we are <u>confident</u> that forgiveness is the only sure way to defeat the Enemy of our soul.

Peter asked the same question, "Lord, how often shall my brother sin against me, and I forgive him? Up to seven times?" "Jesus said to him, "I do not say to you up to seven times, but up to seventy times seven." (Mt. 18:21-12) We stand upon God's promise, "You will keep him in perfect peace whose mind is stayed on You, because he trusts in You." (Jer. 26: 3) Any time the Enemy would try to convince me through my thoughts and feelings that I am still 'mad', I do well to resist him. "Guilt, you are trespassing on the Temple Property of the Most High God. I choose to forgive, and you have no hold on me!" We recall that forgiveness is not based on feelings, but on an act of obedience and the promises of God.

Repeated offenses without remorse or resolution are true challenges to our faith, but God's grace is sufficient even in these things. Jesus did not say to forgive only those who are sorry for what they did; or have asked for forgiveness; or will never do it again. Jesus forgave us while we were yet sinners and ignorant even of our need for forgiveness. How many times have God's people had to suffer to the death, been martyred for their faith, and yet they stood in forgiveness as they were thrown to the lions and used as human torches to light the city of their persecutors? <u>The challenge is to hold a position of forgiveness when the offender does not stop, or even increases his boldness to do us harm.</u> We can do all things ONLY through Christ Who strengthens us. (Phil. 4:13)

Another temptation that leads some into deception comes to those who may believe or feel they are still 'mad at God'. They are still troubled by the question 'Where was He when I needed Him?' or 'Why didn't He stop it?' The Enemy plants these rhetorical questions of 'why' and 'how' in our minds in order to manipulate us back into the cycle of trying to solve the irresolvable conflicts of injustices on our own. He pummels us with 'trying to manage' feelings of resentment and bitterness, continually assaulting us with the notion that these are 'our' feelings simply because we are feeling them, making us feel obligated to defend them.

Confusion and Doubt are only defeated by surrendering our thoughts and feelings and even our 'rights' to justice, to the truth and testimony of Jesus Christ - Who both knows our minds and our hearts perfectly - and the treachery of the Deceiver who is trying to confuse us. We are being tempted to believe that every temptation to sin is 'our own' evil thought coming from our own heart, which the Enemy wants us to conclude is evil. Why would I tempt myself to think evil thoughts? Why would I assume that every thought I think is coming from me, myself? Why? Because we make assumptions and because we do not ponder any other place these thoughts could be coming from but from we ourselves.

Resentment is a spirit which comes in the form of a feeling that comes when we find fault (get angry) with God, and then feel guilty for getting angry with Him. This same feeling of resentment can be directed at any authority figure whom we don't believe is acting with integrity or we feel cannot be trusted to act on our behalf. Resentment comes from feeling guilty for being angry. We end up feeling like we did something wrong and others cannot be trusted to be honest. We decide we have to take care of ourselves. Both Resentment against God and Self-Reliance are familiar spirits who generate their clever thoughts in Hell. These thoughts lead to sin and alienation (separation) from God. Their origin and intention must be identified before we can be confident to send them back to where they came from.

The Enemy can use this vicious circle of abuse and offense to keep us locked in the grip of Confusion and Bitterness for years. He tries to accuse us of not trusting God, and of taking matters into our own hands. The Enemy wants to undermine our faith in God to right the wrongs and deliver us. The Enemy wants us to take matters into our own hands. He wants us to forget that God is the One Who not only went with us into the trial, but is the One Who sustained us through it. He is the One committed - through His Covenant with us - to deliver us out of the fiery trial into the fullness of victory. <u>Our part is to call upon Him, follow Him and trust Him by being obedient to do what He tells us to do.</u>

One of the most difficult trials of all is the one we have come to believe will never end. We 'cave in' at the thought of having to go through a trial that we believe will never end. Living with 'no end in sight' and no hope for positive resolution is difficult and undermines the best of human determination. Without the strength of the Lord, (Eph 6:10) the path of moral resolve and human will power is short lived. It is futile to think that we are any moral or physical or intellectual match for the Devil. There is no way we can outsmart him or outlast him. And because we are no match for the Devil, we are always at the mercy of the Lord - whether we choose to admit it and accept it or not.

For those who do realize that their life and everything related to it remains with and under the care of the Lord, there is rest and hope for justice. This is the portion of those who choose to keep their eyes on Jesus and know the disciple is not above his master. If they persecuted Him, is it any shock that they hate us too? (Jn. 15:18-25) When He died, so did we! We are alive and live now, as dead men, resurrected unto the newness of eternal life. Life and freedom come in knowing Him in whom we live and move and have our being. For the followers of Jesus Christ, He is our portion. He is enough.

In a close examination of the matter, it will be found that both the offender and the offended are victims of Hell's vicious and divisive counsel. It is a malevolent design which sets us up in opposition to ourselves and to each other. As we choose to obey and forgive, we are demonstrating our trust in the faithfulness and justice of God to judge the matter fairly. As we turn the case over to Him, both we and the offender - who was once a victim himself - are eligible to receive a just and righteous settlement for the wrongs committed against each side by the Wicked One.

We do not wrestle against flesh and blood, although the Evil One endeavors to create an irreconcilable conflict between us. (II Cor. 10: 3-4) "For we do not wrestle against flesh and blood, but against principalities, against powers, against the rulers of the darkness of this age, against spiritual hosts of wickedness in the heavenly places." (Eph.6:12) Both the offended and the offender have been wounded, and deceived, and have incurred damage. Both need the justice of God to deliver them from the demonic judgments of the Evil One, who has charged them as breakers of the Law, even though he is the biggest Law breaker of all.

Family members whom I previously held responsible for what happened, and thus became alienated from, can now be reconciled under the new terms of justice as prescribed in the Court of Heaven. Understanding replaces ignorance. We and our 'preceived' enemy have both been wronged. Our real enemy is not flesh and blood, but powers and principalities and spiritual wickedness in high places. Our real enemy is not human.

BUT I STILL DO NOT "FEEL" LIKE I'VE FORGIVEN

Forgiveness based upon feelings adds an element of confusion to the nature of true forgiveness. Many struggle with forgiveness because they do not 'feel' they were sincere enough, or because they do not 'feel' like they did it correctly. Because they still suffer from 'feelings' of doubt and double-mindedness, or are still 'feeling' anger toward someone they have indeed forgiven (by an act of will), they fall for the Enemy's lie that they have not really forgiven; and therefore, their forgiveness is not genuine.

Nowhere in the Bible does it say that forgiveness must be accompanied by feelings, although God's peace will settle into the place where the injustice had once inflamed us. Forgiveness is not a feeling. Forgiveness is an act of one's will - done in obedience to the commandment of God, whether we 'feel like it or not'. And, although we base so much of what we do on how we 'feel', the Bible admonishes us to remember that the just live - not by their feelings - but by faith.

For many who desire to follow God, 'feelings' still override truth and are used as our 'moral compass' to determine the spiritual value, sincerity, or rightness of the things we do. Rather than examining how our behavior is lining up with the Word of God -

under the counsel of the Holy Spirit - we go by how we feel about a situation. When believers use feelings and thoughts as a guide to spirituality, they open themselves up to spirits of Deception that control the Snake Pit. This allows Fear to dictate their thoughts, and teaches them to govern their lives by feelings.

As feelings and thoughts are privy to change from moment to moment, the stability of the soul is compromised by the doubt that emanates from our mind and emotions. That uncertainty creates instability. The soul which functions under the counsel of Doubt (thinking), Fear (feeling), and Confusion (will), is not a reliable instrument to use in defining or determining our spiritual condition. The soul does not operate from a solid and unbiased platform of truth, nor can it provide an accurate or absolute foundation upon which to build a solid relationship with God.

Forgiveness begets forgiveness. Receiving forgiveness from God makes us more inclined to forgive both ourselves and others. Forgiveness helps open our eyes as to the depth of God's love for ourselves and others. Forgiveness breaks the curses and promotes the work of justice, sustaining goodness and creating in us a willingness to forgive the next person in need of it - just as we have been forgiven!

Even as we have been forgiven, we are commanded to forgive. Only then can we come boldly before the throne of grace and mercy to present our case and find help in the time of trouble. Only then will our faith in the Lord Jesus Christ overtake the feelings of fear, purging us from the shame and condemnation of sin. Only then will we have confidence to ask God to remove the judgments which the Enemy has brought upon us for judging others. "And when you stand praying, forgive, if you have anything against any: that your Father also which is in heaven may forgive you your trespasses. But if you do not forgive, neither will your Father which is in heaven forgive your trespasses." (Mark 11:25-26)

JUDGING VERSES DISCERNMENT

We must understand that discerning and judging are not inter-changeable terms. They are not the same thing, although they are often confused with one another. <u>Judging is God's job. Discerning is ours.</u> Jesus warned us not to judge by appearance, but He did instruct us to discern a matter by its fruits. You will know them, not by pronouncing judgment upon them, but by discerning what is the product or fruit coming from their behavior.

Good fruit comes from a good tree, and evil fruit comes from an evil tree. (See Mt.7:17-18) God has given us a method and recourse for addressing evil and identifying its presence. That method is discernment. Many believers are confused about the difference between judging and discerning - and therefore end up failing to speak out against evil or warn others of its presence, for fear of judging or being accused of judging.

As a result, the lines of distinction between the Kingdom of God and the Kingdom of Darkness have become blurred and obscured. Many are pulled into the subtle snares of silence and have failed to discern the presence of the Wicked One. Because we do not discern the real spiritual source and spiritual nature of the matter, we do not take courage to stand up against evil. Because we do not 'call it out' for what it is, or boldly warn those who are confused and caught up in the snares of evil (which masquerade as good), we fail to take a stand for the Truth.

We are intimidated by evil, and answer our critics by 'melting away into the woodwork', mumbling excuses and apologies for not being more tolerant and promises of being more 'politically correct' next time. We must understand that Fear and Confusion use Intimidation to control those who take a stand against wickedness. We say nothing at all in the great and heated debates that would separate the vile from the holy; when, indeed, that is the very thing we have been called to do.

SHAME AND SILENCE

Shame and Fear of being judged, 'blackmail' us into silence, which causes us to hide our sin. Silence would keep us locked in the prison houses of Fear and Shame until we have lost all hope of reconciliation in getting our lives and relationships back.

Knowing the truth sets us free! God has already solved the problem of sin: His solution is for us to simply humble ourselves, repent of the lies we have believed, and accept His provision for sin by admitting (confessing) we have been deceived/tricked. What is left of the matter, except for Pride and Fear to protest to try and stop us from making that confession?

Are we offended, and do we take it personally when the doctor diagnoses us with cancer? Why would we be angry with him for telling us the truth, even though the truth is painful? We would not - unless we had already accepted the cancer as being a rightful part of us. Sin is not a rightful part of me and has no rightful place in me. Sin is a foreign, alien invader that dwells 'in me', as Paul points out.

So, why would we defend sin's presence or be offended by someone who casts out demons, unless we had already embraced sin as a legitimate part of who we are? If we have been deceived into defining our being by what we DO, then it would make sense to be offended and defend our sinful behavior. But if sin is not a legitimate part of us, why do we become defensive by denying it or excusing its operation in us? Why would we not rather rebuke it as an invader in our life? Only because we do not know who we are and have believed the underlying principles of the Pit, the lie that we are what we do.

If we know that sin is not part of our original nature, even though we see ourselves doing sin, we will agree with the Apostle Paul's admonishment to "not let sin rule in us". Romans 6:12 says: "Do not let sin rule as king in your mortal, short-lived, perishable body to make you obey IT, in its lusts, evil passions and cravings." (AMP Bible) What is this that SIN is making me do, ruling over me? And how can I be the sin I am doing if IT is an entity separate from me that is ruling over me and making me do things I do not want to do?

Agreeing that we sinned is the first step in dealing with the sin and critical to it's removal. It is admitting and confessing that it has no rightful place in me. It is foreign to me, the daughter or son of the Most High God. It is not part of my divine nature. It is rather, the thing that is holding me, enslaving me and making me do the things I do not want to do. Getting rid of a tumor or cancer that is growing inside of me is not a matter of 'will power'; it requires a proper diagnoses and aggressive action, resistance and removal. Admitting that we 'sinned' is dealing with sin as God has instructed us to. It is not me, I do not want it, and it has got to go!

When we coddle sin, and make excuses for it we are still being held as its captives. When we agree with the accuser that it is 'our fault', we are assuming the blame. In assuming the blame, we are being deceived/fooled again into agreeing with, it is my fault I am a prisoner, and because I am a prisoner, it is my fault. The truth is, I am being held hostage by something that is creating a war inside of me, the one who wills (wants to) do good. (See Rom.7:23) Assuming the guilt for our sin is not the way to get rid of it. The conviction of the Holy Spirit gives us courage and understanding to see that this thing I just did was not me. It was actually contrary to who I am. I am made in the image of God to love holiness and goodness.

Under the guise of religion and the worldly pressure of taking responsibility for our action (sin), we are agreeing that we deserve to be punished because we are guilty for not being responsible to take the right action in the first place. How can we take responsibility for the plans and intentions of the Enemy to trick us if we do not know about his plan to trick us, or that we are being deceived? God did not reprimand Eve for being deceived. He did not tell her she should have known better. He did not demand that she take 'responsibility' for her actions and He did not redefine her identity by what she had just been tricked into doing. The fact that The Father provided the promise of the coming of the 'Head Crusher' proves that His Children were still worth saving.

Because we were deceived/tricked into letting the thief into our house - by doing something we were tricked into doing - something we did not want to do - does not mean we have to agree with his 'full blown' plan to destroy us. Why would anyone in their right mind knowingly agree with something acting from within them, whose intention is to destroy them? (Mt: 12:29). What else could this be but the work of the Stronger Man Jesus talks about? The stronger man does not come at us pounding down our door, acting like an enemy. He comes in by catching us 'off guard'. He comes knocking on the door of our soul and introduces himself as a 'familiar, old friend of the family come for a visit'. He comes impersonating me to myself by planting thoughts and feelings into my mind and heart that I think are my own. This is how he sneaks into my house to divide it (me) to set me up in opposition to myself and steal my goods. (Lk. 11:17-26) (II Tim.2:24-26).

Why would I ever defend the thief and his breaking into my house and agree that he had a right to steal and kill and destroy me? How does his breaking into my house give him a right to be there? Even if I forgot to lock the door, does that give him a right to come in and steal that which is rightfully mine? Does he have a right to 'trash' my life because I let him in, thinking that he was a friend? Is it my fault he deliberately lied to me? Does the fact that I was tricked disqualify me from crying out for help, or from asking for forgiveness and liberation?

This kind of twisted Self-judgment is the work of none other than Guilt and Self-blame, who are setting me up to agree that what the thief did was my fault, and that I agree with the Prosecution that I deserve to be punished! Our consent with Guilt creates a mentality which allows the Accuser of the Brethren to justify coming against us with his accusations and his demonic judgments. He tries to punish us for the very thing he is guilty of doing.

This also brings up the dubious activity of many who get caught up defending the demon who set them up to take the fall for what he did. As if that is not twisted enough, another counselor from Hell then chimes in and blames us for blaming the Devil for everything we do. He charges us with being unfair in implicating the Devil for tempting us to sin because we should have known better in the first place.

Even after the Devil has done all that he can do to make sure that our destruction will be as devastating as possible, we still 'feel bad' for him. We do not want to be harsh or unforgiving toward him for what he got blamed for doing! How twisted and perverted is that, to take the side of the Prosecution when you are the defendant? We must remember that there is NO GOOD in him, and that we belong to Jesus Christ who truly loves us with an unfathomable love. We are called to believe HIS report as to who we really are, not the Devil's!!

13

THE POWER TO FORGIVE

THE POWER TO FORGIVE

One of the last things Jesus did before He ascended into heaven was to give His disciples power to forgive. "Then Jesus said to them again, 'Peace to you; as the Father has sent Me, I also send you [as my representatives].'" (Jn. 20:21 AMP) "So Jesus said to them again, 'Peace to you! As the Father has sent Me, I also send you'. And when He said this, He breathed on them and said to them, 'Receive the Holy Spirit. If you forgive the sins of any, they are forgiven them. If you retain the sins of any, they are retained.'" (Jn. 20:23)

Of all the powers Jesus gave His disciples, the power to release others from judgment through the forgiveness of sins is by far the most powerful, the most misunderstood, and the least used. Up until that time, no one had disputed the fact that the power to forgive sins rested with God alone. One of the sharpest criticisms Jesus received from the religious sects of His day was His blasphemous presumption to forgive sins. (Mk.2:5-12)

The dispute about Jesus' authority to forgive sins was settled, however, when the Son of God demonstrated His authority to forgive sins while performing miracles of physical healing. The miracles were something only God could do. The fact that Jesus could also do them proved that He had His Father's endorsement. Not only did He preach the Gospel and heal the sick, but He also forgave sins. Healing, deliverance, and forgiveness were confirmations of the True Gospel which were, and are, intrinsic to each other.

In the case of the Paralytic, forgiveness had to come first. This is often the case for those in search of healing. If sickness is perceived as a punishment for something done wrong (sin), then forgiveness given and forgiveness received are essential in releasing one's heart to receive healing. The proof of His authority to forgive sins brought rejoicing and hope to the man's broken heart. The people gladly received Him and His power to forgive sins. (See Mk.2: 12) Those who refused to embrace the miracle were hardened. Those who were hardened were also blinded and failed to realize how much they needed forgiveness themselves.

Only when we understand how much we have been forgiven, can we be entrusted with the power to assist others in receiving forgiveness. Sometimes that forgiveness is for us, sometimes it is for others, and sometimes it is for us to give to others. In John 20, Jesus is giving His followers the authority to do the same work of the Kingdom that He was doing. As His representatives, they were commissioned to heal the sick, cleanse the lepers, raise the dead, cast out demons, preach the gospel and set captives free. Now He added one more assignment to the list: the power to forgive sins and turn the judgment for those sins over to the Righteous Judge. The command to forgive was given with the same level of authority as the powers He had given to us to bind (forbid), and loose (permit) in Matthew 16:19 and Matthew 18:18.

The authority to forgive has been given to those who have been set free through forgiveness to love. Understanding the power of forgiveness makes the way for love and compassion to bring healing and deliverance. This is not stretching the scripture; but rather, this is translating the words of Jesus into exactly what they say. "If you forgive the sins of any, they are forgiven". It does not say you have to limit forgiveness only to those who hurt you, or those who are alive, or those who ask for forgiveness. None of those qualifiers were added to the command. Forgiving was a simple and clear command given as part of the plan of redemption.

Forgiving someone's sins does not make us superior to them or their judge. To the contrary, many times we must humble ourselves and turn our anger over to God. Forgiveness is an act of faith, trusting in the justice of God to right the wrong. Forgiveness means we release the offender from our judgment for the crimes they have committed against us. We are not to be presumptuous in this work of the Kingdom. Forgiveness and reconciliation are the work of the Kingdom! It serves to release others from the judgment of their sin. We have been forgiven. We can initiate the case for forgiveness for others. Just as we have freely received, we can now freely give. Who are we to stand in judgment of another man's servant? (Rom. 14:4) God is the final judge over each of His servants.

For many of us, that will mean He will have to reverse the judgments we have made against ourselves under the counsel of the spirits of Condemnation and Guilt. Why? Because our judgment of ourselves is not our final judgment! Paul says, "In fact, I do not even judge myself. For I know nothing against myself, yet I am not justified by this, but He who judges me is the Lord." (I Cor. 4:3-4)

Jesus is giving us the authority to heal and bring peace to men's souls through forgiveness. If we have the power to hold men in judgment by not forgiving them, surely we have the reciprocal power of releasing them from judgment by forgiving them. Many people that have been forgiven come to repentance and reconciliation shortly thereafter. Our forgiveness releases them from the power of the negative, judgmental, critical words and deeds the

Devil had been using to hold them captive by Bitterness and Unforgiveness. Our unforgiveness of them puts a judgment against them. We are voting with the Enemy to see them judged, punished, and destroyed. Jesus said, "Father, forgive them for they know not what they do." Our forgiveness lifts them up to God to allow Him to be the Judge.

How shocking to see how Satan uses our own words as the agreement he needs to carry the majority vote to push through his agenda to destroy both us, and those who have hurt us, the very ones we have been given the assignment to love! Our words carry the power of agreement. Satan uses our agreement with hardness of heart and unforgiveness to enforce his bitter judgments of sin and death. He gets to make a second move against us by judging us for judging. He uses our tongue to sanction death. "There is death and life in the power of the tongue." (Pr. 18:21) Jesus reminds us of the severity of our words by saying, "For by your word you will be justified, and by your words you will be condemned." (Mt.12:37) We have an incredible privilege and responsibility to set others free through forgiveness. And even as we forgive them, forgiving others is the key to our own forgiveness.

REMITTING AND RETAINING SINS

"Whose so ever sins ye remit, they are remitted unto them and whose so ever sins ye retain, they are retained." (Jn. 20:23 KJV) "Whose so ever…" is the way it is worded in the Old King James. Whose so ever means whoever they are who have sin. All of us have sinned. Again, the Lord's command is not limited to those who recognize their need for forgiveness. The Bible does not restrict or limit this act of forgiveness to only those who are alive. If the people who need forgiveness are dead, they are still alive somewhere. To bring freedom and enforce the full effect of the power of the Cross, Christ gave us the power to release from our judgment those who have died and the crimes they committed against us and our bloodlines before we were even born.

Forgiveness is the key to both "presenting our case", and finding justice. God reminds Isaiah of that by saying that the people have wearied Him with their sins; and then He says to the Prophet, "I, even I, am He that blotteth out thy transgressions for Mine own sake, and will not remember thy sins. Put Me in remembrance: let us plead together: declare thou, that thou mayest be justified. Thy first father hath sinned, and thy teachers have transgressed against me." (Is. 43:25-27 KJV)

God is instructing Isaiah (and us) to remind Him, plead with Him, "let us plead together ...let us contend together: state your case that you may be acquitted (justified)." (Is. 43: 25-27 NKJV) God is inviting us to "present our case, and bring forth our strong reasons", (Is. 41:21 NKJV) so He can have mercy on the situation. In this case, the situation is dealing with the past sins of Isaiah's fathers and teachers.

Forgiving our ancestors for the agreements they made with a lie - and the sin that came out of it - is critical to enforcing the freedom Jesus died to give us, and break the curses in our own lives. And, since forgiveness means to release the offender from our judgment, forgiving others (both those who are here and those who are no longer here) simply means we are releasing them and the crimes they committed against us over to the Righteous Judge for judgment. They must answer to Him, not to us, for things they have done.

Our unwillingness to forgive, on the other hand, causes their sins to be retained. The offender is still held in a place of judgment. In the case of family bloodlines, this causes them, along with us and our families, to be kept in a place of continual demonic judgment. We are still bound to the ancient agreements and deals that our ancestors made with the lies of the Enemy. Satan sees our igno- rance and unwillingness to forgive as the extension of the agreements they made with him. He uses those old, but still legal, agreements to justify the continuation of the consequences and curses of the father's sins down upon the children (us). Because we have not forgiven, released those crimes to God, we are still held in the place of judgment ourselves. The Bible tells us to confess the sins of the fathers which have been visited onto the children to break the generational cord of iniquity. If we do not, the power of those sins to destroy remains. They are still with us. (Ex. 20:5 & Lev. 26:29) By confessing our sins and their sins, "which are with us", we escape the 'generational sins of the fathers' argument the Enemy uses to snare us. Forgiving them releases us from the snare of the Fowler.

When we refuse to forgive others, our unforgiveness is an endorsement of the Enemy's judgments against them. It secures his right to continue carrying those judgments forward onto us. By holding onto the hurt, resentment, anger, bitterness, offense, and our desire to get even or stay mad, we are retaining their sins. Holding them in a place of judgment endorses the Enemy's plan to destroy both them and us. Bitterness and unforgiveness hinder the process of liberation and justice. When we refuse to release (forgive) others held captive to sin and desire to see them punished, we are retaining their sins. Retaining their sins binds us to their sins, and gives them control over our lives. Satan uses the hatred and bitterness he stirs up in our hearts to hold us hostage to the agreements the people we have refused to forgive, have made with the enemy. This ties us into the same judgments and curses he is bringing upon them.

Some say, "Where there is no evidence of repentance or confession of sin, or admission of wrongdoing, we do not have to forgive." That, however, is not what the Bible says. There is not even a small hint that we are to withhold forgiveness from those who have not repented! Forgiveness is a part of the commandment to "Love one another", even our enemies. Did Jesus wait for the mob at the foot of His Cross to repent or apologize before He forgave them? Refusing to forgive them, or waiting until they are 'sorry', or waiting for them to admit they were wrong, locks us into a real and grave place of danger in taking the position of the Judge. "There is one Lawgiver, Who is able to save and destroy. Who are you to judge another?" (Ja 4:12) In judging them, we not only make ourselves the judge, but find ourselves in a difficult position of being judged ourselves.

The Enemy can easily render our refusal, or reluctance to forgive them, as an indirect way of judging them. Unforgiveness puts us in the place of judging them as not worthy of forgiveness. This opens the door for the Enemy to hold us in his judgment for judging them. Though we are told to warn sinners of the wrath and judgment which is to come, we are not authorized nor justified in withholding forgiveness from them. Remember forgiveness means we release them from our judgment, not God's judgment. The final determination of judgment as to one's destination belongs to God. We will be judged ourselves with the same measure of mercy and forgiveness that we rendered to others. (Please note: for those who are saved, the judgment we will experience will not determine our eligibility for heaven but our level of position and rewards in the Kingdom of God.)

"God is a just judge, and God is angry with the wicked every day. If he does not turn back, He will sharpen His sword; He bends His bow and makes it ready." (Ps.7:11-12) When we retain the sins of someone that means we are still holding them in the 'position' of a sinner. We are acting as their judge and they still remain in a position of judgment. When the guilt for sin is retained, that sinner remains under both God's judgment and Satan's. God is the ultimate Judge for all of us. We are not called to judge now, but to forgive (turning the crimes over to the Judge). "Do you not know that the saints will judge the world? Do you not know that we shall judge angels?" (I Cor. 2a & 3a) Yes, but not yet.

We are admonished to forgive one another. Jesus does not use our retention of someone's sins to pronounce judgment upon them, or as a permission to not forgive them. If it were, that would be contrary to the Lord's original commandments to love and forgive. When we forgive someone we are not releasing them from the judgment of God, but handing them over to the judgment of God. God is the only One Who can judge without partiality. To assume that the bad things happening to someone are the consequence of sin or of their being out of the will of God, however, is not always the case. Consider Jesus in the Wilderness. Was He out of the will of God? To conclude the difficulties we are experiencing are a punishment from God for sin, is a slick but effective trick of the Enemy. He tries to convince us the negative things happening in our lives are the consequences of sin and are judgments coming from God. The book of Job was written for the sole purpose of refuting that notion. For all practical purposes, it may well be that the judgments of God have not yet have begun.

Bad things that happen as a result of our sinning are more accurately explained as the result of demonic judgments, than as the result of divine judgment. If God were sending these judgments, then why would He also judge good people? Why would He have to test the faith of anyone, since He already KNOWS everything about them, including the strength of their faith? Though He says, in several places, that "For the righteous God tests the hearts and minds" (Ps. 7:9b), the real test is grounded in the Enemy's challenge to God's ability to keep His sons and daughters believing in His love. In the midst of the fiery trial, Satan tests that love.

And, again, why would Jesus give us the job of judging when He told us not to judge? But, how can we practice church discipline if we are told not to judge one another? Are there ever any scriptural grounds for retaining someone's sins? Only, it would seem, if holding that one in the position of judgment is for chastening and the salvation of their souls. In the matter of church action to be taken against the Corinthian man, Paul admonished the Church at Corinth to "deliver such a one (the man sleeping with his father's wife) to Satan for the destruction of the flesh, that his spirit may be saved in the day of the Lord Jesus." (I Cor. 5:5) Paul's severe admonition would be contradictory to the unchangeable character of God's goodness unless the action would permit the deviant behavior of the man to be corrected.

Our behavior as children was corrected through chastening, discipline, and punishment, not for our destruction, but for our edification. When done in the spirit of love and truth, the child grows up. (Eph. 4:15) Chastening conducted in this manner is the sacred duty of parents and the mark of sonship. This chastening is not meant to destroy the child, but to instruct and qualify the child for citizenship in the Kingdom of God. "For whom the LORD loves He chastens, and scourges every son whom He receives. If you endure chastening, God deals with (us), as with sons, for what son is there whom a father does not chasten?" (Heb. 12:6-7)

Paul is instructing the Corinthian Congregation to bring this man into a position to be chastened by the Lord so that his soul would not be lost in the final condemnation. This pattern of reproof and discipline is to be instituted when we fail to judge (examine) ourselves. "If we would judge ourselves, we would not be judged. But when we are judged, we are chastened by the Lord, that we may not be condemned with the world." (I Cor. 11:31-32) This man is in need of discipline, not encouragement in continuing his shameful, sinful conduct. If indeed, this was the activity of a spirit of Perversion and Lust, they must be exposed. How else will this man see what is going on? How else can he repent and change his mind and confess the sin?

In temporarily retaining this man's sins, Paul is agreeing with God's will in the chastening of the endangered soul. God did not want Satan to end up getting to claim this man's life. God did not want to Judge this man either. He was wanting to chasten him. He needed the church's cooperation, which was to be carried out by their official agreement to turn his flesh over to Satan, for the express purpose of saving him. They were instructed to "turn his flesh over to destruction," in order that his soul and spirit could be delivered from the final judgment of being cut off from God forever. The unified disciplinary action of the church done as an act of obedience to Paul's command, protected them from the individual repercussions Satan would have tried to bring against them for judging the man and not forgiving him. Paul did not tell them to hate him or reject him. They were to distinguish between this man and his behavior. As a created son of God he was being held captive by a spirit of Deception, and a behavior which was completely contrary to the Law of Love.

Obviously, this area of church discipline has been an area of confusion greatly resisted by the Enemy. The reluctance and misperception around church discipline has allowed all manner of leaven (sin) to creep into the house of God and destroy its passion for holiness, its power, and its love for God and others. On the one hand, not discerning the work of Satan and his angel of light brigade in the midst of the church, has failed to expose it. On the other hand, condoning sin has left the church weak and sick. Fear of offending someone and getting sued, have replaced faith in those who are being demonically resisted in their attempt to walk in righteousness. Because we do not distinguish the difference between the person and their behavior that manifests through them, demonic accusations of not being loving, or of being judgmental, have stopped the church short in its attempt to execute beneficial, disciplinary actions on behalf of its members. Peter called out the lie with Ananias and Sapphira. Paul is calling it out here. Both are examples given to emphasize the critical importance of not permitting Divination to rule in the midst of the Church of Jesus Christ.

We are not to condone sin, or overlook it for convenience sake. On the other hand, the misuse and spiritual abuse of the ministry of correction and church discipline, including excommunication etc., have caused much damage to the innocent. Only God Himself knows how many have suffered greatly under the hand of hirelings greedy for gain, and wolves in sheep's clothing who are insecure and controlling. Their false teachings have turned many away from the goodness of God. Paul is here guiding the church between a rock and a hard place . In this very difficult and delicate matter of church discipline, the lump of sin must be surgically removed so the afflicted one can be saved. Just as the doctor must prepare himself/herself for the surgery, they needed to humble themselves lest the Devil judge them for judging. He cited their 'glorying' or turning to look the other way while this man slept with his father's wife was not only, not okay since a "little leaven leavens the whole lump", but also put this man in jeopardy of eternal hell fire.

In Second Corinthians, Paul reminds them to restore "such a one" "in a spirit of meekness" (Gal. 6:1) lest they also be overtaken with demonic backlash and be overcome with grief that is too severe. This punishment which was inflicted by the majority is sufficient for such a man. "Now whom you forgive anything, I also forgive. …lest Satan should take advantage of us; for we are not ignorant of his devices." (II Cor. 2:5-11) The only way this kind of action can be successfully executed is if we do not judge the man ourselves, but allow God to discipline him through our agreement with Him. This agreement allows God to allow the Enemy restricted access to the man's perishable parts, his body, that his eternal parts, his soul and spirit, will be saved. The disciplinary action is meant to bring the man to his senses and call out to God for forgiveness. God then instructs Paul to counsels the other members of the Body to restore the man delivered from the grip of Satan, back into the love and acceptance of their fellowship.

Paul was not suffering personally from this man's sin, nor was he related to him. He was, however, setting a precedent for procedure for chastening, a vital activity in the Body of Christ to protect its individual members. If we are not to judge them, then this is how we are to deal with the situation until they can be restored. If we do not understand how this is properly done, we will be unable to determine what to do. In surgery it is not the objective to kill the patient, though they are exposed to the risk of death. The objective is to heal the patient through deliverance from the malignant growth, obstruction, or dysfunction, that they may regain their health. This procedure must be done in humility to address the area of sin in the church. Before they could deal with this man, they needed to examine and confess their own sins. Only then would they be ready to judge the situation by asking God to chasten the man. This allowed them to keep the command to love and forgive in showing their love and concern for this man's eternal welfare, at the same time they were cleared of the excuse of disregarding this man by saying his sins as none of their business. In matters of eternal welfare, every man's soul was our business. Here we see the incredible and solemn weight of the task given to us to guide others away from the cliffs of sin and destruction, and restore them to truth and freedom through correction, reproof and instructions in righteousness. This, however, does not give us the right to hold them in unforgiveness. "Do unto others as you would have them do unto you" (Mt.7:12) is the simplest rendition of both restoration and forgiveness. Turning him over to Satan was only a desperate measure taken for love's sake, to save the man's soul.

God has given us the power to release others through forgiveness, even though they may not have sinned against us specifically, nor are they part of our bloodline. Jesus did not qualify, or restrict the use of the power to remit sins, (to cancel or hold back from enforcing something or restore something to a previous condition or position) only to those related to us or who had directly sinned against us. There are many offenders who need to be released from the Devil's grip through forgiveness. Restoring that one to a previous position of innocence and forgiveness turns the matter of their liberation over to Heaven's jurisdiction. It is the same thing we do when we turn the crimes committed against us over to the Righteous Judge. We allow Heaven to judge the matter. Retaining and releasing sins is part of the Kingdom business which we, as stewards of and ambassadors for the Kingdom, are commissioned to do. In remitting (releasing and forgiving) their sins, we are turning the crimes that are holding them hostage over to the Court of Heaven, and acting on their behalf for the release of deliverance, healing, and correction.

This power to forgive sins, however, does not give us the 'blanket' power to forgive the sins of the whole world. This power does not absolve a person from their rejection of the Son of God as their means of Salvation. This is a specific power given to us to minster to a specific person in specific situations. Just like the gift of healing does not empower us to heal the sickness of the whole world. It was given to be used for the glory of God in specific situations where the Holy Spirit leads the believer to act.

If we do not remit or release that person from their sins, we essentially hold them in unforgiveness. God is not promoting the retaining the sins of someone as a means of us getting our own justice. The Enemy of our soul, however, honors our authority to "retain their sins" and is delighted to be able to maintain his hold on them. When we fail to turn the crimes committed against the Kingdom of God over to God, we are hindering His right to judge the matter and administer Heaven's justice, while we are simultaneously aligning with the Devil's plan.

Maintaining a position of unforgiveness against an offender prevents God's intervention fin our situation as well. By giving heed to a spirit of bitterness and unforgiveness, we are unwittingly being held in the grip of the Accuser ourselves. He is taking his full liberty to judge us for judging others, in order to present his 'air tight' case against us to the Judge, and declare us guilty for judging others. (A note of clarification on forgiveness: <u>Forgiving someone who has abused you and tried to take your life from you does NOT obligate you to return to them, or continue in that abusive and possibly deadly relationship.</u> We owe our allegiance to the Lord God, and not to some demonized human, who is basically being controlled by the Enemy to destroy us. Continuing in an abusive relationship, be it marriage, business, community alliance, church, or parent/child relationship, is an act of idolatry as we are putting our fear of that person above our loyalty and allegiance to the Lord God. God is our gracious heavenly Father. He does not want to see His child destroyed by Fear and Lies.

Forgiveness is not easy. Exercising our power to forgive, and the blessing that we receive which comes by forgiving others, often comes at great expense to us - even as it did to our Lord. He laid down His life and suffered for us even while we were still hostile enemies to the Kingdom of God. He bids us to follow Him and lay down, not only our lives, but our right to be offended. We are crucified with Christ. All the personal offenses and grievances committed against us, for the sake of the freedom for others, are given as a sacrifice. We count it a privilege to be called to such a place of grace and brokenness in order to participate in the "fellowship" of the sufferings of Christ. (Phil. 3:10)

JUDGE NOT

Forgiveness as a commandment carries with it the power to correct the most severe violations of justice. Forgiveness brings with it the power to release both ourselves and others from the demonic judgments within which we are trapped. It is the official 'prerequisite' for being released ourselves - from the judgments and accusations Satan has made against us for judging others. This release also applies to the release of those things which have been stolen from us, including health and inheritances. God does not enjoy being party to, or a witness to, the crimes that have been committed against us, or our family, any more than a just judge enjoys seeing crime and injustice pillaging his judicial district. God wants the case turned over to Him. It is through forgiveness that the crime and the case are released over to His Court for judgment.

Forgiving others is the prerequisite for the recovery of our own relationships; and for the opportunity to recover things that have been stolen from us. Once we have forgiven those who have sinned against us - by turning the crimes they have committed against us, under the counsel and influence of the Evil One - over to the Court of Heaven, we can petition for the full restoration of justice for ourselves. By forgiving others, we recognize that the things that have been done to us have also been done to them. We have all been the target of injustice from our mutual Enemy who is the Evil One.

Those things stolen can include: peace of mind; our reputation - honor, character, dignity; and rights to life, liberty and the pursuit of our destiny in God. When we forgive, we are automatically freed from the charges Guilt and the Accuser are pressing against us. God, unlike most mediators, knows who started it, and the hearts' intentions of all who were involved in a conflict.

If we forgive, and if we receive God's pardon which He is more than willing to give since He knows we were framed in the first place, the Accuser no longer has anything 'on us'. This allows us to come boldly to ask God to remove the illegal judgments Satan has brought against us under the false pretenses and allegations made by Guilt and FEAR (False Evidence Appearing Real).

We must understand that the Enemy uses any unforgiveness and bitterness, which he himself tempts us to embrace, as his 'right' to bind us and bring upon us the very same thing we judge in others. He uses our unforgiveness as a justification to bring his reciprocal judgments down on us and withhold our blessings - even by twisting the very Words of God to do it.

Matthew 7:1 says, "Judge not lest you be judged for with what judgment you judge, you will be judged." What goes around comes around. <u>Curses come as a result of holding judgments and grudges against others.</u> They originate from disobedience, disappointment and doing things on our own which comes from believing lies and making agreements with the Devil.

Whether we are ignorant or aware, curses come as a result of our agreement with - and participation in - iniquity. Gravity is no respecter of the innocent or ignorant. Just because we do not know the power of gravity or how it works, does not mean we are protected from falling. Neither does the Enemy respect the ignorant or grant a waiver to the unsuspecting for not knowing the power of staying mad. As far as he is concerned, our ignorance is his bliss.

Curses are initiated through sin and the iniquity in our ancestors. They are perpetuated through bitterness and unforgiveness in us, and continued through unbelief and disobedience down into the lives of our posterity. The curses are no respecter of persons. They come to inflict injustices upon the innocent victim, as well as willful perpetrators.

FORGIVING OURSELVES AND THE TRUE GOSPEL

Unforgiveness restrains God's justice and His desire to forgive us, according to the finished work of His Son on the Cross. Satan uses the scripture, as he did against Jesus in the wilderness, to make his counter argument against God's heart to pardon us. Is it not written, "But if you do not forgive men their trespasses, neither will your Father forgive your trespasses."? (Mt.6:15)

Satan legitimizes his petition before the Court using God's own Word, and our holding others responsible, as a means by which to justify his demands. He places his demonic judgments upon us for our disobedience and failure to forgive others. We are confused about why God isn't answering our prayers and why our healing is not coming. We become an easy target for the Enemy's next deception, which is to convince us that God is mad at us. Satan wants to 'checkmate' God in His rescue of us, by convincing us to believe that the bad things that are happening to us are our own fault, and consequences of God's judgment against us for our sin.

The Liar has perpetuated this strategy to break up the relationship between us and God - since the day iniquity was found in him. His hatred for us, and his rebellion against the love of God, has fueled this great fire of hatred and revenge. Satan is determined that we must not ever know or believe the truth about God's love for us. To that end, he sows fear and guilt in our hearts as a means by which to build a wall between us and God's love.

By using our sin and the argument that 'It was my own choice!' the Devil locks us into a defensive position, with absolutely no way to defend ourselves. His accusation for us making a choice, absolutely strikes down any defense we might make in our own behalf. We are caught up in confusion. The Devil's deliberate, legalistic misinterpretation of the Word of God traps us in his cold and calculating rendition of justice and death.

This demonic, 'take-responsibility-it was-your-choice' stance is promoted and perpetuated as the common world view throughout every sector of society: from the human court systems, to the schools, on the streets, in the church, and in the daily raising our children. We do not realize the deadly trap that is set by the world's admonition to take responsibility. Satan uses our desire to be good, law-abiding citizens, to manipulate us, to step right into the responsibility trap. Acting on the false premise that it was our responsibility we give our implied consent to the Enemy's accusations that it was our fault, because we made the choice. It completely washes over the truth about the one who actually initiated the sin, the Deceiver, who deliberately set the trap with which to catch us.

God does not demand that we take responsibility to save ourselves from our sins. He declares that He is Faithful to complete and perfect us, that we are His workmanship created in Christ Jesus unto good works. Our responsibility is to admit to being enticed into sinning by Satan's schemes, and repent. The only action we are obligated or constrained to take is in response to the work of the Holy Spirit compelling us to repent! The Word of God admonishes us to "Confess our trespasses to

one another, and pray for one another that you may be healed."
(Ja.5:16)

The world never, ever hints that we need to repent. It only tells us
to "own our stuff, stop it, and do better!" God is the only One
Who tells us to repent and confess our sins. He knows that many
of the things we are doing, we cannot actually stop doing without
deliverance. (See Rom. 7:20) We cry, along with Paul, "who will
deliver me from this body of death"? God wants to, and has
already made provision to deliver those who follow Him.

One aspect of following Jesus is to take the Devil to Court for the
crimes he has been committing against us since the beginning.
Left to our own devices, we fail to discern his schemes. We resort
back to being guided by our own thoughts and feelings. We are
tempted to return to using our feelings and thoughts, and end up
judging God for abandoning us. We get angry with God and
judge Him for judging us! But, how is this the work of the Holy
Spirit? And if it is not the Holy Spirit, then who is leading us to
adopt these thoughts, and why are we following him?

The real truth is that it is God's desire to remedy the situation and
rescue us from the accusations of the Evil One through the revelation of His truth and forgiveness. All God requires is that we
confess our sins, repent, and acknowledge that we have believed a
lie. How hard and unreasonable is that? Most of us believe,
however, that God is still waiting for us to do something wrong.
We think we must be perfect to make up for our sins before He
will listen to our cries.

The clever way in which the Enemy presents the 'counterfeit
gospel' makes my salvation and sanctification all up to me. He
admonishes us to take responsibility and be good, in order to
make God happy. The Liar makes our good works the centerpiece
and primary means for getting to Heaven. If we fall for these
counterfeit versions of the, 'It's up to me', 'I have to be good, and
get rid of my sin' gospels, we have just fallen for the most evil,

insidious, sophisticated perversion of the glorious Gospel ever crafted by Hell.

Through the promotion of these false gospels, Satan accomplishes his goal of concealing the truth about the love of God, and the power of the Blood of Jesus. There are hundreds of twisted, counterfeit gospels which the Evil One has propagated in the name of Christianity. The fruit of these counterfeit gospels have their origin in Hell, and serve to keep us locked up in the stronghold of Satan's hatred. Believing the lie that the gospel is all-about-sin-and-getting-rid-of-it 'upstages' the true gospel.

The Gospel of Jesus Christ is the gospel of grace and good news. It is all about the Son of God, and the shedding of His blood for the remission of sins. If Satan can make the gospel I follow all about sin, he has fooled me into making my life all about me!!! Making the Gospel 'all about me and my sin' implies that it is up to me to fix myself. This is the same ploy Satan used against Adam and Eve. After they sinned, they felt guilty and ashamed, and hid. They tried to fix the problem of sin and shame by tying fig leaves together to cover their nakedness with their religious efforts. It did not work then. It does not work now.

SIN, THE LAW AND RELIGION – A BRIEF SUMMARY

The Law defined sin. Sin demands a fix. The need to fix sin forms the crux of Religion. Satan needs sin, and uses the Law to enforce the negative effect of sin upon mankind. He uses fear of judgment, and damnation, and the misinterpretation of the Word of God to control the masses that he holds hostage. The Enemy uses the Law to distort the true nature of God, who calls Himself our Heavenly Father.

The Enemy controls us through designated gatekeepers - 'holy men' through whom the sinner must come to receive absolution and forgiveness. These powers of absolution are not given out free of charge. The Enemy sees that fear and guilt make sin a lucrative business and there is money to be made in the redeeming of men's souls. The cost attached to eternal life and absolution of sins is not cheap. Indulgences and pilgrimages and spiritual paraphernalia wring the thirsty souls bound to the Law, of any lasting refreshment or assurance of the unconditional love of God.

Guilt, and fear of Hell, have given the Enemy the formula that he has used for centuries to control the people of God and hold them in a religious bondage to his religious exercises and counterfeit churches. He has used rituals, penance, and religious remedies, including his troop of pious deceivers, to suffocate the true message of the Good News brought through Jesus Christ. He has used the ornate trappings; piercing steeples; the gold-gilded 'fig leaves' of penance; and a liturgy of dead works - to plunder the sheep of God's pasture. All this has only provoked more self-indulgence, anxiety, and religious neurosis.

Clearly these things are not the fruit of the Holy Spirit; therefore, they do NOT originate from God! Guilt strips us of rest, and joy, and peace, and faith in the goodness of God, and replaces it with 'driven-ness', uncertainty, and fear. We are held in the Devil's snare of spiritual abuse, and caught on his hook of self-righteousness. The blind are leading the blind in a never-ending search for a righteousness that has already been given, - over 2000 years ago - to "whosoever will".

In refusing God's forgiveness as the final, free, finished and unearnable gift it is; we have, in fact, rejected Jesus Christ Himself. In adding our good works to the finished work of the Cross, we have added insult to His sacrifice. The liberation He accomplished for us on the Cross has set us free from the demonic judgments assigned to us by the Accuser - including guilt and condemnation. These judgments, declared to be the reasonable punishment for our sins, have been buried under a ton of false (fake) gospels. They have been peddled as the 'golden ticket' to Heaven; when, in fact, these falsehoods are only the shiny promises made to the unsuspecting on their way to destruction.

14

STEPS TO BREAKING THE CURSES

STEP ONE - IDENTIFYING PATTERNS

The first step in breaking a curse is to IDENTIFY it. We allow many of the things that happen to us, simply because we do not recognize them as anything unusual or something we need to resist. Their occurrence has become so familiar that we no longer detect their presence as offensive or evil, much like the hog farmer who has gotten so used to the smell of pigs that, to him, they don't stink any more.

Bad things have become all too familiar; we accept them, and come to expect them. Most of us were not taught well; hence, we have become so acclimated to the way we live that we believe it is 'the way things are, and because this is the way things are, this is the way they must be'. For this reason, we often accept curses as 'normal' and fail to even recognize them, let alone resist them.

We must be aware that all of the information which comes together to make up and represent 'me' is recorded on my DNA - including the trauma 'marks' and bloodguilt. Sickness, poverty, loss, financial setbacks, accidents, assaults, injuries, false accusations, calamities, hardship, hardness of heart, hatred, spiritual and physical difficulties, suicide, violence, pain, mental confusion, diseases, and relationship conflicts come from patterns which have been coded into our bloodlines. Cancer, heart disease, diabetes, obesity, mental illness, immune system diseases, fibromyalgia, multiple chemical sensitivities, chronic fatigue, teeth problems, car accidents, autism, anxiety, OCD, etc., all find their origin and explanation in bloodline curses.

Please note: This is not an exhaustive list, but perhaps a good place to begin to develop awareness but only a few examples of the patterns and problems which come as a consequence of sin. Each one of us is vulnerable to temptations of the Deceiver in unique and specific ways - based upon agreements which our ancestors made! And though we are predisposed to their influence, we are not obligated to act on them. The Lord has not left us without recourse against them, but has made a way for us to overcome them.

But, lest we be ignorant of the Enemy's devices, we must know that wherever a specific door has been left open by sin and iniquity, the Enemy will bring his legalistic form of judgment against those iniquities. This is not the justice God wants for us. God has already made His move, which is the provision for our complete forgiveness and restoration through the sacrifice of His Son, Jesus. The spiritual prescriptions of forgiveness and confession of sin are an integral prerequisite for healing. The Devil has made his move to subvert God's love and forgiveness. The next move is ours.

THE MISSING LINK

Although some of those root causes and the resulting patterns they exhibit may be obscure, others are more easily identified. However, taking a step back to observe the behavior of several generations may be necessary in order to see patterns more clearly. As history 'tracks' life activities over time and generations, deliberate observation makes them more apparent. Taking a spiritual inventory of our family bloodline helps bring to light information which we may not have fully comprehended upon first examination.

Treating physical illnesses as only physical or medical - while omitting the inclusion of the spiritual implication of sin, and its physical effects in/on the body - creates a gap, a missing link between the disease and the healing for that disease. The lack of integration of spiritual truth into the search for the cause and cure for a problem impedes healing and restoration. If we fail to see the spiritual link between sin and sickness, the disconnect remains. When the sin problem is not addressed, the breach is not repaired. Life fails to flourish, allowing disease to invade our lives.

The Lord God Himself speaks clearly of the connection between sickness and disease and health in Exodus 15:26: "And there He tested them, and said, If you diligently heed the voice of the LORD your God and do what is right in His sight, give ear to His commandments and keep all His statutes, I will put none of the diseases on you which I have brought on the Egyptians. For I am the LORD who heals you."

From this scripture, we can clearly see the spiritual link between obedience and health! Obedience to God has always been an essential element in having access to His Divine protection and blessings, including the blessings of health and healing. And even though this connection may be temporarily obscured by God's long suffering tolerance for sin, there is no short cut that will be of lasting benefit for those who deny or downplay the importance of obedience.

That being said, Guilt and Feeling-Guilty-for-not-being-obedient, are the other powerful players which cause resistance to recovery in any kind of physical of spiritual health issues. The Enemy delights in getting us to 'cast our vote' with him - either through disobedience, or to side with Condemnation and Guilt by embracing our 'feelings' over 'faith' in the promises of God. To agree that 'we had it coming' and 'deserve the bad thing that has come upon us' only ties the hands of the Judge - Who must now allow the Deceiver to take even more of what we are so foolishly willing to give away.

Because we often fail to identify the spiritual roots of a physical problem, the solutions are only partial or incomplete. We often fail to see the connection between iniquity and illness, because we fail to see the 'crossover connection' in the integration of the spiritual and the physical worlds. These two worlds blend together to manifest as one experience. Our body and soul are tied together in one response. The spiritual and physical experiences - and their consequences - are pressed together into one expression which I embrace as 'Me'.

In other words, many of our present experiences are made up of thoughts and feelings we rarely address or consider on a conscious level as spiritual in nature, origin, or implication. Most of us are not inclined to follow the Word of God or use it in interpreting our lives or the things that happen to us. Because our first and typical responses to things we experience come from our souls - that is, our mind, will and emotions - we tend to interpret our lives on a physical and emotional level, and leave the spiritual implications of the Word of God out of the equation entirely.

Interpreting our lives and considering the things which happen to us using the spiritual principles of obedience, iniquity, demonic judgment, and the authority of God's Word is not automatic. The things of the Spirit do not come to us naturally.

Although we may sense that spiritual obedience and physical health are linked in some mysterious way, our failure to comprehend the powerful connection between them greatly reduces our likelihood of healing. The recovery of lost and stolen blessings, including health, remain evasive because we do not often see how they are related to sin and the lies that have produced it.

We fail to understand the correlation between what is going on in our lives, and the spiritual condition of our bloodlines; thus, we make judgments that we are not qualified to make. Worse yet, we attribute the bad things happening to us to be the punishment of God for our sin when, in fact, that is far from the truth. This causes a setback in our faith concerning the goodness of God and in our relationship with Him. Knowing that we are loved and in need of a divine intervention in our life is the first step to healing. Forgiveness, including receiving forgiveness for ourselves, is crucial to our restoration.

THE TRANSFERENCE OF THE CURSE

The mysterious connection between Guilt, and sickness, pain and poverty is broken through admission (repentance) and confession. They are often left unexplored in the matters of healing and restoration. Ignorance and unforgiveness allow for the continuation of the transference of the judgment of the curses from one generation down into the next. The things done in the spiritual and natural lives of one generation will be replicated in the spiritual and natural lives of those in the next. What was begun in one dimension will be repeated and expanded and handed down to the next, even crossing over from spiritual to physical and vice versa. Forgiveness - the release of the crime and the offender to the judgment of God - is the only action that will bring justice, break the curse, and stop the degeneration of the human race.

For example, a verbal or emotional judgment against a person in one generation can be brought down upon the descendants of that bloodline, just as easily as judging a contemporary can bring that judgment back on the one who made it. Often the same maladies on someone who was judged, come upon the one who is making the judgment. For example, the one who vows, "I will never _____ like my mother" will find himself/herself doing or saying the identical thing he/she was vowing not to do or say - to the 'letter' as his/her mother did! Those judgments, and the agreements and declarations we make in connection with those agreements, create a pathway - an 'open door', so to speak - for our generational junk to move both down and across our bloodline.

THE ONLY REMEDY

We often fail to understand that what we see or experience is only the 'tip of the iceberg', a small expression or a symptom of what is present in the unseen world of spiritual roots and underlying causes. That unseen world is real and active! The spirits of Fear, Stress, Anxiety, Confusion, Abandonment, Rejection and Self-hatred which come from Guilt, for example, are all spiritual entities which create the issues, and generate the hard core problems - including health issues – that operate in our everyday lives and health.

Understanding that these entities use and manipulate the physical systems and biological functions of our body to distort and undermine our health reveals the true nature of our physical problems to be spiritual in nature and origin. These entities have set up strongholds in our minds and hearts which compromise our immune system and weaken our body's ability to resist disease. A simple medical intervention in such a case will not completely or effectively relieve the condition, although we are tempted to seek a physical remedy for that which appears to be physically broken. We need to look beyond the physical realm to ascertain what is going on in the spiritual realm.

Therefore, it serves us well to expand our search for truth and healing by not limiting our pursuit of answers exclusively to a medical model when addressing health problems. We do well to recognize that medical interventions in and of themselves are not adequate or sufficient in addressing needs of a three part being; nor do we need to accept the inadequacies of our medical system as the final 'signature' on the health of our body or our soul.

Medical remedies are at best partial, and are known to be much more effective when applied within the context of repentance and prayer. As we begin to address the true and underlying causes of our diseases - and the lies which generate the curses behind them - we recognize that calling upon God to restore His truth to our souls, and the confession of sin, are the first steps in the healing of our bodies.

Sickness and disease, however, are not the only places where death and destruction may be manifesting in our bloodlines. Finances, mental functioning, and relationships also offer the Enemy huge opportunities for the devastation of our lives. Every place where we are vulnerable - have a need - gives the Devil another place for the generation and manifestation of curses in our lives.

STEP TWO – WE CONFESS THE SINS OF OUR GENERATIONS

Step two in breaking the curses involves confessing the iniquities that have produced those curses. As Moses and Joshua were about to re-enter the Promised Land, God told them to instruct the people as to how to regain His favor and blessing. God wanted to clear the record, and restore that which had been lost by their unbelieving and disobedient parents in the wilderness.

He commanded them to make no idols, carve no images, and erect no sacred pillars. They were not to engrave stones and worship them. They were to keep the Sabbath and reverence the Lord and His sanctuary. In so doing, if they were obedient, He would give them the rain their land needed to yield its increase. Their threshing floor would supply them with bread to the full, and they would dwell in safety. He would give them peace and freedom from war. They would have remarkable military victories and be fruitful. If they obeyed Him, He would bless them. If they disobeyed Him, however, He warned them that all manner of trouble and calamity would overtake them.

Blessings and curses are part of both the Old and New Testament. In both, obedience remains the prerequisite for blessings, even as disobedience opens the door to the curses. The prescription for blessing has not changed. Obedience is the key to blessing. Forgiveness is the key for breaking the curses.

The curses or demonic judgments manifest themselves as terror and wasting diseases, fever and consumption. They make us vulnerable to sorrow of heart, crop failure and defeat by our enemies. They cause the land to be barren and unfruitful. Plagues and pestilence flourish. They cause the wrath of God to bring desolation and wasting destruction upon our cities and cause our children to be taken from us. (See Deut. 27 & 28) All of these things are still in effect today, as they were then.

Breaking the curses begins with the CONFESSION of the iniquities of the generations past. Leviticus 26:39-46 very clearly instructs those who found themselves eaten up, beaten up and wasting away. "If they will confess their iniquity and the iniquity of their fathers, with their unfaithfulness in which they were unfaithful to Me, and that they also have walked contrary to Me, and that I also have walked contrary to them and have brought them into the land of their enemies, if their uncircumcised hearts are humbled, and they accept their guilt – then I will remember My covenant ..."

Incest, infidelity, abandonment, parental neglect, rejection, failure, favoritism, abuse, anger, violence, bloodshed, extortion, embezzlement, dishonesty, abortion, sexual perversion, lying, bitterness, judgmentalism, gossip, etc., all may have been permitted to operate in our bloodline without our direct permission. God is ready to reverse these judgments and re-establish the blessing and restore His covenant if we return to Him. He only asks that we acknowledge our transgressions as a nation, as a people, and as individuals, in order to regain His blessing.

As New Testament followers of Jesus Christ, He is not asking us to do anything that would deny or detract from grace, or faith, or the merit of the Cross. He is simply asking us to participate with Him in redemption. He is asking us to help Him 'clean up the house' and bring our bloodlines back into fellowship with Him and His holiness.

GETTING OUR LIFE BACK

The principle behind the remedy for re-entering the Promised Land is the same one used in getting our life back. When we see ourselves being "eaten up," and "beaten up," and "wasting away," (Lev. 26:39-45), if we will "confess our iniquity and the iniquity of our fathers which is with us", then God will re-establish the covenant with us. Confessing our fathers' sins as 'sin' sets the record straight and begins the process of reclaiming our own city-souls. This is very similar to the admonition in James 5:16 to "confess [our] trespasses to one another, and pray for one another, that we may be healed." We come back into agreement with God by declaring that those things which separated us and our house from Him were an abomination.

Proverbs 26:2 reminds us that "the curse without a cause does not come." That means there are reasons for what is happening to us. Just as the sins of our forefathers and mothers, and the iniquities they practiced, came down the bloodline to give Satan the opportunity to assault us, the abuse and rejection practiced against us have also affected those who will come after us. The Enemy's assaults against us are deliberate and specific. Our response to them must also be deliberate and specific.

The Holy Spirit is faithful to lead us into all truth. We can ask Him to reveal the specific iniquity that 'blocks the river and clogs the flow' of God's grace and blessings in our lives. He will show us things we may not have noticed - things which are creating significant obstructions in our lives, or the lives of our descendants. As the Holy Spirit reveals to our spirit the "things that pertain to us,"

(I Cor. 2:9-11) the patterns of sin and disobedience that have preceded us become more clear.

We begin to see the destruction which disobedience and rebellion against God have caused. Our hearts are grieved and we want to 'make it right' with a humble apology to God. We admit to and confess the wrongdoing. Those sins and abominations may include things we have not done ourselves - though they are still part of our family's history. Confession is the declaration that God is right. It reinstates His righteous judgments within the context of our lives. We are declaring that God is right and we have been manipulated into believing a lie. Confession brings our will back into agreement with His: 'Thy kingdom come, Thy will be done....'

WE CONFESS

Recognizing the sin and confessing it is not about blaming our ancestors, grandparents, parents, or pointing the finger at others. It is about coming before the Throne of Grace and Mercy, as the authorized representative of our generational bloodline - to use our authority to confess the sins and iniquities of those whose blood we represent. This is the first step in cleaning up the record of wrongs charged to our account.

Specifically, we confess the "sins and iniquities" of our fathers "which are with us". (Lev. 26:39-40) We confess their idolatry in putting other people, places and things - including the work of their own hands and even themselves - in the place of God in their lives. We confess their crafting of 'graven images' and their practices of witchcraft, rebellion and control. We confess their murder, hatred, disobedience, manipulation, spiritual blindness, bitterness, hardness of heart, holding grudges, jealousy, resentments, insecurity and self-reliance as sin and abomination against God's provision for our salvation.

We confess their hatred of one another; abuse of each other; rejection of their children; failure to love and protect each other; violence and strife; pride and bitterness; anger and rage; and murder and bloodshed; and shedding of innocent blood; as sin and abomination against the holiness of God. We confess their religious self-righteousness, and condemnation of others, as sin and abomination against the heart of God.

We confess their reasoning and arguments against God as actions that have broken our family's covenant of trust and reliance upon God. We confess their selfishness and greed, lying and profanity as sin against the goodness and provision of God. <u>Through confession, we turn ourselves back to the power of the Cross as our source of righteousness.</u> Through confession and admission, we settle the old accounts that Satan has been using against us, in our generation. He had hoped to use these accounts to keep us in debt to him for decades, if not centuries to come.

As we confess our family's sins before God, we are taking responsibility - by using the authority we have been given as the authorized representative of our generation - to deal with those sins and the devastating effect they have had upon us and our descendants in obstructing the fulfillment of our destiny and our heritage. We return our hearts to the One True God. As we deal with the deeds of our fathers, we take our place with those who are called to reconcile the world back to God through the Blood of Jesus Christ.

In bringing our generations back to the Cross, we participate in the healing of the desolation of many generations that God talked to Isaiah about in Isaiah 61:4: "And they shall rebuild the old ruins, they shall raise up the former desolations, and they shall repair the ruined cities, the desolations of many generations." "Violence shall no longer be heard in your land, neither wasting nor destruction within your borders; But you shall call your walls Salvation, and your gates Praise." (Is. 60: 18)

When we confess the sins of others, we are coming into agreement with God by admitting that those practices and partnerships with

Darkness were an abomination against the Kingdom of God and His love for us. We reject the agreements our ancestors made with darkness - both knowingly and unknowingly - and declare the restoration of the truth of God's Word and promises over ourselves and our descendants.

We take responsibility by dealing with the iniquities committed both by us and our people, and against us and our people. By confessing those behaviors as 'iniquity' we are coming back into agreement with God. We are dealing with the mess left in our generation, by declaring that the practices of 'sin and iniquity', which came out of fear and disobedience. They must be reconciled through the finished work of the Cross and be dealt with according to truth.

The confession of the sins is the verbal cancellation of the agreements made with the Devil, either by ourselves, or by those who have gone before us. The Devil, in turn, attempts to hold us responsible for those sins. Cancelling the contracts - confession and repentance for our sins, and sins of generations past - is essential in breaking Satan's legalistic grip on us.

Unconfessed sins and crimes committed in one generation, sow abuse and assaults in the next generation. They then reap similar aggression and injustice to those practiced by and against their parents and grandparents. This is also true of the secret crimes and ensuing judgments that come down upon the lives of the descendants of those who were in the occult, practiced witchcraft and participate in Freemasonry. In order for us to have true freedom and experience the life Jesus died to give us, agreements made with the lies - and sin 'born' from those lies - must be confessed and cancelled out. Only then can the crimes be brought to judgment.

Obedience to the Word of God commands us to repent and confess those sins. This allows the full and unhindered execution of the truth and the restoration of justice to our people. For a believer in Jesus Christ, this is the process of, "old things have passed away and all things have become new". (II Cor. 5:17) They are new because those 'old' lifestyles which were built on lies and unbelief are declared to be under the Blood; forgiven and washed away by the Blood of Jesus Christ. Only the atonement made through His Blood can secure justice for us and deliver us from the demonic judgments that Satan would use as his standard for justice. Only as we have been reconciled, can we become reconcilers (II Cor. 5:18-19) and be fruitful extensions of the Vine.

Our confession allows God to cleanse our bloodline; deprogram our souls; and renew our systems according to truth and love. We are asking for mercy, and the restoration of the covenant between God and our family. As a member of that family, we are asking God to cleanse us from the claims Guilt has made upon our souls, and close the doors the Enemy has been using to justify his assault and accusation against us. Again, the demonic life patterns of destruction and judgment are broken through confession and repentance, which allows the Lord to dwell in our midst as He did in the camp of Israel in the days of old. (Deut. 23:14)

$\mathcal{S}$ TEP THREE - REPENTANCE

After we confess those things - which are brought to mind by the Holy Spirit with regard to the sins of our generation - we repent. Repentance means to change our mind. We repent for believing the lies, which have allowed sin and the patterns of iniquity that generated them, to continue to operate in our life and relationships in the first place. We humble ourselves and come back into agreement with the Word of God - by acknowledging our own personal participation in the lie that put us under the domination of Fear.

We cannot repent for, nor 'change' someone else's mind for what they did. That is why God commands us to "confess the sins of our fathers" and "repent" for our own sins ourselves. Repentance is not a transferable activity or obligation. We cannot hire it done nor have someone else repent on our behalf. We receive instruction by the Holy Spirit, who convicts us of believing the lies by showing us the truth. Repentance is our response to the truth. Repentance is our admission that we were deceived into believing lies, and enticed into acting upon those lies. <u>Deliverance and freedom happen when we refuse to deny our sin any longer, or blame others, or try to justify it or seek ways to continue living in it.</u>

Repentance comes when we let go of our 'sacred' opinions and submit ourselves to the Word of God, rightly divided to us by the Holy Spirit. Restoration is not the result of some mysterious act, or some popular practices recommended by a religious expert or denominational dispensation. Repentance releases our souls from the Enemy's 'body of death' operating software, into the freedom Jesus died to give us. In recognizing our need to set the record straight, we are also free to release others from the grievances we have held against them. Offenses, and injustices, and crimes committed against us, can now be brought before the Righteous Judge, with confidence and a clean heart.

We surrender our right to 'get even' and 'settle the score'- by turning the injustice that has been committed against us over to the Lord God. We let go of the mindsets and misperceptions which cloud our memories and manufacture excuses, in an attempt to maintain our own righteousness. Repentance means that we no longer search for and justify explanations and agreements we have made with Reasoning, Religion and Reality. Instead, we rely on the truth to settle the accounts. We trust God to make things right and restore back to us the things which have been stolen from us and our family by the thief.

Repentance begins the process of deprogramming. We are allowing ourselves to re-examine the things we learned while growing up. As we review the concepts and relationships we formed under those strained and dysfunctional circumstances, we realize they were founded upon lies. The process of healing and recovery begins when Jesus Christ - the Wonderful Counselor and Faithful Witness - brings us back to the place of the original pain to show us the truth. <u>The revelation of the truth dispels the power of the lie. The truth sets us free</u> - through the revelation of His presence and His testimony as the "Faithful Witness." (Rev. 1:5)

The revelation of the truth sets us free from the condemnation of the lie and the grip of fear; and gives us the grace to both repent and receive forgiveness. In repenting, we recognize our own participation in the lies - including our ignorant and inadvertent perpetuation of them. By receiving forgiveness, we come out of agreement with the lies Guilt and Condemnation would put upon us by making the transgression our fault. Nothing can keep us from receiving God's forgiveness. Forgiveness is a gift that is freely given. It cannot be earned. Receiving God's forgiveness breaks the downward spiral of demonic judgments the Enemy would use to continue to control the fearful and oppress the forgiven.

Hardness of heart comes with the spirit of Rebellion. Rebellion closes our eyes and ears to the truth. It keeps us from seeing and hearing the truth. (Ez.12:1 & 2) Repentance breaks down the power of Rebellion by giving us the grace to humble ourselves. It breaks the grip of Pride and brings forth the inner transformation, which includes the renewing of our mind that comes through the revelation of the Truth. Humbling ourselves allows us to enter into deeper fellowship with the Holy Spirit and imparts a clearer manifestation of the mind of Christ. As we lay down our 'right to be right', and surrender to the Holy Spirit, we are changed into the likeness of the One Who humbled Himself and laid down His glory to become one of us. (Phil. 1:5-6)

We are His loyal subjects, in need of His defense! We have been translated out of the Kingdom of Darkness into the Kingdom of God's dear Son. (See Col. 1:13) We have been reconciled through the blood of His Cross - so that peace and fellowship might be restored between us and God. We ask Jesus Christ, our Deliverer, to set us free from the contracts and soul ties, and curses which operate in our lives through agreements made with the Kingdom of Darkness and its agents.

Words and deeds that were still alive and active are canceled out as the strongholds created through the sins of the generations past are broken. We are truly free when we realize that we are free to repent and receive the divine revelation of what it means to submit to God. We declare our new allegiance to the King of Kings and the Lord of Lords. Only then can we resist the Devil (Ja. 4:7) and stand in battle, confident of Victory.

STEP FOUR – FORGIVENESS IS THE KEY

Every child is born with an innate sense of right and wrong held within their conscience. When we sin, we are separated from the truth of who we are. Sin separates us from God, from ourselves, and from others. Our innocence becomes violated; and our clear conscience becomes compromised, fractured, seared and troubled.

Whether we have sinned, or someone has sinned against us, the truth is that we are all in need of forgiveness. Forgiveness, and knowledge of the truth, is essential for both clearing our conscience and breaking curses. Forgiveness serves to dissolve patterns of destruction that have come down generational blood-lines, restoring health and blessings to our families.

Unforgiveness and Bitterness hold us in the grip of Pain and injustice. Pain causes the offended one to take matters into their own hands in an attempt to correct the scales of justice and make things fair. Making things fair ('right in our own sight') does not reestablish justice. "Vengeance is Mine", saith the Lord. The crimes committed against the Law of Love can only be addressed through forgiveness. Forgiveness means that we commit the matter to God. When we judge the violation ourselves, we are no longer the plaintiff, we are the judge. When we choose, by faith, to release the offender from our judgment and turn it all back over to God, we acknowledge that we are no longer the Judge.

To forgive someone means that 'I release you from my judgment for the crimes you committed against me. I turn the crimes and injustices over to God and the Court of Heaven'. Even in a human court, we cannot be the plaintiff and the judge in the same case. No man can legally get justice if he sits as his own judge. He must be vindicated by another who has the authority as the judge to make that judgment.

As we forgive, we are no longer usurping the position of judge when we are, in fact, the plaintiff. As we forgive, we permit God to preside in His rightful place as the Judge. We make our appeal to the Highest Court in the universe. We seek heaven's ruling and wait for God to hand down His decision. We choose - by an act of our will - to exercise faith, and trust in God's divine justice to make things right. We do what Jesus did when He said, "Father, forgive them for they do not know what they do." (Lk. 23:34)

The Words of Jesus clearly set forth the terms of personal forgiveness, when He said, "For if you forgive men their trespasses, your heavenly Father will also forgive you. But if you do not forgive men their trespasses, neither will your Father forgive your trespasses." (Matt 6:14-15). Forgiving others makes us eligible to receive forgiveness ourselves. To get forgiveness we must give forgiveness. If Jesus died to assure our forgiveness, who are we to withhold forgiveness from others?

The Law of Retribution is 'pay back' for a crime committed. Reciprocity refers to something done as a mutual exchange, something that works both ways. These Laws demand justice for crimes committed through getting even and causes an equal and opposite action/reaction in our negative human transactions. These principles are set forth in the Old Testament Law of 'an eye for an eye' - which is a combination of the Law of Reciprocity and Retribution. Under these laws, justice is defined as and requires the mutual exchange and pay-back for crimes committed. An eye must be given for an eye taken.

In the New Testament, the Law of Reaping and Sowing expands on the Laws of Retribution and Reciprocity. In the Law of Sowing and Reaping we are told to plant what we want to pick. If I want to pick corn I must plant corn. If we want to 'pick' forgiveness, we must 'plant' forgiveness! Forgiveness must be sowed (given) before forgiveness can be reaped (received). If I want mercy, I must be merciful (give mercy). If we want love we must first plant love.

Unforgiveness is often based upon a misunderstanding of what it means to forgive. In its simplest definition, forgiving someone means we release them from our judgment and turn the judgment of the matter over to the Judge of all the Earth. We trust Him for a fair and righteous settlement of our case - which includes the crime(s) that have been committed against us. Forgiveness allows God to have full freedom to judge the matter and reveal to us all aspects of the situation - including the diabolical activities the Enemy has accomplished behind the scenes.

Forgiving others releases a person from demonic judgments and the bondages created by those judgments. It sets him/her free to choose love and forgiveness for themselves as a way of life. It brings reconciliation to those who have been estranged from the grace of God, and gives them hope and encouragement to repent and believe in freedom for themselves. It not only offers the freedom to break the grip of the lies and old behaviors, it also encourages them to ask for freedom from the judgment that has come upon them for judging others.

Once we have forgiven those who have hurt us, and given the crimes they have committed against us over to the Court of Heaven, we can ask God to remove the judgments that Satan has been holding against us for judging them. We are clean and cleared. The Devil has "nothing on us." (Jn. 14:30) He has nothing he can use to build his case against us. Our freedom was secured at the Cross, and that is enough for God.

Forgiveness brings the case under Heaven's jurisdiction. Turning the case over to the High Court is an appeal which invites and allows the Righteous Judge to rule in men's affairs on Earth. Our forgiveness releases the unforgiven one back to a place of forgiveness, so that reconciliation with God and others is again possible. Lack of forgiveness allows the Enemy to continue to hold that one 'in the grip' of his demonic judgment. Forgiveness brings freedom from the spirit of Fear that had held us as prisoners of Guilt and Bitterness, and provides a way of escape into the place of peace.

$\mathcal{S}$ TEP FIVE – PRESENT YOUR CASE

Now we are ready to present our case and the crimes that have been committed against us, and our bloodline, to the High Court of Heaven. We are given the authority from the Lord to do business for the Kingdom of God here on earth. Specifically, as He directed us through His Word, he has given us the authority to bind, and loose, and forgive. Whatever we bind or forbid, on earth, is forbidden in heaven. Whatever we loose or release and permit, on earth, is released or permitted in heaven.

When we forgive, or give forgiveness, we are releasing the judgment of the 'crimes' committed against us or our people back over to the Righteous Judge. We are relinquishing, letting go of, the bitterness and turning the injustices over to God. To forgive means that we are releasing our option to judge the matter. We are committing it all to God: the offenses, insensitivities, the hurt, the injustice, the right to get even, the anger, the fear, the bitterness and the judgment of the one who caused the pain and injustice. All of the matter becomes His problem. He is the Just Judge.

Many of these crimes and injustices, though specific, are generationally very old. They have lost their 'sting' in the lives of the present generation. This makes the crime and the cause of the current trouble harder to detect, although the concealing of the original source of the current problem does not diminish its power to trigger the same type of injustices and destructive loses again in the present generation. The descendants will find similar things happening in their physical, emotional or behavioral lives as were happening in their ancestors. These crimes have been hidden in the closets of shame and silence for generations. When we realize there is a cause for the things we see and experience, these secrets, though hidden, become worthy of investigation. Only then can the patterns of loss and the manifestations of the curses 'hidden in plain sight' be broken.

Even in our natural world, if crimes have not been submitted to the Court, they cannot be dealt with. When justice is not administered in a timely manner, people become desensitized to crime and injustice begins to prevail. Until the crimes and offenses are brought before the Righteous Judge, the issue cannot be settled or brought to satisfactory resolution. The failure to expedite the matters of injustice leaves the door open to bitterness, discouragement, danger and anarchy.

If generational doors of bitterness and unforgiveness are open, the familiar spirits can come right in. They feel at home in the atmosphere of anger and unbelief. These open doors are the standing agreements that have been made by us or our ancestors that give the familiar spirits the operating privileges they need to continue to repeat the patterns of loss and devastation in the lives of our offspring. We can look for regular and predictable patterns of deterioration, which include the deviation from the standards for blessing that God established in Deuteronomy 27:15-26. By using a simple check list from the sins and crimes named therein, we can to assess the extent of the damage incurred against our family bloodline personally and the human race, in general, in the propagation of sin.

The crimes listed in Deuteronomy include: violence; bloodshed; bribery; treachery; sexual perversion; incest; contempt for parents; idolatry; the practice of witchcraft in various forms; moving and removing landmarks and property lines fraudulently; bestiality; genocide; swindle; cruelty toward children, the defenseless, the blind; deliberately taking advantage of the disadvantaged; domestic, physical, emotional, sexual or verbal abuse; and, generally, any other blatant, specific crimes which have been committed by others in one's bloodline that have not yet been brought to justice.

We are admonished to 'come boldly' to the Throne of Grace and Mercy - as the sons and daughters of God - to find help in time of need. We come as the authorized representative of our bloodline to do business, this day, on behalf of those who have gone before us. We come to obtain forgiveness and justice for the things which have been done or committed against the Law of Love. The list of crimes, despite being old, is still considered viable and active if they have not been dealt with.

We come to the Throne of grace to do business on behalf of our people - in order to contest the illegal activities perpetuated by the familiar spirits which have infested, and infected, and afflicted our families' lives. Those spirits must be brought to trial. We come as the plaintiff to bring the crimes before the Judge. The Holy Spirit is our Counselor; and Jesus Christ is our Advocate, the Faithful Witness who saw it all.

We are asking Him to testify as to what really happened, and to establish the truth. We are in very good 'standing' - as the price for all of our sin, and the removal of all curses, and the healing of all maladies has already been declared done. The price has been paid IN FULL through the shed blood and death of Jesus Christ. He became a curse for us that He might set us free from the curse. "It is finished", He declared, as He hung on that tree. Based upon what He did for us, we can come boldly and humbly before the throne of grace, with full assurance that we will be heard and helped.

We can identify the crimes that seem to be coming down our bloodline by looking carefully at the lives of our ancestors and noting things that specifically 'speak to us' as mean, unjust, wrong, or evil. These are the crimes we identify which need to be dealt with. We acknowledge the acts as sin and abomination committed against the Law of God's love because of maltreatment of each other.

As in any court, the goal is to correctly identify the criminals, name the crimes, bring justice to the victims, and prosecute the perpetrators. Describing the crimes and their ramifications against the innocent will increase our understanding as to the damage the Enemy has done. Be aware that retaliatory curses may also have been put on the perpetrators by the victims! For example, when the 'white man' betrayed the Native Americans and stole their lands and broke the treaties, the Natives may have cursed the white settlers in retaliation. The same is also true of those who descended from the Plantation/Slave owners in the days before emancipation. Cursing the oppressor is not uncommon in any human interaction where offenses and injustices have occurred. Those curses also must be broken.

Injustice and false accusation can be seen in any number of scenarios where slavery, violence, and injustice were practiced. The descendants of plantation owners may find themselves in oppressive and abusive situations. They are now the victims and targets of abuse once practiced by their ancestors against their slaves. The fact that the crimes have never been brought to justice creates a continuous 'cascade' of sin and iniquity, which serves to keep the pain of the original injustices alive like a mysterious virus in the souls of the descendants.

Witchcraft is another vile spirit that attaches itself to the descendants of those who practiced it. Witchcraft is rooted in a spirit of insecurity and the feelings of powerlessness that provoke the victim to take control of his/her circumstances including the people in it. It is often used as a form of control in male/female relationships where divination and false accusation bind the righteous and promote evil.

To be released from a spirit of witchcraft we must forgive the person or group through which the witchcraft has come. In forgiving the humans we are turning the crimes of manipulation, false accusation, control and intimidation committed against us and the demonic spirits of witchcraft, harlotry, leviathan, perversion, seduction and Jezebel that motivate them, over to the Righteous Judge for judgment. Only the Blood of Jesus applied to the sticky web of these spirits can dissolve the snares of witchcraft and restore justice.

 TEP SIX - RELEASE FROM THE JUDGMENTS AND RECOVERY OF LOST BLESSINGS

RECEIVING FORGIVENESS

Forgiving ourselves, and receiving forgiveness, are as crucial to our vindication and our release from the curses of the Accuser, as forgiving others. If we still perceive ourselves to be 'guilty' - even after the Judge pardons us - the Enemy uses that confusion about being forgiven as grounds for protesting the Court's action to release us. We are deceived into going along with the Prosecution, who uses the feeling of guilt to get us to believe 'we had it coming'. This prevents us from receiving the pardon issued by the Judge, Who declared we, the Defendant, 'not guilty'.

The Enemy uses our failure to accept God's forgiveness as the basis for his objection to God's pardon of us. In essence, rejection of God's forgiveness gives the Enemy the right to dispute our vindication and challenge God's ruling to release us by insisting that the pain and punishment we are suffering are deserved - due to our continued agreement with Guilt. When we agree with the feelings of Guilt that we 'did something wrong', we are giving implied consent to the Prosecution's objection by agreeing, 'we deserve to be punished'. This gives the Prosecution cause/justification to continue punishing us.

Freedom from pain and the Enemy's judgments, require that we forgive ourselves for listening to the counsel of Shame and Self-condemnation! Paul instructed us to judge nothing "before the time, until the Lord comes, who will both bring to light the hidden things of darkness and reveal the counsels of the hearts." (I Cor. 4:5) He makes it clear that he is in no position to even judge himself, because the only One who is qualified to rightly judge him, or the situations he finds himself in, and thereby justify him, is the Lord.

We have no more right or wisdom to judge ourselves than Paul did. Many of us already believe a 'lifetime of lies' about ourselves. Our perceptions are skewed, and our judgments are biased. Failure and condemnation have marked our path with sorrow and confusion - until little remains of the truth as to who we are and what has really happened to us. Only God - Who knows the truth and has maintained an unbiased, untainted record of the truth - knows what the Devil has done to undermine us and all of His creation.

Only faith in God's mercy obtains mercy and secures justice for us. Only His testimony will establish our righteous cause. Only His decision can release us from accusations made by injustice, and free us from the demands for our punishment made by the Enemy. Only God can heal our broken hearts and take away the feelings of Anger and Resentment, which Satan has used to accuse us of guilt again and again and again. Only God can heal our broken spirits and set us free from the grip of Death and Destruction and restore to us the joy of our salvation. Only He can "Create in [us] a clean heart," as David prayed. (Psalm 51:1-10)

Part of the redemption and restoration which God purchased for us includes a full and true understanding of our original nature and identity. The Holy Spirit gives us a divine revelation which allows us to comprehend the great price that was paid for our ransom - and returns us to our original state as the sons and daughters of the Most High God.

We have been forgiven and released from the judgments Satan held against us, and the contract Death had on us. Our debt has been forgiven, PAID IN FULL - by God's love. In response to that love, we are called to walk in justice, giving that same forgiveness to others which we ourselves have received. Forgiveness allows us to render that which is due to whom it is due, as we endeavor to "Owe no one anything except to love one another." (Ro. 13: 7-8)

Jesus warns us of the danger of jeopardizing our love and forgiveness by not forgiving those indebted to us. He called that man a "wicked servant" who would not forgive one who was indebted to him - after he himself had been forgiven a much larger debt when not being able to repay it. (See Mt. 18:21-35)

As love is the language of Heaven, Forgiveness becomes its translation and expression on earth. Love is forgiveness; forgiveness is love. No longer are we to apply the cold, hard exacting rule of 'an eye for an eye'. We are called to take the step of faith to love one another - not based upon merit, but based upon loving as God loves us - unconditionally. We let go of resentments, and allow God to be the judge of the hearts of our enemies - because only He knows the truth about what really happened and who started it.

Not forgiving others holds us in the grip of judgment ourselves, and only strengthens the Devil's argument against us, to convince us our suffering comes as the well-deserved result of our sins and God's wrath against us. We conclude that we are guilty; and our punishment - pain, loss, and suffering - is well deserved. Getting me to focus on these demonic judgments as being from God or something 'I had coming' only masks the real truth. It conceals the relationship God has with me, and strains the relationship I have with God.

The Enemy is the one who has been encroaching on my life and family bloodline the entire time! He has used injustice, and every opportunity, to bring his accusation against me and 'pin' the very crimes he has committed against me, on me! The continuation of injustice defers our hope, and creates confusion in our hearts and minds. Receiving the judgment handed down by Guilt crushes me and strips me of any hope for the return of truth and justice.

Unforgiveness, both toward others and ourselves, insures the continuation of the injustices which demons have inflicted upon our ancestors, and creates a sure transition down to our sons and daughters. The negative effect of curses brought on by Guilt and Condemnation continue to keep us bound in the grip of Fear, Pride, Sickness, Hardness of Heart, and bitter Alienation from God.

Feeling cut off from the grace and the forgiveness of God, perpetuates the feelings of pain and separation caused by sin. Rejection drives us to Despair and Confusion strikes down the Law of Love. This allows the roots of Bitterness against God, ourselves, and others to spring up and cause trouble and the defilement of many. (Heb. 12: 12-15)

OVERCOME BY EVIL

When Fear and the spirit of Discouragement become overwhelming, we become frustrated and impatient. We speak things over ourselves and others that we do not mean or want to happen. We must ask God to forgive us for judging ourselves and others - through the negative words we have spoken over ourselves or them - under the counsel of Bitterness and the pressure of Unbelief. Our words are very powerful; they give the Enemy the permission (by agreement) he needs to bind us to the mind sets and difficulties our words have trapped us in.

Speaking negative and demeaning words over ourselves is often done mindlessly, without thought or understanding. Nonetheless, those words are words of death that give the Enemy our 'implied consent' which he uses to bring those curses to pass. Speaking words over ourselves, prompted by Self-judgment, Self-hatred, and Self-bitterness, are one of Satan's most powerful weapons against us, in justifying his claimed right to bring evil upon us. Subconsciously, we still feel bad, and agree that - because we did something bad, we are bad - and thus, worthy of punishment, pain and penalty.

Forgiving ourselves is one of the most overlooked areas for which we are in need of deliverance and forgiveness. We have been locked in the insidious 'prison of Self-condemnation and Self-bitterness and Self-expectation', who have held us hostage in our life our whole life. These are the strongholds of bondage, the prisons of words and expectations which the Holy Spirit wants to 'tear down' in our souls in order to set us free to love ourselves as God does, and stop agreeing with Self-destruction.

Let Him be the judge of you. He will not be as hard on you as you - under the counsel of Hell's accusers - are on yourself. We are God's servants, His sons and daughters. He is the only One Who has the knowledge and wisdom to judge us rightly - because He is the Only One Who knows what really happened. John 20:23 makes it very clear. The power of forgiveness also releases the power to be forgiven. He who would desire forgiveness, must first forgive.

"But if you do not forgive men their trespasses, neither will your Father forgive your trespasses." (Mt. 6:15) In order for God to maintain my righteous cause, I must do His will, not my own. I must do unto others as I would have them do unto me. This is why Lord Himself mandates forgiveness as a prerequisite for obtaining forgiveness for ourselves.

When we obey His command to love and forgive ourselves, He is 'free' - so to speak - to do the same for us. God can answer the Enemy's protest against His forgiveness of us, through the principle of obedience, -"If they obey Me, I will bless them". (Deut. 28:1-14) Can God do any less for us than we would do for others? If we have mercy on them, will not God do the same for us? Forgiveness presents us with the only safe position from which to petition our own case for justice in the crimes committed against us. It also allows us to come with assurance to make our request known for the restoration of our lost and stolen blessings.

Forgiveness means that I release the judgment of the crimes committed against me back to God and allow Him to hear my case and judge the matter. He is the righteous Judge, the only One Who knows the motives of hearts, and all the extenuating circumstances which reality constructed around a matter. To continue to hold on to the offense is to continue to allow those injustices to have power to control us - our moods, dispositions, direction, and destiny.

Forgiveness also becomes an integral part of both breaking the control others have over us, and in breaking the curses in our own lives. As I turn the crimes committed against me over to the Court of Heaven, I am released from the control which others have over me through Hatred, and am moved to a place of safety, outside of the Devil's line of fire. Forgiveness is imperative to freedom, and the restoration of justice - as it makes God's vindication a reality in our personal lives and familial situations.

God is the righteous judge of all the earth. "According to their deeds, accordingly He will repay, fury to His adversaries, recompense to His enemies; ..." (Is. 59:18) All of us have sinned and have been sinned against. Many of us have sustained wounds and assaults against our lives that are too horrible to mention.

We must know that these atrocities have not only hurt us, but grieve the heart of our Heavenly Father, Who permits the will of man to operate. This permission allows the Devil's will to operate which allows the sin and iniquity committed by mankind against one another to grow and multiply. God's final divine remedy is justice. <u>We can move the hand of God's justice by forgiving</u>.

When we refuse to forgive our enemy by choosing to judge the matters ourselves, it interferes with God's intervention. It is an affront to His justice, and puts Him in a position that vilifies His Goodness - because the injustice is allowed to continue by our unconscious agreement with it. Exercising our free will to seek justice on our own causes the exact opposite of the justice we desire; it allows injustice to prevail. The continued injustices open the door to misunderstanding God's goodness, and prevents justice from being served, thus promoting the continuation of human pain and suffering.

Judging God for not dealing with injustice provokes us to make harsh judgments against Him for letting evil prevail. Ultimately, Satan has flipped the tables by using our unforgiveness to temporarily 'tie' God's hands, in the rendering of true justice and in the restoration of our lost blessings. <u>By holding onto unforgiveness and bitterness against God for not judging injustices, we pervert and delay our own vindication from the Lord.</u>

We blame Him for delaying justice in not making our adversaries 'pay'! Satan sets us up in our own mind to feel angry and upset with God. He uses our disappointment to judge God in our hearts for being unfair, and unjust, and indifferent to our plight. Not standing in the truth of knowing Who God is - that He is just - allows the Enemy to call for the judgment of God by using God's own people to create rebellion and riots against Him. How clever is that?

VENGEANCE IS MINE

"Vindicate me, O God, and plead my cause against an ungodly nation; oh, deliver me from the deceitful and unjust man! For You are the God of my strength; Why do You cast me off? Why do I go mourning because of the oppression of the enemy?" (Ps. 43:1-2)

Who will vindicate us? Who will bring us justice? Who will advocate for us? How long must we suffer in the wrongs, the accusations, and the judgments other people hold against us and against our families? "How long, oh Lord, will You forget me forever?" (Ps: 13: 1)

"How long will the long suffering virtue of God allow iniquity to rule in the affairs of men?" the Psalmist asks repeatedly. When will the truth be known so that we can rest in the safety of justice and make sense of our lives?

How many suffer lack, when others have so much? How many feel entitled to things they have stolen from the helpless or innocent, yet have no hint of shame or remorse – even among those who call themselves Christians? Will it ever come to pass that vindication and validation and justice prevail? Yes, if we believe what God says: "'Vengeance is mine. I will repay,' says the Lord." (Ro. 12:19, Lev. 19:18 & Deut. 32:35) We know that God's Word is True, therefore we can trust it. Because we know it, we can believe it - because knowing 'trumps' believing. Therefore, we can know what we know is true - because we are created by God to know and trust Him and recognize His Spirit that bears witness with our spirit!

The question of the restoration of justice and the things lost and stolen, after all, is not a matter of 'if' but 'when'. God will perform what we have asked of Him. He has given us His Word in promising justice and vindication on our behalf. We can get hung up on 'when' and 'why', to the spiritual detriment of our own souls. The promise of justice and peace are settled in the Word of God. They are a promise from Him to us, and He cannot lie. He will do everything He has promised to do. This journey, then, is simply a matter of walking in the revelation of God's goodness; and our innate trust in God's faithfulness to keep His Word.

Bitterness, fear, and the length of the trials are designed by Satan to discourage us - as an enticement to take matters into our own hands. Weariness and doubt cause us to waver at the promises of God. They 'open the doors' of our souls so that we question whether or not God will ever really come through to do what is right and defend us. Doubt says: "If He has not yet, then He won't and if He won't, then it's up to me." Fear says: "If He has not, then He must not want to." Knowing the Truth says: "If He said He would, He will, because God cannot lie!"

The only One Who will maintain my righteous cause and defend my rights, is the One Who sits on the throne, judging in righteousness. "He has prepared His throne for judgment. He shall judge the world in righteousness and He shall administer judgment for the people in uprightness." (Ps. 9:7-8) God asks us to trust Him - to call upon Him, and release the matter to Him.

The cry of Jeremiah from the deepest pit becomes our own:

> "You drew near on the day I called on You, and said, 'Do not fear!' O Lord, You have pleaded the case for my soul; You have redeemed my life. O LORD, You have seen how I am wronged. Judge my case. You have seen all their vengeance, all their schemes against me. ...Repay them, O LORD, according to the work of their hands." (Lam. 3:57-64)

God is jealous over His children and will take vengeance upon our adversaries, who are also His adversaries. He is especially aware of those who trouble and oppress the weak, the innocent, the children, the destitute and downtrodden, the widows, and the fatherless. Even though "The LORD is slow to anger, and great in power, He will not at all acquit the wicked." (Nahum 1:3)

A WAY OF ESCAPE

In order to escape Satan's ceaseless retaliation, we must stay hidden in Christ. We are dead. We were crucified with Christ. (Col. 3:3) We follow Him, and "take every thought captive" (II Cor. 10:4-5) We think those 'thoughts' which are subject to the Word of God and obedient to Christ. Satan twists our devotion into duty, and distorts our relationship with God by making it rule-oriented, using the Law as the measuring rod of our righteousness instead of the Cross.

The Liar tells us the Cross is not enough; there must be more we have to do. He tells us that just being forgiven is too easy. Life is difficult and it is not 'okay' for us to just 'be' okay, forgiven, and following Jesus. By accepting the many thoughts the Tempter puts into our minds - without "taking them captive" and measuring them against the Word of God - we will step into anxiety and confusion, and pursue futility.

If we think that these thoughts are our thoughts simply because they came into our mind, we will quickly lose our identity in Christ to the constant barrage of Hell. We will sink into hopelessness and despair, and miss all the precious and powerful opportunities the Lord has given us to prevail as "more than a conqueror" with Him. (Rom. 8:37) Only the Holy Spirit is able to keep our minds stayed upon the truth of knowing who we already are in Christ Jesus, as we keep "looking unto Jesus, the Author and Finisher of our faith". (Heb. 12:2)

THE POWER OF THE CROSS

Not only does the Cross provide for us a hiding place from judgment; it is the instrument of death and cleansing that God uses to redeem 'whosoever will', from the final judgment of eternal separation. The Cross releases us from the dominion and domination of the 'death grip' of the god of this world. Death no longer has any jurisdiction over us. We are no longer under any obligation to the Devil and need not be intimidated by him.

Jesus, through His death, destroyed him who had the power of death - that is, the Devil "and released those who through fear of death were all their lifetime subject to bondage." (Heb. 2:15) "He has delivered us from the power of darkness and translated us into the kingdom of the Son of His love, in Whom we have redemption through His blood, the forgiveness of sins." (Col. 1:13)

The only death which now concerns us is in reckoning the old man dead. Our death ends all obligations to the Evil One, as well as his control over us within his Evil system. (See Rom. 6:11-12) Our agreement with the lie is thus null and void. The 'old man' is 'reckoned dead'. Our death allows God to pluck us out of the kingdom of Darkness, and translate us into the Kingdom of His Dear Son. Our death ends the argument Satan makes for our soul, and renders further discussion on the matter of our righteousness obsolete.

Confession and repentance discharge sin's dominion over us. They cancel the agreements we have made with the Enemy, either through ignorance, or by forced confessions he obtained by manipulating us while we were detained in Hell's concentration camp. Our realigned agreement with God through admission and confession of our sin (behavior which originated from being enticed to believe the lies of the Enemy), sets us free and reinstates us in our relationship with Him.

Repentance and confession make a way for God's forgiveness, thereby providing a way of escape from the wrath to come. All of the unresolved conflicts and outstanding debts; all of the open accounts and unfinished business Satan counted against us are settled. His claims to our soul, and his 'ownership' of the goods and gifts God had given us, are rejected, and his power over us is removed.

Justice has been established for us. True liberty is ours. "Therefore if the Son makes you free, you shall be free indeed." Whom the Son sets free "is free indeed". (Jn. 8:36) These are not just empty words, irrelevant to modern twenty-first century man. Faith in the work of the Cross, and the redemption it carries, are as pertinent and imperative to our salvation today as they were to the early church believers. Our eternal survival and the restoration of justice are found in the Cross, and released through the Word of the risen Lamb of God.

The redeeming power of the Cross can renew broken hearts and heal diseased bodies. It can bring beauty for ashes and joy for mourning. (See Is. 61:1-4) It cannot work, however, if we choose to disregard it or deny our need for it. Even though Jesus Christ died so that we and our descendants might live an abundant life, His desire for us to do well and live abundantly does not happen automatically. We must accept Him and allow His Holy Spirit to apply the power of the Cross to our individual needs deeply and daily.

A SUMMARY FOR RECOVERING YOUR LOST BLESSINGS

To remove the curse, come as the authorized representative of your family to:

1) Identify the generational sin or iniquity (the crimes committed against the Law of Love).

2) Identify the corresponding agreements you and/or your family made with lies.

3) Confess the sins of your generations, and their agreements made with the lies.

4) Repent for your own sin and change your mind about the lies you believed.

5) Cancel out your personal agreements with those lies, using the Word of God.

6) Declare those specific sins and agreements to be an abomination against God.

7) Forgive your ancestors for believing the lies that opened doors for the curses.

8) Forgive any others still living who have committed offenses against you.

9) Receive God's forgiveness for yourself / Reject the Accuser's verdict of guilty

BRING YOUR CASE BEFORE THE HIGH COURT OF HEAVEN:

10) Name the specific crimes committed against your family before Heaven's Court.

11) Ask for the testimony of Jesus, the Faithful Witness, to testify on your behalf.

12) Use any other scriptural promises to support your case and confidence in God.

13) Ask God to judge the specific Liars and Thieves who worked to destroy you.

14) Call for the removal of the demonic judgments brought upon your bloodline.

15) Identify the patterns of destruction that have come from demonic judgments.

16) Confess them as coming from believing lies and agreements made with fear.

17) Repent for the lies and declare the truth over you and your family.

18) Ask God to delete the marks of trauma & patterns of iniquity left on your DNA.

19) Ask for the restoration of specific things lost: justice, truth, honor, health, etc.

20) Ask for the revelation of Jesus Christ and His truth to set your people free.

Breaking generational curses involves several steps, including the CONFESSION of SINS and REPENTANCE. (Use the Prayer for Release from the Sins of the Generations found in the back of any of our manuals or at www.liferecovery.com)

After the patterns are recognized and the iniquities are confessed, the next step is FORGIVENESS. Forgiveness releases the crimes committed against us to the Court of Heaven for judgment, and closes Satan's case against us. His demand for blood, and his claimed right to continue to violate us who are the temple property of the Most High God, are rendered null and void. The Blood of Jesus more than satisfies the Devil's demand for our blood; and the death of Jesus more than answers the Devil's demand for our death. You can pray these prayers for yourself or on behalf of others in your family. (Use the Prayers for Forgiveness and the Release from Self-hatred and Self-rejection, the Prayer for Self-Acceptance, the Prayer for Forgiveness of Others, and the Prayer for Forgiveness of God, all found in the back of any of our manuals or at www.liferecovery.com)

PRAYER FOR PRESENTING OUR CASE TO THE COURT OF HEAVEN

This prayer is an outline, like the one Jesus gave us in the Our Father. Just as 'The Our Father' is not to be used as a religious exercise or as part of a magic formula, these prayers provide us with a basic framework as we prepare to come before the Court of Heaven to present our case. We are the plaintiff or petitioner. Jesus Christ is our Advocate (Attorney), and also our Faithful Witness because He saw exactly what happened. He also steps in as our substitute, in that He took the punishment for our healing and deliverance by becoming a curse for us. We are here to bring our case before the Righteous Judge Who has greatly desired to judge our situation and vindicate us in the crimes the Enemy has committed against us and our ancestors for a long time.

Dear Lord Jesus, Son of the Living God, I come before You and the Court of Heaven right now to do business, this day, on behalf of myself and my family, as the authorized representative of my generational bloodlines. I come boldly, according to Your Word, as your son [daughter], made in Your image and brought forth by Your own will and truth. I come on behalf of myself and my ancestors [here you can speak the names of your parent using their full names], to confess and cancel out the agreements we made, both knowingly and unknowingly, with the Evil One. I now want to present the crimes which have been committed against us under the hand of Satan's wrath; and close the doors of bitterness and unforgiveness Satan has been using to continue to bring these works of Darkness down upon me and my children. On our behalf, I seek mercy and release from the Enemy's demands against us and his Law of Reciprocity in his [an eye for an eye] judgments against us. I come to present the crimes committed against us through his hatred for us to the Court of the Righteous Judge.

As part of my request for forgiveness, I choose to forgive and release from my judgment _____ [name the person] for _____ [name the crimes] - abuse, abandonment, rejection, cruelty, insensitivity, murder, etc. - any place where the law of love was violated - that they have committed against me and/or my people under the counsel of the Evil One. I forgive them and release them from my judgment, as I choose to turn the judgment of these crimes over to the Righteous Judge Who sits on the bench of the High Court of Heaven. I present my case and ask the Court and the Righteous Judge to hear my complaint against my real enemy, the Evil One, who calls himself the god of this world. I present my complaint against him for the crimes he has committed against me and my children, including those who are part of my family's bloodline.

I ask for the restoration of justice, truth, mercy, joy, righteousness, peace, purity, health and healing, my honor, reputation, confidence, sound mind, etc. and the blessings of God to me and my offspring. I also petition the Court to give each of us who yet remain alive, including those who were used as an enemy against me, a deep and holy revelation of Jesus Christ and His love and salvation.

I ask the Court to rule against the Enemy, and render him powerless and strip him of those things that belong to me and my family, and forbid him to continue in his degeneration of our bloodline. I ask that You would lock him up in Your Judgment Pit until the time of Your Final Judgment upon him and his evil world system.

PRAYER FOR THE REMOVAL OF THE JUDGMENTS AND THE RESTORATION OF LOST BLESSINGS

Now you are ready to pray for the removal of the judgments and the restoration of lost blessings.

I also come before the High Court of Heaven to present my case for the removal of the demonic judgments which the Enemy has put upon me and my bloodline for the sins we committed against You while under the influence of his deception. I ask for the removal of every curse - including those brought against us by the familiar spirits, the angels of light, the spirits who bind us in soul-ties, spirits of religion, deception, divination, witchcraft, spirits of accident, assault, and injury, disease, self-condemnation and the demon keepers of the vows. [Vow Keepers hold us to the vows we have so foolishly made under the counsel of deception].

I petition for the restoration of all that has been stolen from me and my bloodline including, _____, [fill in specific things you want back]: my honor; justice; the truth; peace; health; relationships, especially with my spouse and children; and for divine deliverance from the curses. I remind the Court that Jesus Christ became a curse for us to set us free from the curses, and by His stripes we are healed. I have come to receive forgiveness, healing and freedom from the curses through the confession of my sins, and through the Blood of Jesus Christ, who died for my restoration.

I ask that You, Lord, God, would reveal the lies that the Enemy has used to bind us to the torture racks of Hell's irresolvable conflicts (to find fault with us that he might accuse us for the things he has done). The Serpent has deceived us, as he did our First Parents. I ask You to forgive us who stand in Your presence asking for Your mercy. I ask You to turn away the Prosecution's accusations and arguments against us in these matters of injustice, and restore Your truth and justice and the Joy of Your Salvation to us.

We ask You to forgive us for agreeing with the spirit of Fear and Guilt and coming into agreement with their solutions to solve the treacherous conflicts they have set up in our lives. I ask You to deliver us from the Accuser of the Brethren who finds fault with us for not being able to resolve the demonic dilemmas or escape the diabolical snares he deliberately set up for the express purpose of corrupting us and destroying Your Image in us.

I ask You to forgive us for not receiving Your forgiveness which has opened up the door for the Accuser's objection in You carrying out Your full pardon of us. I ask that the Court would make note of these schemes the Accuser has put upon us in his deliberate attempt to deceive and destroy us in his effort to try and separate us from Your love, Lord God.

I also ask for the Faithful Witness, Jesus Christ, to testify to the truth as to what really happened to us and our bloodline, in this hijacking of our souls. Jesus knows it all, including the Enemy's evil intention against us even beginning in the womb. He knows we are no match for the wiles of the Wicked One and has promised to never leave us or forsake us.

We ask for Your healing of our bodies, including our DNA. We ask for the _____ [Ask for anything specific and appropriate in the restoration of things pertaining to your health or stolen from you and *your generations.] May Your Mercy and Justice deliver us from the Evil One and restore unto us the revelation of your peace and love that we might continue to hope in Your Goodness.*

We are Your workmanship, created in Christ Jesus unto good works. Thank you for Your Word which declares that You are Faithful to complete the work You have begun in us and that You will never leave us or forsake us. We know Your Love never fails. We rest our hope fully upon the strength of Your promises. We are Yours and we thank You for delivering us from the sway and persuasion of the Wicked One. We thank You for vindicating us and for ruling in favor of Your Justice in rescuing and restoring us from this present evil world. Amen!

KNOWING THE GROUND RULES

- Knowing there is a war going on between God and Satan for the souls of man
- Knowing there is one rule in the war - "whom we yield ourselves servant to obey, his slave we become"
- Knowing Satan has two objectives in this war: first to corrupt our concept of God
- Knowing Satan's second objective is to corrupt our concept of ourselves and who we are
- Knowing there are only two kingdoms: God's and Satan's (I have no kingdom)
- Knowing we are made in the image of God
- Knowing at the moment of conception we were thrown into the Snake Pit of Life
- Knowing we have been programmed by the "Body of Death" operating software
- Knowing Satan works to obscure our divine nature, made in the Image of God

- Knowing Satan psychologically recondition us to believe we are what we do
- Knowing Satan's objective is to separate us from the Love of the Heavenly Father
- Knowing Satan's aim is to trick us into believing the lies of the Pit to get us to sin
- Knowing an agreement with the Enemy must be made before he can do anything
- Knowing others can make those agreements for us, even without our knowing
- Knowing if we are doing things we do not want to do we are being controlled
- Knowing Satan makes the lie look like the truth to us to bring us into bondage
- Knowing the truth sets us free, and lies bring us into bondage
- Knowing iniquity and sin are part of our legacy through the sins of the fathers
- Knowing they were tricked into believing the lies that bring forth the fruit of sin
- Knowing these lies bring us into bondage to sin and separate us from God
- Knowing the Enemy wants to alienates us in our relationship with God
- Knowing the Enemy's definition of Justice demands an "eye for an eye"
- Knowing that God is the Just and Righteous Judge Who will not acquit the guilty
- Knowing that justice on earth has fallen in the streets and has been compromised
- Knowing the accumulation of iniquity and injustice perpetuates the curses
- Knowing demonic judgments create patterns of dysfunction in our bloodlines
- Knowing iniquity requires a divine response

KNOWING MY RIGHTS

- Knowing I am made in the image of God and my divine nature is my first nature
- Knowing I am redeemed through the Blood of Jesus Christ given for my ransom
- Knowing I am called by Jesus Christ to follow Him
- Knowing I have a new inheritance in Christ Jesus available to me as His child
- Knowing I am a blood bought child, heir to eternal life and the promises of God
- Knowing I have an Enemy who desires to corrupt the image of God in me
- Knowing I've been hijack and the Enemy is holding my soul hostage to fear
- Knowing the Enemy has impersonated me to myself (First Person Impersonator)
- Knowing he is the 'Strong Man' that Jesus warned us would come to divide our house
- Knowing I have been deceived into thinking I am what I feel, think, say, and do
- Knowing I have been falsely accused by the Accuser who sounds like "me"
- Knowing he uses my hatred of sin and feelings of guilt to alienate me from myself
- Knowing I have sinned against myself by believing his lies
- Knowing he finds me guilty for the things he's tricked me into doing
- Knowing I must forgive myself in order to receive God's forgiveness
- Knowing I must forgive others in order to be forgiven

GOING TO COURT

- Knowing the Devil and his activities are illegal in my life
- Knowing the Devil is the Accuser of all of the sons and daughters of God
- Knowing that I am no match for the Devil, either to overpower or outwit him
- Knowing I have a Savior Who died in my place
- Knowing I have Jesus Christ as my Advocate, Defender and my Savior
- Knowing He will successfully plead my case
- Knowing Jesus Christ is the "Faithful Witness", He knows the truth
- Knowing He was there, at the scene of the crime when I was assaulted
- Knowing I have been lied to, and lied about
- Knowing Jesus Christ will testify to the truth in my behalf
- Knowing I have a just and righteous Judge
- Knowing the Accuser of the brethren is a criminal and a liar
- Knowing he intends to divide my house and set me up in opposition to myself
- Knowing the Devil builds his case against me using my own sin as evidence
- Knowing the Devil uses my own words and actions against me to prove I'm guilty
- Knowing his intent is to prove me guilty of the very thing he did himself
- Knowing my agreements with him are not mandatory, I can cancel them
- Knowing the evidence he uses against me only stands if I agree with the charges
- Knowing that the Liar will be exposed and convicted

THE ADVERSARY'S CLAIMS

- Knowing my agreement with the lie brings me under the power of the Liar
- Knowing I have sinned, been tricked, deceived into believing the lie
- Knowing I made a choice to agree with it under the counsel of deception
- Knowing the Enemy will use my sin as evidence against me
- Knowing he will build his case against me using the agreements I made
- Knowing I have done bad things because I was deceived, not because I am bad
- Knowing it is not wise for me to even judge my own self as bad or good
- Knowing I must repent of judging others and myself in matters of conduct
- Knowing the Devil sets me up to test my faith in the promises of God
- Knowing that both God and the Enemy are working in the same place
- Knowing they are working at the same time to do the opposite thing in my life
- Knowing the Devil demands that God judge me
- Knowing that I have many times tried to quit what I could not stop
- Knowing that if I am doing the thing "I do not want to do", it is not me doing it
- Knowing I need deliverance, not more self-control or will power
- Knowing the Enemy will tempt me to hate myself based on the things I am doing
- Knowing the thing I did or have done is not who I am

- Knowing because I come from a sinful generation, I too am marked with iniquity
- Knowing I am under an avalanche of generational sin and iniquity and bloodguilt
- Knowing this brings the curses and generational patterns of destruction on me
- Knowing there are open accounts, vows, and agreements with sin and iniquity
- Knowing the Enemy uses these sins to bring his demonic judgments against me
- Knowing Satan claims the right to prosecute me
- Knowing Satan's claims to my life as a believer in Jesus Christ are illegal
- Knowing If I believe his lies I am held in bondage to them

PREPARING MY DEFENSE

- Knowing If others have sinned against me; I must forgive
- Knowing If I am suffering for the sins of others; I must forgive
- Knowing If I am suffering for the sins I did not commit; I must forgive
- Knowing If I have sinned; I must forgive myself
- Knowing I cannot save myself; I need a Savior
- Knowing I cannot judge others; I release their crimes against me, to God
- Knowing I am an authorized representative for my generation,
- Knowing I can stand in for my ancestors and bring their past crimes to Court
- Knowing I can do business on behalf of my ancestors, I confess
- Knowing I can do business on behalf of my descendants; I pray for their release

- Knowing I can confess their iniquity; I can confess our sin to God
- Knowing I can confess and repent of my own iniquity; I receive freedom
- Knowing that even if my heart condemns me, God knows my heart;
- Knowing He knows the truth about everything
- Knowing He keeps truth and justice for all generations

MY PETITION

- Knowing I can petition the Court of Heaven for a righteous and just settlement
- Knowing I can release my enemies from my own judgment and still get justice
- Knowing that I can trust the righteous Judge of all the Earth to do what is right
- Knowing I can trust the Court of Heaven to vindicate me
- Knowing I can receive justice, mercy and the reestablishment of truth
- Knowing I have been vindicated and was restored 2000 years ago at the Cross
- Knowing I can bring my bloodline back to the Cross of Calvary
- Knowing God can cleanse my bloodline with the Blood of the Cross
- Knowing we are cleansed from wickedness by the Blood of Christ
- Knowing it was for the purpose of reconciliation that Christ died;
- Knowing that all things will be restored back to Him
- Knowing that I am a vital participant in the restoration of justice

- Knowing that all things work for good to those who love God
- Knowing that I am destined for the throne to rule and reign with God
- Knowing these fiery trials have purified my soul and refined my faith
- Knowing I am more than a conqueror in Him
- Knowing that my life has been hid with Christ in God
- Knowing that in Him I live and move and have my being
- Knowing that all is well with my soul and all God says is true
- Knowing that in all my afflictions, He was afflicted with me
- Knowing that the truth set me free
- Knowing I am forgiven and to me this grace has been given
- Knowing I am a son or daughter of the Most High
- Knowing I can declare along with all the redeemed, the manifold wisdom of God
- Knowing we are to make known the manifold wisdom of God to the rulers of Hell
- Knowing the church is called to make known the fellowship of the mystery
- Knowing we will rule and reign with Christ
- Knowing I am destined to live with Him forever in Heaven,
- Knowing every knee will bow and every tongue will confess that the Lord is God
- Knowing God is just and has the last move,
- Knowing We win, I say: Amen, Amen, Amen.

ABOUT THE AUTHOR

Marjorie Cole, founder of Life Recovery, Inc. a prayer and counseling ministry, and author of numerous books, manuals, and cd's
has worked as a teacher and counselor for more than 30 years. An
excellent bible teacher and conference speaker, she has traveled
both nationally and internationally. Her video and audio teachings are seen throughout the world including Eastern Europe,
Romania, the African nations, the Middle East and Europe.

Marjorie has worked as a counselor in both Christian and secular
settings including Minnesota Teen Challenge where she wrote the
book, "Taking the Devil to Court". She has a master's degree in
counseling psychology and chemical dependency counseling.

Using a biblical approach to counseling and truth as the basis for
freedom, she has developed Life Recovery, Inc., a systematic,
comprehensive approach to healing and deliverance that has
helped thousands of people apply scriptural principles to their
lives, bringing them to truth and a new freedom in Christ. Those
principles include understanding spiritual warfare, deliverance,
inner-healing, breaking generational curses, and discipleship.

Marjorie, along with her husband Jarry Cole who pastors True
Light Church, host Rescue Radio, a weekly podcast. They have
been in the ministry for over forty years.

Among the many other literary works by Marjorie Cole include "God On Trial - Opening Arguments" a radio drama series that exposes the war between God and Satan for the souls of men that explores the question of God's right to rule the world.

Go to www.liferecovery.com for a complete listing.

facebook.com/LifeRecoveryInc

twitter.com/liferecoveryinc

youtube.com/LiferecoveryInc

CRAVINGS -Why Do I Do What I Don't Want To Do?

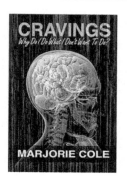

Craving is defined as a strong desire to have something, to demand, to force, through deviousness. We are torn between self-indulgence and self-control, often spending our lives trying to quit something we cannot seem to stop.

Freedom from the failure and dysfunction brought on by addictions begins with knowing the truth about "who I am". Cravings takes us beyond the surface of addictions and typical "do-more management strategies" and "try harder" self-help methods, into the deeper context of spiritual warfare. It exposes the lies we believe and the operation of demonic programming that controls our souls. The book offers a biblical, in depth look at the spiritual battle that goes on inside of us that makes deliverance a real part of our healing and recovery.

Taking The Devil to Court - Present Your Case (Revised)

"Taking the Devil to Court" is a basic primer in understanding spiritual warfare. It sets the stage for giving the reader a deeper understanding of the "real life" drama of spiritual warfare and lays a biblical foundation that will adequately explain the most difficult of spiritual entanglements and encounters. "Taking the Devil to Court" is a basic, "must read" for anyone wanting freedom for themselves or for those working to "set captives free".

Several new chapters have been added to address the issues of DNA, programming, and dealing with demonic "alters". "Taking the Devil to Court" also clearly addresses the subtle "first person impersonations of the "strongman" Jesus warned about in Matthew 12:29 and Luke 11, so often overlooked in traditional Christian counseling. Without understanding how the Enemy masquerades as our very thoughts, we will not be able to take every thought captive and make it subject to Christ. (II Cor. 10:3-5).

———

Check out www.liferecovery.com for more books, cd's, podcasts, blogs, and videos.

Made in the USA
Middletown, DE
15 February 2022

61166444R00176